# Income and Wealth

# Income and Wealth

## ALAN REYNOLDS

GREENWOOD GUIDES TO BUSINESS AND ECONOMICS
Wesley B. Truitt, Series Editor

**GREENWOOD PRESS**
WESTPORT, CONNECTICUT • LONDON

**Library of Congress Cataloging-in-Publication Data**

Reynolds, Alan.
   Income and wealth / Alan Reynolds.
      p. cm. — (Greenwood guides to business and economics,
      ISSN 1559–2367)
   Includes bibliographical references and index.
   ISBN 0–313–33688–1 (alk. paper)
   1. Income—United States.   2. Wealth—United States.   3. Income
distribution—United States.   I. Title.
   HC110.I5R478 2006
   339.2'20973—dc22       2006021343

British Library Cataloguing-in-Publication Data is available.

Library of Congress Catalog Card Number: 2006021343
ISBN: 0–313–33688–1
ISSN: 1559–2367

First published in 2006

Greenwood Press, 88 Post Road West, Westport, CT 06881
An imprint of Greenwood Publishing Group, Inc.
www.greenwood.com

Printed in the United States of America

The paper used in this book complies with the
Permanent Paper Standard issued by the National
Information Standards Organization (Z39.48–1984).

10   9   8   7   6   5   4   3   2   1

# Contents

# Illustrations

## TABLES

**FIGURES**

# Series Foreword

Scanning the pages of the newspaper on any given day, you'll find headlines like these:

"OPEC Points to Supply Chains as Cause of Price Hikes"
"Business Groups Warn of Danger of Takeover Proposals"
"U.S. Durable Goods Orders Jump 3.3%"
"Dollar Hits Two-Year High Versus Yen"
"Credibility of WTO at Stake in Trade Talks"
"U.S. GDP Growth Slows While Fed Fears Inflation Growth"

If this seems like gibberish to you, then you are in good company. To most people, the language of economics is mysterious, intimidating, impenetrable. But with economic forces profoundly influencing our daily lives, being familiar with the ideas and principles of business and economics is vital to our welfare. From fluctuating interest rates to rising gasoline prices to corporate misconduct to the vicissitudes of the stock market to the rippling effects of protests and strikes overseas or natural disasters closer to home, "the economy" is not an abstraction. As Robert Duvall, president and CEO of the National Council on Economic Education, has forcefully argued, "Young people in our country need to know that economic education is not an option. Economic literacy is a vital skill, just as vital as reading literacy."[1] Understanding economics is a skill that will help you interpret current events that are playing out on a global scale, or in your checkbook, ultimately helping you make wiser choices about how you manage your financial resources—today and tomorrow.

It is the goal of this series, Greenwood Guides to Business and Economics, to promote economic literacy and improve economic decision-making. All seven books in the series are written for the general reader, high school and college student, or the business manager, entrepreneur, or graduate student in business and economics looking for a handy refresher. They have been written by experts in their respective fields for nonexpert readers. The approach throughout is at a "basic" level to maximize understanding and demystify how our business-driven economy really works.

Each book in the series is an essential guide to the topic of that volume, providing an introduction to its respective subject area. The series as a whole constitutes a library of information, up-to-date data, definitions of terms, and resources, covering all aspects of economic activity. Volumes feature such elements as timelines, glossaries, and examples and illustrations that bring the concepts to life and present them in a historical and cultural context.

The selection of the seven titles and their authors has been the work of an Editorial Advisory Board, whose members are the following: Alan Carsrud, Florida International University; Alan Reynolds, Cato Institute; Robert Spich, University of California, Los Angeles; Wesley Truitt, Loyola Marymount University; Walter E. Williams, George Mason University; and Charles Wolf Jr., RAND Corporation.

As series editor, I served as chairman of the Editorial Advisory Board and want to express my appreciation to each of these distinguished individuals for their dedicated service in helping to bring this important series to reality.

The seven volumes in the series are as follows:

*The Corporation* by Wesley B. Truitt, Loyola Marymount University

*Entrepreneurship* by Alan L. Carsrud, Florida International University

*Globalization* by Robert Spich and Christopher Thornberg, UCLA

*Income and Wealth* by Alan Reynolds, Cato Institute

*Money* by Mark Dobeck and Euel Elliott, University of Texas at Dallas

*The National Economy* by Bradley A. Hansen, University of Mary Washington

*The Stock Market* by Rik W. Hafer, Southern Illinois University–Edwardsville, and Scott E. Hein, Texas Tech University

Special thanks to our senior editor at Greenwood, Nick Philipson, for conceiving the idea of the series and for sponsoring it within Greenwood Press.

The overriding purpose of each of these books and the series as a whole is, as Walter Williams so aptly put it, to "push back the frontiers of ignorance."

Wesley B. Truitt, Series Editor

**NOTE**

1. Quoted in Gary H. Stern, "Do We Know Enough about Economics?" *The Region*, Federal Reserve Bank of Minneapolis (December 1998).

# Introduction

We are all prone to draw invidious comparisons between ourselves and our neighbors. Such comparisons give us much edifying satisfaction when they can be twisted to our advantage.
—Wesley Clair Mitchell, *The Backward Art of Spending Money* (1937)

This is a book about the *growth* and *distribution* of income and wealth in the United States. It is about who earns what, who owns what, and why. And it is about how income and wealth have or have not changed over the years.

Growth relates to improvement in living standards over various periods of time. It has been widely reported, for example, that average wages did not rise at all for twenty-five or thirty years in real terms, after adjusting for inflation. And it has been widely reported that typical household income or wealth did not rise for just as many years. Such statements appear continually in newspapers, magazines, academic books and articles as if they were unquestionable facts. Yet they are actually just estimates. And because such estimates are often contradicted by other statistics, it takes some effort to find out why.

What is described as "average" is not necessarily typical. What is described as a household or family may be one person or many. What should or should not be counted as income, wages, or wealth is remarkably controversial and critically important. How wages and wealth are adjusted for inflation can make a huge difference. So can the choice of years being compared, such as starting with a cyclical peak like 1979 and ending near recession, such as 2002.

In addition to tackling many tricky questions about the growth of average incomes, the issue of income distribution or inequality also involves concepts and statistics that will need to be more carefully examined than they usually are.

You may have read that "real average family income" has barely increased for many years, or that all the gains went to the top 10 percent. But words such as "real," "average," "family" and "income" have several different meanings, and it turns out to matter quite a lot which ones we use.

You may have read that corporate chief executive officers (CEOs) earn 500 times as much as an average worker, or even 1000 times as much. But where did those figures come from? Are the "averages" really typical of either CEOs or workers? These are the types of questions we will be grappling with, but it is just a tiny sampling.

The book is literally crammed full of quotations from the popular press and from academic economists. This is not just because I am notoriously irritable and argumentative; I would argue irritably with anyone who would say such a thing. Actually, the quotations are to show that this is no arcane academic issue, but something that is often on the front page of the nation's leading newspapers, the cover story of major magazines, and a favorite topic of the nation's most influential columnists and editorial writers. Using their actual words and numbers seems fairer than paraphrasing and makes it clear that such words and numbers have been used by real people rather than "straw men."

Quotations from real people should help place the arguments and evidence in the context in which income and wealth statistics are most often presented—namely, as marketing devices intended to *persuade* people to support various sorts of advice about government policies.

Such policy persuasion runs the gamut from banning imports and immigrants on the right, to capping incomes earned in disfavored occupations (corporate CEOs) on the left. Ever since I first began writing about economic issues in 1971, it often seemed as though "income distribution" was the trump card most often played to obstruct or promote public policies, regardless of other merits or defects those policies might have. If environmentalists argue for increasing taxes on gasoline to discourage waste, they are sure to be opposed by interest groups arguing this would place a disproportionate burden on the poor. If health specialists argue for a higher tax on cigarettes that too will be opposed by interest groups arguing that cigarette taxes are unfair because poor people are more inclined to smoke. If tax specialists devise a reform likely to reduce inefficient distortions and disincentives, somebody is sure to trot out a crude "distribution table" suggesting the program must be thwarted because it might leave someone better-off.[1]

The reasons people give for supporting public policies always sound high-minded, but such salesmanship is not always entirely candid. Ethanol producers might actually be greens in disguise, but that may not be the real reason they spend so much lobbying for ethanol subsidies. As Richard Wagner suggested, "the creation and operation of public programs is guided less by wishes and high motives than by interests and strong motives."[2]

## INEQUALITY REDEFINED

Most income is earned or stolen—not "distributed." A tiny fraction *is* distributed by means-tested government transfers (mostly Medicaid, not cash), but it accounts for less than 10 percent of the federal budget. So what is this "income distribution" story all about?

Expressing concern about income inequality is not at all the same as being concerned about poverty. Everyone except Ebenezer Scrooge is concerned about poverty, and he was a fictional character. To be terribly concerned about inequality allows a person to be absolutely indifferent about whether an apparent increase in inequality is because too many Americans are becoming rich because some became poorer.

Recent academic studies about income inequality have been almost entirely devoted to income distribution *within* the top 10 percent or top 1 percent—how the extremely rich have been racing ahead of the merely very rich.[3] This is something quite new and seemingly rather odd.

In the early 1970s (I first joined this debate in a *New York Times* op ed in 1972), the issue of income distribution was almost entirely focused on those *below the poverty line* or in the *bottom fifth* of the income distribution. "We have virtually nothing to say about the very rich," Christopher Jencks wisely wrote in the radical 1972 book *Inequality*, because "their incomes have a negligible effect on statistical analysis of income distribution."[4] It was not about hurting the rich but helping the poor.

In 1988, Frank Levy's *Dollars and Dreams* continued to define the income distribution issue mainly in terms of difficulties facing those *at the bottom*. "Much of the growing inequality," he wrote, "was due to the continued increase in female-headed families, a trend which redefined the nature of the lowest quintile. But after 1979, inequality was reinforced by a deep recession and declining means-tested benefits, both of which undermined the lowest quintiles. . . . In the bottom quintile 44 percent of families now have no earner."[5]

Starting around 1992, however, inequality began to be *redefined* in such a way that nearly all the attention shifted away from the troubles of the bottom quintile to the high incomes of increasingly tiny number of people at the top. Some economists began using a sample of income-tax data to focus on increases in income among the top 1 percent of taxpayers (now about 1.3 million). Others fretted over the stock option windfalls of 100–500 top corporate executives. If poor people were mentioned at all, it seemed an afterthought. By 2006 the "national income" pie was being sliced into wafer-thin slices. Nearly all of us—between 80 and 99 percent—were supposedly being victimized in some inexplicable way by the earnings and stock market gains of the top one-hundredth of one percent (0.01%), or 13,000.

Before we assume that the existence of a very small number of very rich people poses a problem for anyone else, it might help to think about any actual super-rich person and then ask ourselves how that person's affluence detracts in any way from the living standards of anyone else.

The two young founders of Google, Larry Page and Sergey Brin, quickly made something like $12 billion each by greatly facilitating our information, education, and shopping efficiency. Why should anyone care how much money the founders of Google, Apple, or Microsoft made? Some might object that they earned a larger *share* of income, but in what sense can we regard *their* income as shared? Google is something new—without Google there could be no income from Google. The Google founders have their income and you have yours. What they earn has nothing to do with how much or little you can earn, except that their inventions may help you earn more (personally, I feel as though I owe them a really big check).

The new emphasis on shares of income earned by the very highest income groups appears to reflect zero-sum reasoning—as if one person's gains must be at someone else's expense. Real income is regarded as a given amount, which might just as well be divided up this way or that.

The authors of *The State of Working America* write as though there was some sort of fixed salary pool: "Much more of the nation's salary income became concentrated at the top, leaving less to be divided among the larger work force."[6] *New York Times* columnist Paul Krugman says, "if the rich get more, that leaves less for everyone else."[7] Discussing changes in wealth over time, Edward Wolff wrote that "middle-aged households gained at the expense of both younger and older households" and therefore referred to the young and old as "less privileged age cohorts"—as though one person's savings must be at someone else's expense, and the young had been denied the privilege of becoming middle-aged.[8]

All of these comments imply that some people can improve their living standards only at the expense of others. Yet there is no reason to suppose that a raise or promotion for Smith will somehow result in a pay cut or job loss for Jones. If greater numbers of people end up earning higher salaries by acquiring valuable skills in college or on the job, that does not "leave less to be divided" among others. If more entrepreneurs start successful new businesses, that does not "leave less for everyone else."

## A PREVIEW

The following chapters demonstrate that popular and academic discussions of income and wealth inequality and wage stagnation have often been muddled by misunderstanding of a few basic concepts and measurements.

The first chapter deals with concepts and measures. When we read that something happened to the real incomes of average households, it turns out to matter quite a lot what is or is not counted as income, and exactly how income was adjusted for inflation. The mix of "households" now includes many more young and elderly singles than in the past, which understates the gains in household income. Top income groups have no ceiling so the mean average is much higher than typical (median) income. When comparing median rather than mean averages, the increase in real income from 1989 to 2004 was no faster in the top 10 percent than it was in the bottom 20 percent or bottom 40 percent.

The second chapter is mostly about work. When households are sorted by income into higher and lower fifths, we find the top fifth has nearly six times as many full-time workers as the bottom fifth. Substantial differences in incomes are largely explained by the number of workers per household, their age, and education. Some figures from the Census Bureau and Congressional Budget Office help unravel recent claims that 80–99 percent of Americans have experienced no increase in real income since 1973.

The third chapter looks into perennial reports that the middle-class is shrinking. The percentage of households earning an inflation-adjusted income between $30,000 and $50,000 has indeed gone down over the past—thirty to forty years, but the increased percentage earning more than $50,000 is even larger. A larger percentage of Americans earning more income is frequently confused with the rich getting richer, although it actually means more people are getting rich. The bar defining the amount of money needed to be counted among the top 20 percent was pushed up, which naturally raises the average of income above that higher bar.

The fourth chapter questions the frequently repeated claim that average real wages have not increased since 1973. That "average weekly wage" mixes part-time and full-time jobs together and then adjusts that mish-mosh with an old price index known to exaggerate inflation. Average real wages and benefits rose by 40 percent from 1973 to 2004.[9] The broadest measures of living standards—real consumption per person—increased by 74 percent from 1980 to 2004.

The fifth chapter about the "top 1 percent" (in terms of income) is perhaps the most difficult but definitely the most important. Estimates of the rising share of income earned by the top 1.3 million taxpayers come from a sample of individual income-tax returns. But such estimates cannot be compared before and after 1986 because massive changes in tax laws changed what is reported as income to the IRS. Billions in business income was shifted from the corporate to the individual tax return, and most middle-income savings have moved off the tax return into tax-deferred accounts. Most studies exclude rising income from Social Security and other transfer payments, which further exaggerates the amount and the growth of income at the top 1 percent. Between 1986 and 2003, however, there was no clear upward trend in the income share of the top 1 percent.

The sixth chapter relates to the fifth, because stock options of CEOs were a trendy explanation for the top 1 percent's rising income share while stock prices soared from 1996 to 2000. But incomes of the top 100–500 CEOs fell by 48–53 percent from 2000 to 2003, according to two critics of CEO pay. Stock options distributed broadly among millions of *nonexecutives* are a much more plausible explanation of why the taxable incomes of 1.3 million taxpayers (like that of a few hundred CEOs) rose and fell with stock prices. Claims that average CEO pay is 400–1000 times as much as that of average workers have been based on appalling estimates. Stock options have nothing to do with wage inequality anyway, because the cost of stock options is borne entirely by stockholders, not workers.

The seventh chapter is about the distribution of wealth. A rising percentage of families with a net worth above $1 million indicates that wealth is becoming more widely dispersed. A rising percentage of families own stocks, and homes and valuable "human capital" (college degrees). Older people always have the most *financial* capital because it takes many years to accumulate wealth and because we need savings to supplement our rapidly depreciating *human* capital.

The eighth chapter introduces inequality of *consumption* as a better measure of living standards than one year's income. People can consume out of past income (savings) or future income (debt), or with in-kind transfer payments such as Medicaid and food stamps. Gini coefficients show from 1986 to 2001 consumption inequality declined and wage inequality was unchanged. Two major press reports in 2005 suggesting income mobility had diminished were based on scanty evidence shown to be incorrect. Studies comparing differences in the earnings of siblings indicate that inequalities between U.S. families do not persist for even one generation.

Chapter nine deals with "causes and cures"—that is, with various proposals to fix wage or income inequality, usually by the indirect approach of tinkering with the job market. Before the doctor can cure something, it usually helps to figure out if the patient is sick and if so what the disease might be. In this case, many proposed cures seem totally disconnected with the assumed causes. They seem based on some oft-repeated mythology about the good old days when more men got their hands dirty and more women sat at a sewing machine all day.

In reality, the loss of manufacturing jobs in recent years was greater in Japan, Germany and China than in the United States. And U.S. manufactured output has doubled since 1979. The fastest-growing service jobs pay much better than manufacturing jobs. And labor's share of national income was no higher in those good old days when more workers belonged to unions.

The textbook trade-off between "equity and efficiency" is really about incentives and economic growth. And that trade-off can be huge. It is doubtless true that income in fast-growing economies like India, China, and South Korea is now "distributed" (earned) far less equally than in such dismal places as Ethiopia, Burundi, and Tanzania where there is very little income to distribute. But it is doubtful that anyone in India or China thinks Ethiopia or Burundi made the better trade-off.

That was just a very small sampling of what lies ahead. There is more, much more.

Some readers will doubtless be tempted to pigeonhole all nine chapters into a single word or two. If that is unavoidable, alas, then the correct word would not be liberal or conservative but "skeptical." I accept nothing as an article of faith. I want to hear the logic and see the evidence. And you should demand nothing less. In the absence of logic and evidence you should not give a hoot about my opinion. Reality is not a matter of opinion. Raw opinion is like math errors or typos—understandable human error, but uninformative. To err is human, to understand is hard work.

## NOTES

1. Distribution tables are terribly static, partial equilibrium exercises, which assume nobody reacts to taxes and are therefore useless for long-run analysis. An example in Chapter Nine uses capital taxes to show how much this matters. See Kevin A. Hassett and R. Glenn Hubbard, eds., *Inequality and Tax Policy* (Washington, DC: The AEI Press, 2001).

2. Richard E. Wagner, *To Promote the General Welfare* (San Francisco: Pacific Research Institute, 1980), p. 17.

3. Hilary Hoynes and Nada Eissa are rare exceptions. For example, see Hilary W. Hoynes, Marianne E. Page, and Ann Huff Stevens, "Poverty in America: Trends and Explanations," *Journal of Economic Literature* Vol. XLIV(2) (Winter 2006); and Nada Eissa's home page: http://www.georgetown.edu/faculty/noe/.

4. Christopher Jencks et al., *Inequality: A Reassessment of the Effect of Family and Schooling in America* (New York: Basic Books, 1972), p. 13.

5. Frank Levy, *Dollars and Dreams* (New York: W.W. Norton, 1988), pp. 197–98.

6. Lawrence Mishel, Jared Bernstein, and Sylvia Allegretto, *The State of Working America, 2004–2005* (Washington, DC: Economic Policy Institute, 2005), p. 60.

7. Paul Krugman, "For Richer: How the Permissive Capitalism of the Boom Destroyed American Equality," *New York Times Magazine*, October 20, 2002.

8. Edward N. Wolff, *Top Heavy* (New York: Twentieth Century Fund Press, 1998), pp. 15–16.

9. Real compensation per hour, nonfarm business sector. Economics Report of the President: 2006, Table B-49.

# One

# Concepts and Measures

The control of statistics is one of the critical functions of power in a democratic society. The numbers define the limits of the possible; they confer the awesome mathematical legitimacy of "fact" upon some parts of reality and deny it to others.
—Michael Harrington, *The New American Poverty* (1984)

It often seems difficult to pick up a newspaper without being confronted with some depressing new statistic or study purporting to show how little real incomes have grown for average families, or how huge a share of income or wealth went to the top 1 percent or top 10 percent. Such statistics are rarely as clear or simple as they may seem. They are sometimes quite deceptive, but in complex ways not easy to discover. This chapter introduces a few basic concepts and measurement techniques and shows how the facts can vary greatly depending on various ways of defining real income, or family, or "average."

Suppose you picked up the newspaper and read that "average income among working families barely increased at all in real terms from 1979 to 2002." That seems like a perfectly straightforward factual statement, and a shocking one. Whether or not it is an *accurate* and *meaningful* statement, however, depends on five subtle details:

- What does "average" mean? A *median* average means half earn more and half less. A *mean* average simply adds up everyone's income and divides by the number of families. Neither average is necessarily typical.

- What does "working" mean? Some people work part-time, or for only a few months in the summer, or both. It dilutes the average if their incomes are combined with full-time, full-year workers.
- What does "family" mean? In some studies a family can mean just one person. In other studies a family can mean anyone filing an individual income-tax return, which might be four people in one family (my eldest granddaughter filed a tax return at age 5) or it might be a law firm, hedge fund, or bank.
- What does "real" income mean? To convert *nominal* income or wages into *real* income or wages in different year we need to divide today's dollar figure by some price index. The consumer price index (CPI-U) is notorious for *overstating* inflation and therefore *understating* real gains in income or wealth.
- What does the choice of years mean? 1979 was a cyclical peak followed by three years of inflationary recession; 2002 was the first year after a recession and terrorist attack. Any weakness in income between those dates was partly *cyclical* rather than a secular trend, and concentrated in 1980–1982 rather than later.

Even the seemingly simple task of comparing average real income over a period of years turns out to involve several complex concepts and measurement problems. It is not as easy as it looks. As one of my teachers used to say, "If economics is that simple why do we pay professors to teach it to our kids?"

Getting the numbers right is not a matter of trivial nitpicking. Consider the issue of which price index to use when estimating the growth of real income or wages over a long period of years. The familiar consumer price index from the Bureau of Labor Statistics (BLS) appears to show the cost of living rising by 222 percent from 1977 to 2005. But the same index has been updated to today's higher statistical standards starting with 1977, and that updated consumer price index (CPI-U-RS) shows only a 184 percent rise through 2005.[1] The BLS has also been developing an even better "chain-weighted" CPI since 2000, but it is too new to be of much use. Chain-weighted means that if people switch from buying apples to oranges when the price of apples goes up then apples will be considered less important (get a smaller weight) in the index. The Commerce Department's Bureau of Economic Analysis (BEA) has a similar chain-weighted index for personal consumption expenditures (PCE deflator), and it shows an even smaller 175 percent rise from 1977 to 2005. In calculating overall growth of real income or wages from 1977 to 2005, the "real" gain would be understated by 38–47 percent if using the CPI-U rather than either of the two updated measures of inflation. That is not exactly small change. There is really no excuse for using the old CPI-U (or its narrower cousin, CPI-W) to measure long-term changes in real income or wages except laziness or intent to deceive. Whenever you find "real" income or wages being defined in terms of the archaic CPI in this book, that is because somebody else presented the numbers that way and I was too lazy to redo them. But you can redo them yourself.

Most price indexes and many other statistics can be found in the online version of the *Economic Report of the President*.[2] To convert a median weekly wage of $262 for the year 1980 into the purchasing power of the year 2000, just find the PCE deflator of 52.078 for 1980 from table B-7. Divide $262 by 52.078 then multiply by 100 and the 1980 wage of $262 becomes $503 in 2000 dollars.

Some of the same questions raised about the real growth of average incomes also apply to the distribution of incomes. Whenever you come across dramatic statistics about the distribution of average family income, ask what is meant by average, family, and income. And watch to see if the dates being compared are between cyclical high points and cyclical slumps. Income distribution tends to be equalized by recessions, because stock market losses and business failures reduce top incomes even more than the lowest incomes. Unlike statistics about income growth (which begin with cyclical booms), select statistics about income distribution may begin with recession years in order to demonstrate how rising stock prices and prosperity cause "inequality."

But there are many more subtle complexities, involving assumptions and estimates, which often makes it a big chore to figure out how various income distribution figures were spun. It can be fun, though, like solving a mystery.

## QUIZZICAL QUINTILES

When people express concern about increasing inequality, they mean the average income among, say, the top 10 or 20 percent has grown more rapidly than average income among the bottom 20 percent (quintile) or bottom 10 percent (decile), thus leaving the top group with a larger percentage share of total incomes of everyone in the country.

But "average" income can be measured in different ways. An arithmetic or "mean" average simply adds up all the income and divides by the number of households or families in each group (such as the bottom 25 percent, or quartile). A "median" average is a mid-point—the point at which half of the group earns more and half earns less.

How income is "distributed" (earned) among families depends on how we choose to measure income, family, and income distribution. There are many different choices, and they can make a big difference.

Most discussions of income distribution are based on dividing households, families, workers, or taxpayers into groups, such as the top and bottom "quintiles" (fifths). The total income in each quintile is then divided by the number of, say, households to arrive at a *mean* (not median) average for each group.

What do we mean by income? The most commonly reported figures exclude transfer payments (such as Social Security and Medicaid) and taxes. They refer hypothetically to what income distribution would be if the government did not take money from some people and give it to others (and if doing so had no effect on incentives to earn and report income).

What do we mean by family? In Census Bureau terminology a family consists of two or more related individuals living together, such as mother and son, husband and wife, or two young sisters sharing an apartment. A household, however, can consist of one "unrelated individual" living alone. Single-person households have, in fact, become increasingly common in recent years and particularly prevalent within the lower income groups. In some studies, including the Federal Reserve's Survey of Consumer Finances (SCF), singles are counted as "single-person families" rather than as households. That can be confusing. What appears to be a low-income "family" in some statistics may be a college student who receives uncounted gifts from parents.

Table 1.1 shows that the composition of households and families changed quite dramatically over just two decades. As a result, what may at first appear to be a worrisome trend in some measures of the growth or distribution of incomes can often be partly explained by changing demographics. The fact that more people are postponing marriage until they are older than 30 creates more "single, nonelderly" households, for example. And the fact that the population is rapidly aging creates more "single elderly" households. Very young and very old single people typically have lower incomes than

**TABLE 1.1**
**Distribution of Persons by Family Type**

|                                | 1981 (%) | 2001 (%) |
|--------------------------------|----------|----------|
| Single nonelderly              | 5.1      | 7.1      |
| Single elderly                 | 3.0      | 4.1      |
| Nonelderly couples             | 16.6     | 16.5     |
| Elderly couples                | 7.2      | 6.6      |
| Married couples with children  | 51.3     | 43.0     |
| Single-mother families         | 6.4      | 6.0      |
| Other families with children   | 4.7      | 8.4      |
| Other families without children| 5.6      | 8.5      |

*Source:* http://www.bls.gov/opub/mlr/2005/04/art2abs.htm.

middle-aged, college-educated married couples. But the cost of living is generally lower for single people, so real income per capita (per person) will rise more than real income per household when a rising share of households consists of one person. Because singles and elderly couples now account for a larger share of households than they did two or three decades ago, that change in demographics alone can make it appear as though there are more lower-income households. But such comparisons across decades have to be handled with care, because the meaning of "families" changes over time.

Changes in median *household* income—the income level in the middle, with half of the households above and half below—are the figures that news reports typically use when discussing growth of "family" incomes.

Figure 1.1 shows that the real, inflation-adjusted median income among four-person *families* is significantly larger than median "household" income and has also grown at a substantially faster pace. There is also less inequality of family income than of household income, as will be shown later in this chapter. We cannot use median household income to describe typical "families," even if the meaning of "typical family" was clearer than it is. Because households include far fewer four-person families (two parents and two children) than in the past, and many more one-person households, the apparently slower growth of median *household* income has become increasingly misleading. Income growth among "traditional families" has clearly been stronger than the household figures suggest. But income growth among one-person households may also have been stronger than the household figures suggest. It is the changing mixture of one-person and multiperson households that makes it unavoidably misleading to compare household incomes over many years.

In *Consumption and Social Welfare*, Daniel Slesnick of the University of Texas notes, "Median family income is a reasonable index of social welfare only if the family in the middle of the income distribution is representative of the entire population."[3] *Newsweek* columnist Robert Samuelson explains, "The median household was once imagined as a family of Mom, Dad, and two kids. But "typical" no longer exists. There are more singles, childless couples, and retirees. Smaller households tend to have lower incomes. They drag down the overall median. So do more poor immigrant households."[4]

The addition of large numbers of poor, uneducated immigrants in recent years must have the statistical effect of making the U.S. poverty rate higher than it would otherwise be, for example, regardless of its impact on wages of less-skilled native-born Americans. Immigration of young people who have not completed high school also has the statistical effect of making high-school "dropout" rates look much higher than otherwise, although many

**FIGURE 1.1**
**Real Median Income of 4-Person Families and Households**
**1975–2003**

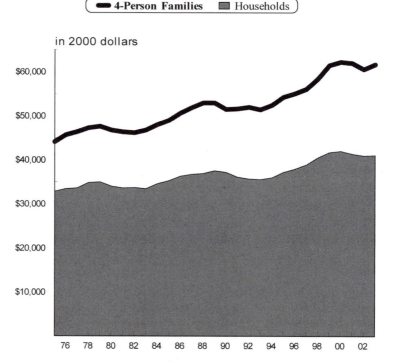

*Note:* Adjusted for Inflation with PCE Deflator.
*Source:* http://www.census.gov/hhes/income/4person.html.

such youths never attended school in the United States. This does not mean low-income immigration is undesirable for the immigrants themselves or for those who are not foreign-born. It simply means we have to take this effect into account when examining statistics. If many more low-income people moved into the city where you live, for example, that must make the city's average income lower than otherwise. Yet it need not have any effect at all on your income or that of your neighbors. Even median averages can mislead. And mean averages are often more misleading.

## KEEPING THE GINI IN THE BOTTLE

Several statistical measures attempt to summarize the degree of inequality with a single number, but do so with substantial ambiguity.[5] The most popular of such summary measures is the Gini coefficient devised by

Corrado Gini in 1912. It is derived from the Lorenz curve devised by Max Lorenz in 1905. The Lorenz curve is a graph with the cumulative share of households or families on the horizontal axis, starting with the 20 percent (quintile) with the lowest income, then the second lowest, and so on. The vertical axis shows the cumulative share of the quintiles' total income, 0–100 percent.

Perfect equality would mean that the first 20 percent of households would receive 20 percent of all income, 40 percent would receive 40 percent, and so on. Each quintile would have 20 percent of the income. In that case of perfect equality, the Lorenz curve would not be a curve at all—it would be a diagonal, 45-degree line. In reality, however, actual distribution of income and wealth have never been equal in any society. So the Lorenz curve is always *shaped like a bow*. Think of the curve as a bow and perfect equality (the diagonal line) as the string of the bow.

Figure 1.2 draws a Lorenz curve for pretax, pretransfer money income of U.S. households (not families). The relative size of the bowed Lorenz curve underneath the diagonal line, when compared with the total triangle below that straight line, is the Gini coefficient (also called the Gini index or ratio). The wider the gap between the bow and the string, the larger is the Gini coefficient and the greater is the degree of inequality according to this measure.

Once you find the shares of income earned by each of the five quintiles from www.census.gov, there are online calculators that will convert those figures into a single Gini coefficient.[6]

Those coefficients are calculated in pretransfer, pretax terms, which we could call the "conventional" measure. Yet the Census Bureau has calculated fourteen other Gini coefficients going back to 1979 by adding various transfer payments and subtracting various taxes. For simplicity, we will focus on the conventional measure of money income and the second-broadest measure "postransfer aftertax income."

The conventional figure shows the U.S. Gini coefficient for households rising from 0.425 in 1986 to 0.466 in 2004 (largely because of the 1993 sampling changes), which is why many economists and journalists believe there was an indisputably large increase in inequality between those years.

"The standard measure of inequality is the Gini coefficient," wrote Dan Seligman of *Forbes*. Citing one of several Gini coefficients he concluded, "The reality is that measured inequality has been rising steadily for close to thirty years and hit successive new highs in the Carter, Reagan, elder Bush and Clinton administrations before doing the exact same thing under the younger Bush." Seligman added, "It rose more under Clinton—from 0.433 to 0.462—than under any of those other chaps." Both Republicans and

**FIGURE 1.2**

**Lorenz Curve for U.S. Households, Pretax & Pretransfer Money Income, 2004**

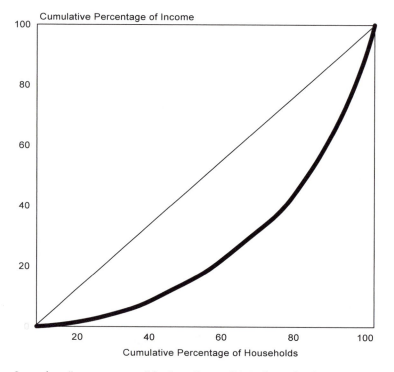

Cumulative Percentage of Households

*Source:* http://www.census.gov/hhes/www/income/histinc/h02ar.html.

Democrats abuse inequality statistics to score political points, as can also be seen by equally dubious references to the Reagan Administration throughout this book. It is usually prudent to assume such politicized statistics are highly suspect.

Mr. Seligman's comment results from comparing Gini coefficients before and after 1993, for example, when Mr. Clinton took office. But in that same year, as the Economic Policy Institute (EPI) points out, "a change in survey methodology led to a sharp rise in measured inequality."[7] The Census Bureau changed its sampling methods in ways designed to collect more data on high incomes, which makes it disingenuous to compare Gini coefficients before and after 1993. From 1993 to 2004, the conventional Gini coefficient increased very little—from 0.454 in 1993 to 0.459 in 1997 and 0.466 in 2004.[8] The Gini for families increased even less—from 0.429 in 1993 to 0.438 in 2004. Although the conventional Gini appeared to rise "more under

Clinton," that was a statistical illusion caused by a major change in the way the survey was conducted.

One of the most commonly repeated statements about this topic is, as Leonard Burman of the Urban Institute put it, that "the trend toward rising inequality has continued unabated."[9]

Judged by more than one Gini coefficient, however, the evidence of rising inequality since the mid-1980s is somewhat ambiguous. Top income shares are highly cyclical, particularly if income includes capital gains from stock trading, so some measures of inequality appear to "worsen" after recessions end.

The widespread belief in the existence of a long-term trend toward inequality will be explored from various angles throughout the book. The following chapter, in fact, offers several demographic reasons why we should have expected the income gap between top and bottom quintiles to widen over time. In this and other chapters, however, we will also discover that whether or not there has actually been a relentless "trend toward rising inequality" largely depends on (1) how we choose to measure real income or consumption, (2) which dates we choose to compare, (3) whether we measure the income of the top quintile by using a mean or median average, and (4) whether or not we take account of the change in Census sampling in 1993 and some distortions created by the 1986 tax reform.

Table 1.2 shows the Census Bureau's estimated Gini ratios for households and families from 1992 to 2004, before transfer payments are added to incomes at the bottom or taxes are removed at the top. Note that inequality is greater for households than families by this measure. But neither series shows much upward movement for a dozen years—aside from that one-time jump in 1993 caused by a change in sampling methods.

As is customary, the figures in Table 1.2 do not account for taxes and transfer payments. The Census Bureau's broadest measure of income, which does adjust for taxes and transfers, greatly reduces the household Gini coefficient to 0.40 in 2004.[10] Since the table shows that family income is more equal than household income, a Gini coefficient for families would be much lower than 0.40 if transfer payments and taxes were taken into account.

When the household Gini coefficient is adjusted for transfers and taxes, there is no clear upward trend over relatively prosperous recent years (that is, aside from the "equalizing" stagflation of 1980–1981). It was 0.409 in 1986, 0.408 in 1989, 0.412 in 2001, and 0.394 in 2002 and 2003.[11] Since the 1993 "change in survey methodology led to a sharp rise in measured inequality," as the EPI explained, the fact that the post-tax, post-transfer Gini index was lower in 2003 than it was in 1989 is one reason to question claims that "the trend toward rising inequality has continued unabated."

**TABLE 1.2**
**Census Bureau Gini Ratios for Pretax, Pretransfer Money Income**

| Year | Households | Families |
|------|-----------|----------|
| 2004 | .466 | .438 |
| 2003 | .464 | .436 |
| 2002 | .466 | .434 |
| 2001 | .462 | .435 |
| 2000 | .458 | .433 |
| 1999 | .456 | .429 |
| 1998 | .459 | .430 |
| 1997 | .455 | .429 |
| 1996 | .450 | .425 |
| 1995 | .456 | .421 |
| 1994 | .456 | .426 |
| 1993 | .454 | .429 |
| 1992 | .433 | .404 |

*Source:* http://www.census.gov/hhes/www/income/histinc/histinctb .html.

A Gini coefficient based on what consumers spend shows much less inequality than any measure based on a snapshot of annual income (which may be temporarily high or low). A Bureau of Labor Statistics study estimates that the Gini coefficient for consumption spending was only 0.316 in 1986 and it *fell* to 0.307 by 2001.[12] This measure also casts some doubt on the view that such broad measures of inequality have continually increased, although there may be other measures that support that view.

All summary measures, such as the Gini index, can be misleading. As a Census Bureau study points out,

The Gini index...is more sensitive to changes in the middle of the earnings distribution rather than the tails. This is because it is derived from the Lorenz curve, which expresses the relationship between the cumulated percentage of aggregate earnings and the cumulated percentage of earners. An increase or decrease in earnings in the middle of the distribution will have a greater impact on the measure than a similar change at either end since there are more earners in the middle ranks.[13]

Similarly, Anthony Atkinson of the London School of Economics also noted, "the Gini coefficient attaches more weight to transfers affecting middle income classes."[14] Since transfers are often not even counted in the United States, however, that point may be moot.

Gini indexes are often used to compare inequality between countries, so the fact that the U.S. government is unique in providing most targeted aid to the poor in the form of *in-kind benefits* (such as Medicaid, food stamps, and housing allowances) and a nominal "refund" for taxes not paid (the EITC) can greatly distort international comparisons unless such in-kind benefits are counted as income (as they rarely are).

Even if Gini indexes did account for all transfer payments and taxes they would nonetheless suffer serious flaws. Two Lorenz curves can have quite *different shapes,* for example, yet still yield the same Gini coefficient.

Alan Blinder of Princeton University used the figures in Table 1.3 to show how two quite different distributions of income could nonetheless produce the same Gini index.[15] Distribution B in the third column is no less egalitarian than Distribution A, if we take the Gini coefficient seriously, yet the fact that the top quintile has a smaller share under Distribution B would be of little comfort to the lowest quintile, which also has a smaller share. Table 1.3 illustrates why concern about "inequality" is not at all the same as concern about the poor.

The switch from Distribution A to Distribution B is not just hypothetical. The share of income going to both the bottom quintile and the top 5 percent fell between 2000 and 2003, because both the highest and lowest incomes are particularly vulnerable to recession (in 2001). A top Bush Administration official proudly described that cyclical setback as "a decline in inequality," which was somewhat ludicrous despite being technically and politically correct.[16]

Another serious but little-noticed problem with Gini indexes is also common to all discussions about the share of income going to top income groups, such as the top 1, 5, 10, or 20 percent. These income shares are *mean* averages, not medians. A mean is not a meaningful average of income in top groups; it does not represent what is typical of the group and it

**TABLE 1.3**
**Comparison of Income Distributions Producing the Same Gini Index**

| Income Share of | Distribution A (%) | Distribution B (%) |
| --- | --- | --- |
| Lowest quintile | 3.6 | 0.6 |
| Second quintile | 8.9 | 11.9 |
| Middle quintile | 15.0 | 15.0 |
| Fourth quintile | 23.2 | 26.2 |
| Top quintile | 49.4 | 46.4 |
| Approximate GINI | 0.423 | 0.423 |

*Source:* Alan Blinder, Princeton University.

cannot be properly compared with average income in the lower four quintiles.

## MEAN INCOME MISLEADS

When national income is divided into quintiles, or into smaller groups such as the top 10 percent, the figures always refer to *mean* averages within each group. This turns out to be quite misleading when comparing top income groups to the others because the mean income of top groups (unlike other groups) is much larger than the median.

Dividing people into lower and higher classes involves an ordinal ranking from zero to the very highest income. When estimating a *central tendency* for top income groups with this sort of data, a *mean* average is inappropriate. A *median* average would be a far better way of describing what is normal or typical for the whole group.[17] This is *not* a problem for the bottom four quintiles, because (as Table 1.4 shows) the mean average in those groups is very close to the median.

Income *within* the top 1, 5, 10, or 20 percent, by contrast, is not evenly distributed between a floor and ceiling because there is no ceiling. Most households in such top groups are clustered near the bottom of a wide range of incomes with a very small number at the upper tail of the distribution (above $1 million a year, for example). The distribution in top income group resembles a ski jump—with the high point of the jump starting at the lowest income defining the group and then quickly falling to become almost flat where incomes are very high. Many more households earn $200,000, for example, than the number earning $20 million, yet both are weighted equally within a mean average.

**TABLE 1.4**
**Before-Tax Household Income (in 2004 dollars)**

| Percentile of Income | 1989 Mean ($) | 1989 Median ($) | 2004 Mean ($) | 2004 Median ($) | % Change in Median 1989–2004 (%) |
|---|---|---|---|---|---|
| Less than 20% | 8,746 | 9,173 | 10,800 | 11,100 | 21.0 |
| 20–39.9 | 21,653 | 21,439 | 26,100 | 25,700 | 19.9 |
| 40–59.9 | 38,079 | 38,292 | 43,400 | 43,200 | 12.8 |
| 60–89.9 | 60,158 | 59,731 | 69,100 | 68,100 | 14.0 |
| 89–89.9 | 89,017 | 87,250 | 106,500 | 104,700 | 20.0 |
| Top 10% | 254,818 | 153,168 | 302,100 | 184,800 | 20.7 |

*Source:* Survey of Consumer Finances, http://www.federalreserve.gov/pubs/oss/oss2/scfindex.html. 1989 figures converted to 2004 dollars with CPI-U.

The mean average of income in any top income group is not comparable to the mean average in groups bounded by an upper and lower range, and is not really a meaningful average at all.

If average real income for some top income group rose by 10 percent in one year it would indicate that *some* households with higher incomes outweighed those with lower incomes. But it would *not* show that *most* members of that group earned 10 percent more, that "typical" members of the group earned 10 percent more, or that gains among those who did have higher earnings averaged 10 percent. Despite these serious anomalies, mean income within top groups nonetheless remains the precarious statistical foundation for *all* discussions of "inequality" of income and wealth.

Table 1.2, from the Federal Reserve Board's SCF, identifies both mean and median income by quintile (e.g., 20–39.9% is the second lowest quintile), with the top group split into two deciles of 10 percent each. Mean income for the top 10 percent is about two-thirds larger than median income, showing how mean averages *greatly exaggerate* the level of typical incomes of top income groups.

The last column of Table 1.4 shows changes in *median* real income from 1989 to 2004. Unlike the widely reported increases in *mean* income for top income groups, the 20.7 percent increase in *median* income for the top 10 percent was roughly the same as the increases in the poorest two quintiles (the bottom 40 percent). The sizable across-the-board increases in median income since the cyclical peak of 1989 indicate widespread economic progress despite recessions in 1990–1991 and 2001.

Median income for all households was $43,200 in 2004 according to the SCF, and mean income was $70,700. It would be extremely misleading to say the higher mean income describes an "average" family. Yet it is equally mistaken to say that a mean average describes an "average family" within the top 10 percent. That is because every top income group, such as the top 10 percent, encompasses a very wide range of incomes that starts from a relatively modest threshold level and rises to include a small number of astonishingly high incomes.

*New York* magazine's 2004 survey on who earns what in Manhattan identified three famous hedge fund managers who earned between $550 million and $1.02 billion. For that same year, the Census Bureau defined the top 5 percent of households (not families) as everyone earning more than $157,185. Blending together all incomes from $157,195 to $1,020,000,000 and then dividing that total by the number of households (113,146,000) produces a hodge-podge "average" of $264,387.[18] But such an "average" tells us virtually nothing about the *typical* level of income among those 5.7 million households. Mean averages also tell us virutally nothing about typical *increases* in income among those 5.7 million housheolds over a period of years.

Measuring the growth of incomes or the inequality of incomes is a little like Olympic figure skating—full of dangerous leaps and twirls and not nearly as easy as it looks. Yet the growth and inequality of incomes are topics that seem to inspire many people to form very strong opinions about very weak statistics. There will be ample room left for different opinons after we sort through a few more messy statistics. Since opinions are easy and facts are difficult, any opinons based on sound logic and honest evidence deserve considerable respect.

## NOTES

1. Bureau of Labor Statistics, "CPI Research Series Using Current Methods (CPI-U-RS)." http://www.bls.gov/cpi/cpirsdc.htm.

2. *Economic Report of the President* (Washington, DC: U.S. Government Printing Office, February 2006), tables B-16 and B-62. http://www.gpoaccess.gov/eop/.

3. Daniel T. Slesnick, *Consumption and Social Welfare* (New York: Cambridge University Press, 2001), p. 5.

4. Robert J. Samuelson, "The Changing Face of Poverty," *Newsweek*, October 18, 2004. http://www.msnbc.msn.com/id/6214398/site/newsweek/.

5. The Census Bureau provides variance of the log of income, mean logarithmic deviation of income, and Theil, Gini, and three Atkinson indexes. http://www.census.gov/hhes/www/income/histinc/ie6.html.

6. To calculate a Gini coefficient online with a free calculator, go to http://www.wessa.net/co.wasp *or* http://www.poorcity.richcity.org/calculator.htm.

7. Lawrence Mishel, Jared Bernstein, and Sylvia Allegretto, *The State of Working America 2004/2005* (Ithaca, NY: Cornell University Press, 2005), note to figure 1I, table 1.12, pp. 66–67.

8. U.S. Census Bureau, *Income, Poverty, and Health Insurance Coverage in the United States: 2004*, table A-3, p. 40.

9. Nell Henderson, "Income Gap Narrower by Treasury's Measure," *Washington Post*, March 23, 2006.

10. U.S. Census Bureau, "The Effects of Government Taxes and Transfers on Poverty: 2004" (February 8, 2005), table 2. http://www.census.gov/hhes/www/poverty/effect2004/effect2004.html.

11. U.S. Census Bureau, "Historical Income Tables—Experimental Measures" (December 20, 2005), table RDI-5 (Index of Income Concentration (Gini Index), by Definition of Income: 1979 to 2003). http://www.census.gov/hhes/www/income/histinc/rdi5.html.

12. David S. Johnson, Timothy M. Smeeding, and Barbara Boyle Torrey, "Economic Inequality through the Prisms of Income and Consumption," *Monthly Labor Review*, vol. 128(4) (April 2005), table 3. http://www.bls.gov/opub/mlr/2005/04/art2abs.htm.

13. U.S. Census Bureau, "Current Population Reports, Series P60-183," *Studies in the Distribution of Income* (Washington, D.C.: U.S. Government Printing Office, 1992), p. 52.

14. Anthony B. Atkinson, "On the Measurement of Inequality" (1970) in *Social Justice and Public Policy* (Cambridge, MA: MIT Press, 1983), p. 25.

15. Alan S. Blinder, "Commentary," in *Inequality and Tax Policy*, eds. Kevin A. Hassett and R. Glenn Hubbard (Washington, DC: The AEI Press, 2001), p. 40.

16. Henderson, "Income Gap Narrower."

17. "When a variable is normally distributed, its distribution is completely characterized by the mean and the standard deviation.... The statistic most appropriate for describing the central tendency of scores in an ordinal scale is the median." Sidney Siegel, *Nonparametric Statistics for the Behavioral Sciences* (New York: McGraw-Hill, 1956), pp. 12, 25. The Census Bureau reported a relatively large standard error for the top quintile of 0.34 in 2004.

18. U.S. Census Bureau, "*Historical Income Tables—Households*," tables H-1 to H-3 (all races), http://www.census.gov/hhes/www/income/histinc/h02ar.html.

# Two

# Work Matters

The richest fifth of families supplied over 30 percent of the total weeks worked in the economy...while the poorest fifth supplied only 7.5 percent. Thus, on a per-week-of-work basis, the income ratio between rich and poor was only 2-to-1. This certainly does not seem like an unreasonable degree of inequality.

—Alan Blinder in M. Feldstein, *The American Economy in Transition* (1980)

---

The top fifth of households has nearly six times as many full-time workers as the bottom fifth. Wages rise faster than inflation in the long run while transfer payments do not, so gaps between two-earner households at the top and no-earner households at the bottom grow wider over time. Substantial differences in incomes are largely explained by the number of workers per household, their age, and education. Sensational claims that 80–99 percent of Americans have experienced no increase in real income since 1973 are contradicted by data from the Census Bureau and Congressional Budget Office.

---

Most income in the top fifth (quintile) of households is from two or more people working full time. Most income in the bottom fifth is from government transfer payments. Some transfer payments are received in kind (Medicaid, food stamps, housing, and energy assistance) and some, in cash (Social Security, Supplemental Security Income, Temporary Assistance to Needy Families, the Earned Income Tax Credit, and disability and unemployment benefits).

Income from work invariably rises faster than inflation in the long run. That is what we mean by an increase in *real* wages, which, in turn, is the main reason average real incomes normally rise from one decade to the next. Full-time workers typically experience an increase in *real* wages or salaries (raises and promotions) as they gain age and experience.

Income from government transfer payments, on the other hand, does not usually rise in real terms. Social Security is adjusted to stay even with inflation, which leaves Social Security income unchanged in real terms. Many other transfer payments are not automatically adjusted for inflation, and their real purchasing power has declined at times. Because transfer payments are not expected to rise in real terms, as wages and salaries usually do over the course of a business cycle, the gap in real income between households dependent on transfer payments and households with two full-time workers should be expected to grow wider and wider over time. Nobody should have been terribly surprised or alarmed if the gap between average income in the top and bottom quintiles widened during periods of prosperity, when wages and benefits are most likely to rise in real terms.

The main reason income in the top quintile should be *expected* to rise more rapidly than in the bottom quintile is simply because there are many more workers at the top than at the bottom.

There are nearly six times as many full-time year-round workers in the top quintile as there are in the bottom quintile, according to the Census Bureau.[1] The bottom quintile, by contrast, is largely dependent on transfer payments, and cash transfers do *not* normally rise faster than inflation.[2] It follows inexorably that real income gains among the bottom quintile cannot possibly keep up with real income gains in the top quintile during prosperous periods like the late 1980s and late 1990s when real labor compensation rose in real terms.

The Bureau of Labor Statistics, for example, reports that the average number of *earners* in 2003 was 0.6 in the lowest quintile, 1 in the second, 1.4 in the third, 1.7 in the fourth and 2.0 in the top quintile. This is not just because there are more retired, disabled, and unemployed people in the bottom quintile. It is also because there are simply *fewer people* per households in the bottom quintile—because so many young and elderly households in the bottom income group consist of just one person. There are just 1.8 *persons per household* in the lowest quintile, 2.3 in the second, 2.5 in the third, 2.8 in the fourth, and 3.1 in the top quintile. According to the BLS Survey of Consumer Expenditures, there are nearly three times as many *people* in the top quintile as in the bottom quintile, and four times as many *workers.*[3]

Similarly, the Census Bureau rounded down to zero the average number of workers in the lowest income quintile in 2004 because 56.4 percent of bottom-quintile households had *no* workers all year, not even a part-time worker for a few weeks. There was roughly one worker per household in the second and third quintiles, by the Census count, and at least two workers per household in the top two quintiles. The Census also makes an important distinction between those who work part time and/or for just part of the year and those who work full time year round. In the lowest quintile, the number of people who worked full time all year amounted to less than 3 million compared with 9.2 million in the second, 12.7 million in the third, 15.1 million in the fourth, and 16.4 million in the top quintile.[4] While the top quintile has only four times as many workers as the bottom quintile, according to the Census Bureau, it has 5.5 times as many full-time, year round workers. If income among the quintiles were divided by hours worked, the difference between the top and bottom quintiles would not be very great. Many years ago, Alan Blinder of Princeton estimated that "on a per-week-of-work basis, the ratio between rich and poor was only 2 to 1."[5]

The fact that there are many more workers in the top fifth of households than in lower fifths has not always been appreciated by those who think it sounds easy to simply take income from the top and spread it around more evenly. The influential 1972 book, *Inequality* by Christopher Jencks, Herbert Gintis, and others, argued that even if "the most productive fifth of all workers accounts for half of the Gross National Product, it does not follow that they need to receive half the income. A third or a quarter might well suffice. . ."[6] Yet the top fifth produces and receives half the income (before taxes) by providing 5.5 times as many full-time workers as the bottom fifth. If the top 20 percent received just 25 percent of total income, their abnormally high work effort would become abnormally foolish. Since there are at least two workers per household in the top 20 percent, and 5.5 times as many full-time workers as there are in the bottom 20 percent, to divide household income almost equally would amount to asking "the most productive fifth of all workers" to work for nothing or less than nothing. Why would they do that?

With very few workers in the bottom quintile—because of retirement, unemployment, disability, or indolence—living standards in that group are *extremely* dependent on the generosity of taxpayers. In addition to the Census Bureau's familiar surveys on "money income," the Bureau also offers fourteen other definitions that add or subtract various items that affect living standards, such as taxes and government transfer payments in the form of cash or in-kind benefits.

In 2001, mean income in the bottom quintile was $10,096, but that figure dropped to $2,834 if cash transfers were excluded. Average money income in the bottom fifth consisted of that $2,834 of income from work and savings, plus $6,498 from non-means-tested cash benefits (mostly Social Security and disability); plus $850 from means-tested cash benefits such as Supplemental Security Income (SSI) and Temporary Assistance to Needy Families (TANF); plus $154 from the Earned Income Tax Credit (EITC). All of that added up to $10,336—slightly higher than the official measure, which excludes the EITC among other differences. Transfers thus accounted for 72.6 percent of money income among the lowest quintile in 2001. However, in addition to cash transfers there are also "in-kind" transfers that clearly affect living standards, and free up cash for other uses. To the $10,336 we should therefore add $868 from Medicare, $850 from Medicaid, and $692 for miscellaneous noncash benefits that are means-tested. Total cash and in-kind income therefore amounted to $12,746, and government cash and in-kind transfers accounted for 77.8 percent of that total.[7]

Aside from in-kind transfers, the second quintile received 22.3 percent of money income from transfers that year, the third quintile, 6 percent; the fourth, 5 percent; and the top quintile, 1.9 percent. It does not matter much that 2001 was a recession year: The bottom quintile also received 69.7 percent of their cash income from transfers in 2000.

If valuable in-kind benefits are included, such as Medicaid, food stamps, and housing and energy assistance, government transfer payments account for more than three-fourths of the real income of the bottom 20 percent of households.

To note that there are very few workers among the lowest-income households is not to pass judgment. There are usually good reasons why people do not work, such as old age, legitimate physical or mental disability, or long-term unemployment. There are also less-admirable but perfectly understandable reasons why some people do not work, such as alcoholism or heroin addiction. And there are less-admirable reasons why actual income of some people with no *visible* means of support is simply not reported—such as gambling, tax evasion, and criminal activities. Whatever the reasons, legitimate work in the formal economy accounts for such a trivial portion of the income and benefits of those in the lowest quintile that they cannot possibly share in the real income gains when typical salaries and benefits for two-earner families in the top quintile are rising in real terms.

Those who happen to fall into the bottom fifth of the income distribution in any particular year are typically quite dependent on government benefits (such as unemployment or temporary disability benefits). Those in that situation for several years or more are even more dependent on such benefits (such as Supplemental Security Income). They do not experience the equivalent of raises and promotions that are commonplace among two-earner couples in their prime earning years.

Initial Social Security benefits keep pace with the general rise of wages, but all subsequent benefits just keep pace with inflation. Other transfer payments, many of which have benefits set at the state level, have at times declined in real terms.

The situation in the top quintile is inherently different. Most of these households consist of married couples with two or more workers, typically working full time all year. They are often at the stage of life when raises and promotions are most common.

With two full-time workers among the top quintile, and usually none at the bottom, the gap between two-earner households and no-earner household *must* grow continually wider unless real incomes of workers rarely rise (allegations that typical workers have experienced chronic "wage stagnation" since 1973 or 1980 are untrue, but a later chapter will deal with that topic).

If salaries and employee benefits generally rise faster than inflation, while government transfer payments do not, then the gap between two-earner families at the top and no-earner households at the bottom must necessarily widen over time.

In fact, the prevalence of at least two workers per household is strikingly higher in both of the top two quintiles. This should not be entirely surprising because there are many more young students and old single-person households in the bottom quintile than in the top. Single-person households in the bottom quintile are not necessarily poor, even temporarily, since young couples and graduate students often receive parental support and widows may own valuable homes and other assets.

When it comes to explaining the widening gap between top and bottom quintiles, the key point is that those in the lowest quintile receive little of their income from work, for various reasons including retirement, disability, and substance abuse. They instead rely quite heavily on Social Security and disability checks, Supplemental Security Income (SSI), Temporary Assistance to Needy Families (TANF) and other transfer payments. Social Security is indexed to keep pace with inflation, unlike some other transfer payments, but such income does not normally increase in *real* terms as wages, salaries and employee benefits do.

Figure 2.1 compares the average growth of *real* income since 1980 among households with *two* earners to that of households with no earners. Think of the dark line as representing average (mean) income among households in the top quintile and the bars at the bottom as representing households in the bottom quintile. Since most households in the top quintile have two earners and most in the bottom quintile have no earners, the widening gap that is clearly apparent in the graph is also apparent when comparing mean income

**FIGURE 2.1**
**Mean Household Income by Number of Earners**

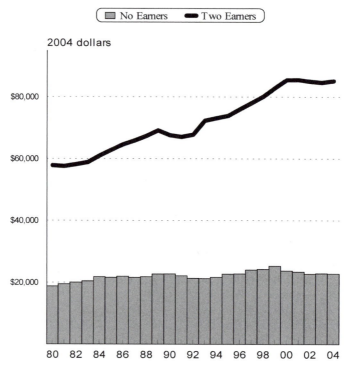

*Source:* http://www.census.gov/hhes/www/income/histinc/h12ar.html.

between the top and bottom quintiles. The only way that mean income of the top quintile could not have increased relative to mean income of the bottom quintile would be if many in the top group had stopped working, or if two-earner families had not experienced any real salary gains.

If inequality is defined in the traditional manner as the gap between average income in the top and bottom quintiles, then differences in the number of workers in those quintiles go a very long way toward explaining why there is such a gap and also why it has grown wider over time.

## THE ELUSIVE WORKING POOR

As Abba Lerner pointed out in 1961, "the lowest fifth are not all such poor people. Some of them are well-to-do men who happen to have done badly in business this year."[8] Small businesses aside, quite a few individuals counted among the bottom fifth in any one year are facing transitory difficulties and have assets and an established credit record they can draw upon. Yet virtually all of the *persistently* poor and near-poor are nonetheless included within the bottom quintile.

The fact that there are very few *workers* per household among those in the bottom quintile, and fewer still who work full time for a full year, appears contradicted by many books and articles written about the "working poor." This apparent contradiction arises because those who write about the working poor families have defined "working" and "poor" and "families" in uniquely uninformative ways. Working is sometimes defined to include any work at all, even a few hours for a few weeks. Even Bureau of Labor Statistics studies define working as being in the labor force for six months out of the year, whether employed or not ("labor force participation" includes being unemployed but more-or-less looking for a job).[9]

The redefinition of what it means to be poor is even more strained than the redefinition of what it means to be working. In discussions about the working poor, a poor person is almost always defined as anyone (including 16-year old students) who earns an hourly wage that would be insufficient to support a family of four. And one-person households (including college students) are redefined as one-person families.

Those who define poverty in this strange way surely realize that most people who earn a wage sufficient to keep four people out of poverty are *not* supporting more than one person and are, on the contrary, frequently claimed as dependents on someone else's tax return. If one out of four of the nation's primary breadwinners were actually earning too little to keep their families out of poverty, then the poverty rate would be 25 percent even if all the poor were working (as they definitely are not). Yet Table 693 of *The Statistical Abstract of the United States* (2006) shows the poverty rate was 12.5 percent in 2003, down from 15.3 percent in 1993. And Table 699 shows the poverty rate among married couples was 5.4 percent.

The working poor can be found in Table 697, which shows that in 2003 the poverty rate among full-time year-round workers over the age of 16 was just 2.6 percent. But that figure is exaggerated. If the figures are adjusted to account for the earned income tax credit and noncash transfers (such as food stamps and subsidized housing), the poverty rate among full-time year-round workers was 1.8 percent in 2004, according to the Census Bureau.[10] The working poor do exist, but their numbers are very small. Even if we included everyone who worked part-time for at least half of the year, and those who were at least looking for a job, the poverty rate among that group of marginal workers was 5.3 percent in 2002 and 2003, and would have been considerably lower if the EITC and food stamps were considered (such anti-poverty programs can reduce poverty only if economists bother to count them).[11]

The Bureau of Labor Statistics defines a "full-time worker" in terms of labor force participation, which means it includes *unemployed* people who tell a pollster that they are looking for a full-time job. Even the 2.6 percent poverty rate among "full-time workers" does not mean that many full-time workers were actually poor despite collecting a paycheck. On the contrary, it often means they were unemployed for many months, which implies *temporary* distress rather than chronic poverty.

In *The Betrayal of Work*, Beth Shulman focused the whole book around a claim that "in the late nineties, one out of every four workers earned less than $8.70 an hour. For these thirty million Americans, this amounts to an annual income of $18,100 if they were working full time, the government-defined poverty level for a family of four."[12] One of the two books she cites to support that claim says, "In 1998, among people between age 25 and 64 who worked full-time and full-year, a total of 9,772,000 persons, or 11.3 percent of the total, earned less than $8.50 an hour."[13] The main reason that 11.3 percent figure was nowhere near "one out of four" is that this particular researcher (unlike others) took care to exclude part-time workers and teens with summer jobs.

The Working Poor Families Project "with the support of the Annie E. Casey, Ford and Rockefeller Foundations" came up with an imaginative way of redefining working poor to mean any family with a *relatively* low income, regardless how little they worked. "To be considered low-income, a family of four earned less than $36,784 in 2002 (far less than the median income of $62,732 for a family of four)."[14]

An economist from Chicago used to tell an apocryphal joke about a local politician who had supposedly said, "No American family should ever have to get by on less than the median income." Half of all families always get by on less than the median income, because that is what median means. Yet the Working Poor Families Project defined any income below 60 percent of median income as poor. If median income doubled in real terms, that *relative* definition of poverty would also double. And because that definition of poverty was based on earnings alone—regardless of the Earned Income Tax Credit, Medicaid, and other transfer payments—the problem was defined in a way that ensured it could *never* be solved.

## REALITY IS NOT A MATTER OF OPINION

During a spirited exchange with *American Prospect* editor Robert Kuttner, Paul Krugman wrote, "I am not prepared to be indulgent toward . . . factual assertions that can be flatly disproved by spending a few minutes with the Statistical Abstract of the United States."[15] He had a point. The *Statistical*

*Abstract* is indeed a handy source of many facts, as we just found when discussing the working poor. And it is readily available at any library or as a free download from www.census.gov.[16] The tables are numbered and the sources clearly named, so any reader can easily check most of the following references to those tables. Each table in the *Statistical Abstract* also identifies its sources, which makes it easy to update data online.

Some of the most interesting information in the 2006 edition is found in Section 12, Labor Force, Employment, and Earnings. Table 636, for example, describes "Workers Paid Hourly Wage Rates." It turns out that 73.9 million workers were paid by the hour in 2004, but only three-fourths (55.7 million) worked full time and 22 percent were under the age of 25.

Table 589, "Employed Civilians," shows there were 139.3 million workers in 2003, or 127.6 million if we arbitrarily exclude the self-employed and those working in agriculture (it is commonplace to exclude agriculture and the armed services, even though work is work). The number of full-time workers was 101.2 million.

Looking at tables 632 and 589 together, we discover that only *55 percent* of all full-time wage and salary workers (55.7 million divided by 101.2 million) were paid by the hour. When we examine "average wages" in later chapters, do not forget that nearly half of all full-time employees earn no wages at all. They earn salaries. Researchers try to convert annual salaries into hourly wages, but that is treacherous because hours vary widely and surveys do not report them accurately (a nine-to-five schedule is thirty-five hours a week, for example, but people may call it forty hours out of habit).

## WHO EARNS WHAT AND WHY?

The *Statistical Abstract* also provides some fascinating information in section 13 (Income, Expenditures, and Wealth). What this section shows is that substantial differences in household income can be explained by (1) the number of workers in the household, (2) their age, and (3) their education.

Table 681, for example, shows that in 2003 the median income of married-couple households was $62,281 while the median income of unrelated households was $20,160. That is why the changing demographics in Table 1.1, showing a relative increase in the number of single households, helps explain why measures of household income include relatively more low-income households than in the past. Married couples earn *three times* as much as single people. That is partly because singles are often very young or very old and because single households cannot possibly have two salaries. Regardless whether or not one regards this source of inequality as unfair, couples do need more income than singles. Two can not live as cheaply as one.

Within that married-couple elite, table 683 shows that in 2003 the median income among married couples in which the husband worked full-time year round and the wife also worked at least part-time was $81,255. The median income among families in which the wife worked but the husband did not was $43,931. And the median income among families in which neither spouse worked was $27,190.

In short, incomes of couples when both spouses worked was *three times* larger than among couples in which neither spouse worked. But that gap is actually much narrower because of income and payroll taxes extracted from those who work and in-kind benefits distributed to many who do not work.

Whether or not one regards this source of inequality as unfair, it certainly provides some incentive for at least one spouse to keep working, at least part-time for part of the year. If more work did not typically bring more income, why would anybody work?

Age is another factor that helps explain why some earn more than others in any particular year, largely because on-the-job training is valuable and tends to be rewarded with raises and promotions. Table 681 of the *Statistical Abstract* shows that median income of families in which the household head is 45 to 54 years old was $70,149 in 2003, while the median income of those younger than age 25 was $26,198. The income of mature, experienced people after decades of raises and promotions is 2.7 times as large as the income of inexperienced youngsters.

Whether or not one regards this source of inequality as unfair, it nonetheless offers some comfort that those under the age of 25 in any particular year will not remain in that "underprivileged" situation forever. In fact, much of the distinction between poor and rich is actually just describing the same people at different stages in their lives.

Formal education also explains sizable differences in income, of course. Table 675 shows that in 2003 the median income of households (not families) headed by someone with a doctorate degree was $96,830 while the comparable median income for high school graduates was $36,835, and the median for those with less than a ninth grade education was $18,787.

In short, those with a doctorate degree typically earn *5.2 times* as much as those with only a grade-school education. Whether or not one regards this source of inequality as unfair, it certainly provides some incentive for people to remain in high school and perhaps to invest time and money in higher education. If additional schooling did not usually help to increase personal income, fewer people would bother to become better educated.

So far we have learned that (1) families with two people working earn about three times as much before taxes as those with nobody working, (2) experienced middle-aged employees earn almost three times as much as young novices, and that (3) people with advanced college degrees earn more than five times as much as those with very little schooling.

There are many other ways that people might be grouped and categorized, but income differences between such groups would still have to take into account the number of people per household, the number of workers, their age, and their education. The Census Bureau likes to group people on the basis of where their ancestors lived, for example. This makes it possible to discover that median income among Americans whose past or present generations came here from the highly varied nations of Asia is higher than the incomes of those rooted in such different "Hispanic" places as Cuba, Brazil, Puerto Rico, and El Salvador. To unravel possible reasons for such differences economists have to first "control" for many "variables" such as differences in work, age and education between these diverse groups. Then there would be many other factors to consider, such as the fact that English is commonly spoken in some Asian nations or that some cultures are less likely to encourage women to work.

Similarly, average incomes of African American males are still substantially lower than for non-Hispanic white males, although this is much less true of females. Again, such income comparisons between groups need to be adjusted for number of people per household, number of workers, their age, and education. When using household data, one would have to take account of the fact that black marriage rates have declined in recent years, so other households are more likely to include two people and two incomes. After controlling for a variety of such variables, whatever remains unaccounted for (the residual) may be attributed to current discrimination, the legacy of past discrimination, or cultural differences.[17] This book does not attempt to sort out all such complex differences between subgroups of households. Our central topics are the growth and distribution of income and wealth among all households, families, employees, or taxpayers.

Differences in incomes between men and women pose another difficult topic that is beyond the scope of this book. Among full-time, year-round workers, median earnings of women were only 56.6 percent as high as those of men in 1973, but rose to become 76.5 percent as high by 2004.[18] To investigate either the remaining gap or the fact that it narrowed so rapidly would require controlling for differences in education and on-the-job training. Interestingly, the academic literature on the growth and distribution of income has often focused only on inequality and/or slow growth of *male* earnings. Meanwhile, median earnings of full-time women employees rose by more than a third in real, inflation-adjusted terms—from $23,350 in 1973 (in 2004 dollars) to $31,223 in 2004. Various competing theories of male wages (such a declining unionization, globalization, or skill-based technical change) are generally inconsistent with the rapid growth of female earnings.[19]

## CHANGING DEMOGRAPHICS AND DISTRIBUTIONS

To observe that big differences in income can be largely explained by the number of full-time workers in a household, their education and experience does not explain why those differences have widened if, in fact, they have (which partly depends on how income or consumption is measured and over which years). Commenting a brief op-ed I once wrote on this topic, a critic complained that I had "ignored a key issue," because "these types of analyses reveal nothing about the key question of whether inequality has increased *over time*."[20] I was not addressing the "problem" of rise in inequality at the time, but even in that context, the critic was wrong. It is a factual question whether or not demographic changes reveal very much about changes in income distribution, but they would "reveal nothing" only if nothing changed.

If the number of highly educated people in the top fifth increased over time, or the number of dropouts in the bottom fifth increased, would we really expect that to "reveal nothing" about how much income was earned in those top and bottom income groups? If the number of two-earner couples in the top fifth of households increased from one decade to the next, would that really "reveal nothing" about how much income was earned in the latter decade by households in the top fifth?

In fact, the numbers of workers in the top two quintiles, their education, and age have indeed changed *over time* in ways that should have widened the earnings gap between them and the lowest quintile.

- The female "labor force participation rate" (the percentage over the age of 16 who are either working or looking for work) rose from 44.7 percent in 1973 to 60 percent in 1999, before leveling-off.[21] This mirrored an increase in the percentage of two-earner married couples concentrated in the top two quintiles.

- A rising percentage of workers are college-educated and, as Lawrence Mishel observes, "[H]igh earners tend to marry other relatively high earners (some say increasingly so)."[22] The result is a growing number of households with two high-earners, which raises the thresholds defining top income groups and results in "inequality"—relatively rapid growth of mean income within those groups.

- Immigration in recent decades has been bifurcated—adding large numbers of people with very little education and a small number with graduate degrees. That was almost certain to increase measured income inequality, at least initially. Countries that import millions of poor people are bound to end up with more poor people than otherwise, regardless of any impact on wages of nonimmigrants.

- Aging of the baby-boom generation might likewise be expected to increase inequality during their preretirement years, because a larger portion of the population has been reaching middle age, when earnings usually peak.

Differences in the number of workers per household and their age and education account for a substantial portion of the differences in income in any given year. Changes in those variables likewise account for at least some of the changes in income distribution from one decade to the next. There is much more to be explained, particularly when it comes to the very rich and very poor. But the amount of income people earn is nonetheless strongly related to the quantity and quality of the work effort they supply. Work matters.

## REAL INCOME GROWTH

Aside from examining reasons why household incomes differ (are unequal), the second major theme of this book concerns the rate of growth of real income (or real wages) over some long period of years. Such periods sometimes begin with a cyclical peak, such as 1973 or 1979, which is misleading unless they also end with a cyclical peak, such as 1989 or 2000. The *Statistical Abstract* is not entirely adequate for tackling this topic, but the *Economic Report of the President* may be helpful. The newest and most detailed information is available online at the Web sites of the Census Bureau (www.census.gov) and Bureau of Labor Statistics (www.bls.gov).

Table 2.1, from the Census Bureau Web site, shows the mean average of household incomes in 2004 dollars by quintiles (fifths), with the last column showing the top 5 percent. To keep it visually uncomplicated, the figures are limited to every five years except for 1967 and 2004, which were the earliest and latest available. These figures generally show *real income rising at all income levels. Wall Street Journal* writer David Wessel said, "The 1990s were different. Nearly all workers did better than they did in the 1980s—even those at the bottom."[23] Actually, the increase in real income for lowest two quintiles between 1980 and 1990 was not so bad when you consider that 1980 was followed by two recession years and that 1990 was also a recession while 2000 was a prerecession peak. The 2004 income figures for all income groups had not yet regained the cyclical peak of 2000, but cyclical recoveries are rarely that fast. It was not until 1996 that median household income regained the level reached in 1989—reaching $42,544 in 1996 (in 2004 dollars), compared with $42,524 in 1989.

As is customarily the case, the figures in Table 2.1 are *pretax* and *pretransfer*. They do *not* add Social Security and many other transfer payments to incomes at the bottom and they do not subtract taxes from incomes

**TABLE 2.1**

**Average Household Income by Quintile (and Top 5 Percent) Census Bureau (Estimates in 2004 Dollars)**

|      | Lowest 20% | Second | Middle | Third  | Top 20% | Top 5%  |
|------|-----------|--------|--------|--------|---------|---------|
| 1967 | $7,668    | 21,246 | 33,918 | 47,457 | 85,406  | 134,722 |
| 1970 | 8,392     | 22,733 | 36,606 | 51,599 | 91,348  | 140,208 |
| 1975 | 9,002     | 22,113 | 36,280 | 52,718 | 93,076  | 141,245 |
| 1980 | 9,358     | 23,291 | 38,434 | 56,622 | 100,958 | 150,869 |
| 1985 | 9,400     | 23,821 | 39,540 | 59,477 | 111,100 | 171,379 |
| 1990 | 10,043    | 25,268 | 41,736 | 62,925 | 122,116 | 194,456 |
| 1995 | 10,272    | 25,106 | 41,980 | 64,533 | 134,671 | 232,423 |
| 2000 | 11,141    | 27,818 | 46,325 | 72,014 | 156,053 | 276,855 |
| 2004 | 10,264    | 26,241 | 44,455 | 70,085 | 151,593 | 264,387 |

*Source:* U.S. Census Bureau. http://www.census.gov/hhes/www/income/histinc/h03ar.html.

at the top. As will be shown in later chapters, taking account of transfer payments (or of the consumer spending made possible by such transfers) greatly increases measured real income among the lowest 20 percent particularly if in-kind transfers are counted as well as cash. Taking account of taxes greatly reduces actual income in the higher income groups—what is left after paying income and payroll taxes.

Even the unadjusted Census Bureau figures in Table 2.1 show *accelerating* real income gains among the bottom 80 percent from 1970 to 2000. Average income in the bottom four quintiles rose from $29,832 in 1970 to $31,926 in 1980, $34,993 in 1990, and $39,325 in 2000. In other words, real income among the bottom 80 percent rose 7 percent from 1970 to 1980, 9.6 percent from 1980 to 1990, and 12.4 percent from 1990 to 2000. Yet many economists and economic journalists continued writing that the bottom 80 percent was "barely creeping ahead"—or even falling—at a time when Census Bureau surveys show that real incomes of the bottom 80 percent were actually rising at a faster and faster pace.

In a 2004 article in the *Nation*, for example, Paul Krugman wrote that, "According to estimates by the economists Thomas Piketty and Emmanuel Saez–confirmed by data from the Congressional Budget Office—between 1973 and 2000 the average real income of the bottom 90 percent of American taxpayers actually fell by 7 percent."[24] That claim could not possibly be "confirmed by data from the Congressional Budget Office," because CBO estimates only go back to 1979. Between 1973 and 2000, according to the CBO, the average real income of the bottom 80 percent of American taxpayers actually *rose* by 12 percent before taxes and 15 percent after taxes.

The CBO estimates for real after-tax income are shown in Table 2.2 in a format intentionally similar to the previous table of Census Bureau figures, to make it easier to see that different definitions of income compiled from different information produce quite different results.[25] The CBO uses a sample of tax returns rather than a survey of households. And the CBO includes transfer payment received in cash and in kind—making incomes of the lowest 20 percent in 2003 more than 37 percent larger than in the Census figures.

Despite the fact that these are after-tax estimates, the CBO estimates for the top 5 percent are nonetheless larger than the Census survey. That is because the CBO counts *taxable* capital gains as income and allocates most corporate profits (and taxes) to high-income groups. In the CBO estimates, capital gains add to measured income when someone sells stock or other assets for more than what they paid for them, but only if such sales show up on tax returns (unlike capital gains accumulating inside a tax-deferred IRA or 401-k plan, or most gains from home sales).

Some CBO additions to top incomes will be questioned in Chapter Five, about the "top 1 percent." Despite such statistical ambiguities, however, it is clear that the CBO figures *do not* confirm Mr. Krugman's startling claim that "the average real income of the bottom 90 percent of American tax-payers actually fell" from 1973 to 2000. On the contrary, the CBO's estimates of real after-tax income rose in every income group since 1979, which was confirmed by Census estimates of pretax income in the previous table. By the year 2000, in fact, the top 20 percent had an average income as high as only the top 5 percent did in 1979, according to the CBO.

Steven Rattner, a managing principal of the Quadrangle Group LLC (a private investment firm that manages $4 billion), wrote in *Business Week*, "We can debate a lot of economic data but not income inequality." He too

**TABLE 2.2**
**Average After-Tax Household Income by Quintile (and Top 5 Percent)**
**Congressional Budget Office (Estimates in 2003 Dollars)**

|      | Lowest 20% | Second | Middle | Third  | Top 20% | Top 5%  |
| ---- | ---------- | ------ | ------ | ------ | ------- | ------- |
| 1979 | $13,500    | 27,300 | 38,900 | 50,900 | 89,700  | 149,600 |
| 1985 | 12,200     | 25,800 | 38,300 | 62,100 | 103,100 | 189,300 |
| 1990 | 13,100     | 27,200 | 38,900 | 54,500 | 112,200 | 210,100 |
| 1995 | 14,100     | 28,700 | 41,500 | 56,800 | 116,400 | 217,000 |
| 2000 | 14,600     | 30,900 | 44,700 | 63,300 | 151,100 | 319,900 |
| 2003 | 14,100     | 30,800 | 44,800 | 63,600 | 138,500 | 270,200 |

*Source:* Congressional Budget Office. http://www.cbo.gov/ftpdoc.cfm?index=7000&type=1.

cited data from Piketty and Saez as evidence of "the glacial progress of all but a few."[26] Those estimates were presented as indisputable facts, something nobody could possibly debate.

*New York Times* writer David Cay Johnston, in his 2003 book *Perfectly Legal*, claimed,

[T]he only significant income gains over three decades [1970 to 2000] went to a very narrow slice at the top. . . . Four out of five Americans were making less or were no better off in 2000 than in 1970. . . . The incomes of the richest 1 percent, and especially the top-earning 13,400 American families, have soared while the bottom 80 percent of Americans have seen their incomes stagnate for three decades.[27]

Like Paul Krugman and Steven Rattner, Mr. Johnston relied on estimates from private economists Piketty and Saez, which he mischaracterized as "official government data." Tables 2.1 and 2.2, by contrast, actually are official government data, not academic estimates, and they both show substantial gains of real income in *all* of the bottom four quintiles since 1967 (Census) or 1979 (CBO). The Piketty-Saez study will be examined briefly below and (along with three similar studies) it will be analyzed in more detail in later chapters. At this point, it is sufficient to note that the U.S. Census Bureau and Congressional Budget Office would have to be *entirely wrong* if statements about 80–90 percent of Americans experiencing little or no real increase in incomes since 1970 or 1973 were even remotely close to being accurate.

### REALITY IN A FOOTNOTE

Mr. Krugman's highly improbable claim that real incomes have stagnated since 1973 for all but the top 10 percent was later outdone by an even more outlandish claim that real incomes stagnated for all but the top 1 percent. The AFL-CIO Web site reprinted a graph from an updated version of the Piketty-Saez paper (where it is labeled Figure A1) ostensibly showing average real income soaring for the top 1 percent but stagnating "for everybody else."[28] Unfortunately, AFL-CIO neglected to reprint a critical footnote from the Piketty-Saez graph. That footnote explained that the graphical illusion of income stagnation among the bottom 99 percent of was the result of selecting faulty statistics to minimize their real income growth: "From 1973 to 2000, the average income of the bottom 99 percent would have grown by about 40 percent in real terms instead of stagnating (as displayed in the figure above) if we had included all transfers (+7 percent effect), used the CPI-U-RS (+13 percent effect), and especially defined income per capita (20 percent effect)."

By confining the facts to a footnote, the graph in Piketty-Saez conveyed the false impression that nearly all U.S. households had experienced *stagnating* real incomes since 1973, rather than a 40 percent increase. It appears that the Piketty-Saez estimates have been widely reported but narrowly understood.

The income share of the top 1 percent is a *ratio*, with estimated income in that group as the numerator and the sum of that amount plus incomes of the bottom 99 percent as the denominator. We cannot possibly know what *share* the *top* income groups receive unless we know how much money is earned by the *bottom* 90–99 percent.

The footnote in Piketty-Saez explained a few devices for understating the *growth* of real income among the bottom 99 percent over a long period of time, 1973 to 2000. But the *level* of real income among the bottom 90 percent in the year 2000 was also understated in somewhat different ways. Underestimating the denominator of the ratio makes the share going to the numerator (the top 1 percent) look much larger.

According to the unique Piketty-Saez measure and definition of income for the year 2000, "the median income, as well as the average [mean] income for the bottom 90% of tax units is quite low, around $25,000."[29] That number is too low to be believed. To say that 90 percent of all "tax units" had a *median* income of $25,076 in 2000 is to say that *45 percent* (half of the 90 percent) earned less than that. If you believe Krugman and others who say the Piketty-Saez estimates measure family income (they do not), then these estimates say that 45 percent of American families had incomes below $25,000 during the cyclical peak year of 2000. Yet the Census Bureau estimates that only 19.2 percent of U.S. *families* (or 27.5 percent of households) earned less than $25,000 in 2000.[30] As we found to be the case with related claims that 80–90 percent had no real income gains from 1973 to 2000, the Piketty-Saez estimate that 45 percent earned less than $25,000 a year is totally inconsistent with Census Bureau estimates.

Median family income in the year 2000 was $50,732, according to the Census Bureau. Since half earned more than $50,732, it would have been impossible for 45 percent to have earned less than $25,000. The *mean* average was $65,773 for families, $57,135 for households. Yet the tax-based estimates of Mr. Saez result in both mean and median averages for 90 percent of U.S. "tax units" that were not even half as large as the mean and median for *all* households or families.

We can debate a lot of economic data, as Mr. Rattner said, and we should. The Piketty-Saez data he cited is inconsistent with that of the Census Bureau, Federal Reserve Board (Survey of Consumer Finances), and the CBO.

Mr. Saez offers two inadequate explanations: "First, our income definition does not include any government transfers. Second, CPS income is reported at the household level which is larger than the tax unit we consider."

Transfer payments are indeed critically important to the bottom 20 percent, but the small amount of transfers reported on income tax returns is much too small in comparison to gross income reported to the IRS, which was nearly $6.3 trillion in 2000 after adding back the adjustments. Unemployment benefits reported to the IRS were $44 billion, for example, and Earned Income Tax Credit refunds were $34 billion. Bigger transfer payments from Social Security are largely unreported to the IRS because senior couples with an income above $18,400 did not have to file a return in 2005, when average benefits were $12,000. But most transfers are too concentrated in the poorest quintile to begin to explain a $25,000 median income for 90 percent of reporting taxpayers.

Mr. Saez's second explanation for the low $25,000 figure relies on the distinction between a tax unit and a household. Two employed singles living together constitute two tax units, so their household income could be twice as large as their income per tax unit. Cutting many household incomes in two might make a significant difference. Yet those who cite Piketty-Saez in the popular press *never* explain that these estimates do not describe the incomes of households or families. Paul Krugman, for example, wrote, "According to Piketty and Saez . . . in 1998 the top 0.01 percent received more than 3 percent of all income. That meant that the 13,000 richest families in America had almost as much income as the 20 million poorest households."[31] Piketty and Saez estimates do not refer to either families or households; they refer to tax units.

Another obvious problem with income data for "tax units" is that not everyone reports all their income. In 2002, reported adjusted gross income (AGI) was $961 billion smaller than a *comparable* measure of personal income, leaving 13.7 percent of personal income unaccounted for.[32] A later chapter about "the top 1 percent" explains why all of these tax-based estimates of income distribution are misleading.

Whatever the explanation, the fact that the Piketty-Saez estimates imply that 45 percent of Americans earned less than $25,000 in the year 2000 reflects flaws in those estimates rather flaws than in the U.S. economy.

It is difficult to imagine how so many learned people came to believe that 80 or 90 percent of the American people had experienced virtually no increase in real incomes for 25–30 years. It may have something to do with what Chapter 4 calls "the wage stagnation thesis"—a related yet distinctly different claim that average real wages (rather than incomes) have been supposedly stagnant since 1973. It may also have something to do with the old-fashioned focus of many researchers on male incomes, as though the impressive rise of women's incomes does not matter.

Regardless of controversies yet to be discussed regarding the real growth of average wages and salaries, when it comes to total income (including investment income and transfer payments), the false belief that the bottom 80 or 90 percent has made no progress since 1973 appears to be based on little more than a zero-sum obsession with *relative* income shares. Simply because those in the bottom 80 percent did not have a rising *share* of the rising real income, these analysts incorrectly thought the bottom 80 or 90 percent made no progress at all.

Whenever someone asserts that the top 1 percent earned 15 percent of this or the top 10 percent earned 44 percent of that, the first question to ask is "percent of what?" Any alleged share of the top 1 percent or top 10 percent is a *ratio* of income in that group to the income of everyone. Any ratio has both a numerator and a denominator. To make the ratio look large, one simply has to add as much as possible to the incomes of the top group and subtract as much as possible from the incomes of everyone else.

Studies that use income tax data to estimate income distribution usually exclude transfer payments from the denominator and enlarge the numerator by including taxable capital gains and a rising amount of profit that used to be reported under the corporate income tax. Such clever calculations do make shares at the top look larger, but they have the unwanted side effect of also making shares at the top more *cyclical*. Profits among Subchapter-S corporations, partnerships and LLCs can quickly turn into losses in recessions when top investors' capital gains likewise disappear. As a paradoxical result, the only time lower income groups can be said to be doing *relatively* well—in terms of their share of total income—is when the economy is in a recession. This is not because recessions are beneficial to people with low or modest incomes, of course, but because recessions cause even greater *percentage* losses in the volatile income of small businesses and investors.

Table 2.2, based on CBO income tax data, shows that between the year 2000 and 2003 the mean average of after-tax income fell by $500 (3.4 percent) for the lowest 20 percent but real incomes fell by $49,700 (15.5 percent) for those in the top 5 percent. Treasury Secretary John Snow cited similar figures in order to boast that "there has been a decline in inequality."[33] If inequality is measured by taxable income shares, then a three-year collapse in stock prices after March 2000 and a recession and terrorist attack in 2001 did indeed produce "a decline in inequality." By the Treasury's calculation the top 5 percent earned 15.4 percent of after-tax income in 2003—down from 19 percent in 2000. Yet the fact that the poor also suffered a multiyear setback from the recession, as they always do, should make us think twice about assuming that a "decline in inequality" is always a good thing.

When income is defined to include taxable capital gains and/or the profits of businesses filing under the individual tax code, recessions prove particularly effective at shrinking income shares at the top. And anything that reduces the share of measured income reported among the uppermost income groups must raise the *relative* shares of the bottom 90–99 percent even though nearly everyone's real income declines in the process. It would be nonsense to conclude that recessions are beneficial to the poor or middle class simply because recessions reduce the share of income received by those at the top. Yet that would merely be an extreme example of the sort of conceptual errors that routinely arise from defining prosperity in purely relative, zero-sum terms.

When something seems too good to be true, it usually is not. And when income statistics seem too *bad* to be true, they usually are not.

## NOTES

1. U.S. Census Bureau, "Percent Distribution of Households, by Selected Characteristics within Income Quintile and Top 5 Percent in 2004" (June 24, 2005), table HINC-05. http://pubdb3.census.gov/macro/032005/hhinc/new05_000.htm.

2. Congressional Budget Office, "Changes in Participation in Means-Tested Programs" (April 20, 2005). Figure 2 in this CBO study shows average monthly benefits falling since 1977 for AFDC/TANF, and unchanged in real terms since 1993 for SSI and since 1995 for the EITC (which is rarely counted as income in income distribution studies).

3. Bureau of Labor Statistics, "Consumer Expenditures in 2003" (June 2005), table1. http://www.bls.gov/cex/home.htm.

4. U.S. Census Bureau, "Percent Distribution of Households" (June 24, 2005).

5. Alan S. Blinder, "The Level and Distribution of Economic Well-Being," in *The American Economy in Transition*, ed. Martin Feldstein (Chicago: NBER, University of Chicago Press, 1980), p. 436.

6. Jencks et al., *Inequality*, p. 10.

7. U.S. Census Bureau, "Historical Income Tables—Experimental Measures" (May 13, 2004), table RDI-8, http://www.census.gov/hhes/income/histinc/rdi8.html.

8. Abba P. Lerner, *Everybody's Business* (New York: Harper Torchbooks, 1961), p. 97.

9. Bureau of Labor Statistics, "The ratio of the working poor to all individuals in the labor force for at least 27 weeks was 5.3 percent," *A Profile of the Working Poor, 2003* (March 2005), Report 983.

10. U.S. Census Bureau, "The Effects of Government Taxes and Transfers on Poverty: 2004" (February 8, 2005), table 4. http://www.census.gov/hhes/www/poverty/effect2004/effect2004.html.

11. Editorial, "Rate of Working Poor Unchanged in 2003," *Monthly Labor Review*, vol. 128(4) (April 12, 2005). http://www.bls.gov/opub/ted/2005/apr/wk2/art02.htm.

12. Beth Shulman, *The Betrayal of Work* (New York: The New Press, 2003), pp. 25–26.

13. Paul Osterman, "Employers in the Low-Wage/Low-Skill Labor Market," in Richard Kazis and Marc S. Miller, eds., *Low-Wage Workers in the New Economy* (Washington, DC: The Urban Institute Press, 2001), p. 69.

14. Tom Waldron, Brandon Roberts and Andrew Reamer, *Working Hard, Falling Short* (October 2004), p. ii. http://www.qecf.org/publications/data/working_hard_new.pdf.

15. Paul Krugman, "Of Economists and Liberals," *American Prospect*, vol. 7(6) (November–December 1996).

16. The 2006 edition of the *Statistical Abstract of the United States* can be downloaded at http://www.census.gov/prod/www/statistical-abstract.htm.

17. The legacy of past discrimination is discussed in Roland G. Fyer, Jr., and Glenn C. Loury, "Affirmative Action and Its Mythology," *Journal of Economic Perspectives*, vol. 20(3) (Summer 2005); Thomas Sowell emphasized cultural explanations in "Crippled by Their Culture," *Wall Street Journal*, April 26, 2005.

18. U.S. Census Bureau, *Income, Poverty, and Health Insurance Coverage in the United States: 2004*, table A-2, p. 38.

19. Richard B. Friedman, "How Much Has De-Unionization Contributed to the Rise in Male Earnings Inequality," in *Uneven Tides*, eds. Sheldon Danziger and Peter Gottschalk (New York: Russell Sage Foundation, 1994).

20. Jared Bernstein, Lawrence Mishel, and Chauna Brocht, "Any Way You Cut It: Income Inequality Is on the Rise Regardless How It's Measured," (briefing paper, Economic Policy Institute, September 2000), p. 1. http://www.epinet.org/content.cfm/briefingpapers_inequality_inequality.

21. *Economic Report of the President* (2005), table B-39.

22. Lawrence Mishel, "Waging Inequality," *American Prospect Online*, February 24, 2005, http://americanprospect.org/web/page.ww?section=rootandname=ViewWebandarticleId=9238

23. David Wessel, "Is Inequality over Wages Worsening?" *Wall Street Journal*, January 19, 2006.

24. Paul Krugman, "The Death of Horatio Alger," *Nation*, January 5, 2004. http://www.thenation.com/doc/20040105/krugman.

25. Congressional Budget Office, "Historical Effective Federal Tax Rates: 1979 to 2003," spreadsheet table 1C (December 2005). http://www.cbo.gov/ftpdoc.cfm?index=7000andtype=1.

26. Steven Rattner, "The Rich Get (Much) Richer; The Top 1% Takes a Fatter Slice Now Than at Any Time since the 1920s," *Business Week*, August 8, 2005.

27. David Cay Johnston, *Perfectly Legal: The Cover Campaign to Rig Our Tax System to Benefit the Super-Rich and Cheat Everybody Else* (New York: Portfolio, 2003), pp. 39, 307.

28. AFL-CIO website. http://www.aflcio.org/corporatewatch/paywatch/retirementsecurity/index.cfm.

29. Emmanuel Saez, "Reported Incomes and Marginal Tax Rates, 1960–2000: Evidence and Policy Implications," *NBER Working Paper* 10273 (January 2004), p. 17.

30. *Statistical Abstract of the United States* (2006), tables 673 and 678. To put Mr. Saez's $25,000 estimate in perspective, an income below $17,603 for a family of four was officially poor in 2000.

31. Krugman, "For Richer."

32. *SOI Tax Stats—SOI Bulletin—Historical Tables and Appendix*, table 6: Total Adjusted Gross Income Estimated from National Income and Product Accounts (NIPA) and as Reported on Individual Income Tax Returns per Statistics of Income, Tax Years 1950–2002. http://www.irs.gov/taxstats/article/0,,id=115033,00.html.

33. Henderson, "Income Gap Narrower."

# Three

# A Vanishing Middle Class?

The mixture of bad economic news . . . along with a perception that the Reagan administration's economic policies favored the rich, spawned a number of publications suggesting that . . . past industrial policies were leading to a decline in the middle class.
—Paul Ryscavage, *Economic Inequality in America* (1999)

By almost any measure the middle class is smaller now than it was in 1973 . . . There is now a pervasive sense that the American Dream has gone astray, that children can expect to live worse that their parents.
—Paul Krugman, *Peddling Prosperity* (1994)

From 1983 to 2004 there were numerous reports that showed alarm at the percentage of households earning between $30,000 and $50,000 having gone down. Yet the decline was due to the fact that the percentage earning more than $50,000 had gone up. A larger percentage of Americans earning more income is frequently confused with the rich getting richer, although it actually means more people are getting rich. With many more people moving up, the minimum income needed to be counted among the top 20 percent also moved up. Since higher and higher real incomes were required, average incomes above those higher threshold was bound to rise. Too many formerly "middle-class" couples were becoming rich, by the standards of the previous generation; they could no longer all fit within the top 20 percent. The bar defining entry into each of the top income groups was pushed up by more people crowding it from below.

Periodic claims that the middle class is "shrinking" or "vanishing" have appeared every few years for more than two decades. In July 1983, for example, Robert Kuttner wrote "The Declining Middle" in *The Atlantic*. On February 5, 1984, Lester Thurow wrote "The Disappearance of the Middle Class" in the *New York Times*. On September 22, 1986, David Wessel wrote "U.S. Rich and Poor Increase in Numbers: Middle Loses Ground" in the *Wall Street Journal*.

Such stories continued to be reported every few years—each of them seemingly unaware that the same theme had been repeatedly reported (and repeatedly debunked) many times before. The persistence of this story offers a useful lesson in the misuse and misunderstanding of even the simplest income distribution statistics.

To prove the middle class is shrinking, declining, disappearing, or vanishing, these alarmed reports invariably define the middle in fixed terms, such as those with an inflation-adjusted income between $35,000 and $50,000. Such a fixed definition ensures that the proportion of households in that middle group *must* decline with a rise in general prosperity, because prosperity causes a rising *percentage* of families to earn *more* than $50,000.

In 2004, the *Washington Post* rediscovered this old theme, devoting nearly three pages to a major front-page feature on "The Vanishing Middle-Class Job." The *Post* launched this with great fanfare as "the first in an occasional series about the changes roiling the middle of the American workforce."[1] This was nothing new, of course. "In 1984, 1988, and 1992," noted columnist Bruce Bartlett, "the *Post* ran innumerable reports about the imminent disappearance of the middle class."[2]

In the 2004 version there were seven colorful graphs, one of which summarized the article's theme: "In 1967 nearly a quarter (22.3 percent) of households made between $35,000 and $49,999 in inflation-adjusted terms. But that share was down to 15 percent by 2003." But that same graph showed that the percentage of U.S. households with a real income *higher* than $50,000 rose from 24.9 in 1967 to 44.1 percent in 2003. And the percentage with income lower than $35,000 fell from 52.8 percent to 40.9 percent. The article could have been more aptly titled, "The Vanishing Lower-Class Job."

Another graph said, "The percentage of households earning close to the median income has fallen steadily over three decades." What was "close to the median" income, however, did not stay the same; it rose with economic progress. Measured in 2004 dollars, median household income rose 30 percent from 1967 to 2004—from $34,234 in 1967 to $44,389, in 2004 dollars.[3]

Any unchanged definition of "the middle class" can always be shown to vanish over the years, simply because *more people are making more money.* The fact that one of the nation's leading newspapers imagined that this was some sort of social crisis shows how easily confused some people are when looking at income statistics.

The statistical fallacy behind the "vanishing" middle class has been exposed repeatedly by many people, not just me. At the end of 2005, for example, a *Wall Street Journal* article by Stephen Moore and Lincoln Anderson noted that "in 1967 only one in 25 families earned an income of $100,000 or more in real income, whereas now [in 2004], one in six do. The percentage of families that have an income of more than $75,000 a year has tripled from 9% to 27%."[4] Such undisputable facts about a rising percentage of families earning higher salaries are clear, and clearly a good thing. Yet those same facts have been repeatedly described as a "vanishing middle class" for more than twenty years. If the past is any guide, young journalists are likely to reinvent this quaint fallacy in the future.

In a seemingly sophisticated variation on this same theme, *The State of Working America* from the Economic Policy Institute (EPI) notes that 31.3 percent of American families earned more than $75,000 in 2002, compared with only 11.1 percent who earned that much (in constant dollars) in 1969, and only 18.3 percent in 1979. The authors fret that "the pace at which families were shifting into the highest group—those earning more than $100,000—sped up in both the 1980s and 1990s." As a result, "the share at the top of the income distribution –over 200% of the median—grew fairly consistently over this period.... Thus, by this measure, America's broad middle class has been shrinking."[5] The alleged problem, by this measure, turns out to be that *too many* families were earning too much money. But why was that a problem?

## TOO MANY RICH PEOPLE

Such complaints—deploring the rapidly rising percentage of families earning more than $50,000–100,000 a year—are persistent yet inexplicable. A larger percentage of Americans earning more income is apparently being confused with a quite different concept of "inequality"—namely, the same number or percentage of people earning more money.

In an Urban Institute anthology about low-earners, for example, Anthony Carnevale and Stephen Rose began their chapter by correctly noting that "the share of workers in less-skilled retail and personal service (counter) jobs stayed remarkably constant from 1959 to the present." That was an accurate and effective refutation of slogans about "McJobs" or "the Wal-Martization of America," which suggest that a rising share of U.S. workers have been displaced from "good jobs" (on assembly lines and sweat shops) into retailing and counter jobs. Carnevale and Rose were nonetheless troubled by the exact opposite of "Wal-Martization"—namely, too many people moving up into high-paid jobs. The real inequality problem, in their view, was that "the number of workers earning over $50,000 went from 13 percent of all workers to 18 percent."[6]

Since the share of less-skilled jobs remained about the same while the share of high-skilled jobs grew rapidly, that must indeed produce a statistical impression of "pulling apart" (to borrow the title of an EPI book). Yet there is no sense in which a larger percentage of workers earning higher incomes can possibly have a harmful effect on other people with "less-skilled" jobs. The fact that a growing percentage of Americans invested time and money to acquire college degrees, for example, did not mean their higher salaries were "at the expense of" immigrants and others who did not finish high school.

In later chapters, we will find this same fundamental error repeatedly infecting much of the popular and academic discussion about increasing inequality of both wealth and income. That is, the fact that larger numbers of people have left what used to be thought of as "middle class," and become relatively well-off by the standards of an earlier generation, is often confused with the "rich getting richer"—i.e., a small minority becoming better-off than before.

Even academic specialists in poverty research make this same mistake—confusing *larger numbers* of Americans joining the ranks of "the rich" with the idea of the same number of rich becoming even richer.

In 1989, three prominent researchers affiliated with the University of Wisconsin's Institute for Research on Poverty, Sheldon Danziger, Peter Gottschalk, and Eugene Smolensky, published a paper on "How the Rich Have Fared, 1973–87."[7] (New York's Russell Sage Foundation funded this study, among many others describing high incomes and wealth as inherently problematic).

"Since the 1973 cyclical peak," the authors found, "the ranks of the rich have more than doubled." They defined families to include single people (normally called a household rather than a family). And they defined "rich" to mean households with incomes nine times higher than the poverty line—e.g., $95,000 for a family of four in 1987.

Their conclusion was that "[t]he proportion rich increased from 3.1 to 3.7 percent [of all households] during the 1973–79 peak-to-peak years . . . and rose to 6.9 percent by 1987."

Danziger, Gottschalk, and Smolensky evidently thought their readers should be alarmed to learn that too many U.S. families were joining "the ranks of the rich." Yet this was just another way of expressing the identical complaint of those who have repeatedly worried about a "vanishing" middle class. In both cases, the percentage of families earning "middle class" incomes declined because more of them were earning more than some arbitrary ceiling of $50,000–100,000 being used to define a middle-income group.

Danziger, Gottschalk, and Smolensky also worried that "about 50 percent of the income growth experienced by the top decile [ten percent] reflected higher earnings by wives." Working wives were earning too much money, pushing family incomes higher. As a result of so many more women and households joining "the ranks of the rich," they concluded, "inequality increased and is now higher than at any time since 1973."

If the percentage of households joining *the ranks of the rich* kept doubling every fourteen years, as it reportedly did from 1973 to 1987, then ranks of the rich would exceed 28 percent of all households by 2015. Would that be considered an alarming or ominous development?

Suppose the percentage of American families who earned more than nine times the poverty level eventually exceeded 50 percent. Would that too be a matter of concern? Would it be cited as proof that the American Dream of upward mobility was just a quaint myth?

This same "problem"—more families becoming rich and fewer of them remaining middle-class—is usually described in *relative* rather than absolute terms. Instead of complaining that a larger *percentage* of households or families is earning more than $95,000 or $100,000, it is customary to speak in terms of the *share* of income received by, say, the top 5 percent. What is not commonly understood, however, is that this same phenomenon of a larger *percentage* of households becoming rich (by the standards of the past) must also increase the apparent *share* of income received by, say, the top 5 percent. That is because many incomes that were high enough to be counted among the top 5 percent in 1973 or 1987 are not nearly high enough today, so they have been dropped out of the average. Any average of all incomes above $150,000, for example, is almost certain to be larger than an earlier average of all incomes above $100,000 because incomes between $100,000 and $150,000 are no longer diluting the average.

Census figures on household income differ from those used by Danziger, Gottschalk, and Smolensky, but are sufficiently similar to illustrate how the upward progress of a larger percentage of households into the ranks of what used to be considered rich has the statistical effect of raising the *share* of income reported in any top income group.

Danziger, Gottschalk, and Smolensky estimated that the percentage of households earning more than $95,000 in constant 1987 dollars (about $164,000 in 2004 dollars) had increased from 3.1 percent in 1973 to 6.9 percent by 1987. In 1973, even incomes that were well below $95,000 in 1985 dollars would have fit quite comfortably within the top 5 percent in

1973. By 1987, however, it would have been mathematically impossible to fit 6.9 percent of households into the top 5 percent. Many households that earned about $96,000 in both 1973 and 1987 would have been counted among the top 5 percent in 1973, but not in 1987. The income *threshold* or *floor* defining the top 5 percent had to be raised by 20.7 percent from 1973 to 1987, because so many more families were earning more than $95,000 in 1987 than in 1973. They could no longer all fit within just 5 percent of the total population.

Measured in constant 2004 dollars, an income above $106,615 would suffice to put households in the top 5 percent in 1973, but they would have needed $128,690 to make it into that elite group by 1987 and $157,185 by 2004.[8] If the Census Bureau had continued to include all income above $106,615 within the top 5 percent in 2004, as they did in 1973, then mean income would surely be substantially smaller than it actually was in 2004 when the actual average was no longer diluted (as it was in 1973) by incomes between $106,615 and $157,185. This leads us to another important reason why it is inappropriate to compare mean income in the bottom four quartiles with mean income of any top income groups. It is not just that top income groups alone have *no ceiling*, as discussed in the previous chapter, but also that the floor defining membership in top income groups has been substantially increased by the rising *percentage* of households earning what used to be considered a very high income.

## THRESHOLD ILLUSION

As a larger *percentage* of households joined "the ranks of the rich" there were soon "too many rich people" to fit within the top 5 percent or top 20 percent. The bar had to be raised, and that, in turn, has inspired what I call "threshold illusion." That is, a rising mean income among the top 5–20 percent has been routinely misinterpreted as indicating that income gains were confined to only that top group. In reality, rising incomes among those with incomes *below* the rising threshold have caused the definition of top income groups to *exclude* incomes that had formerly been among the top group (such as incomes between $106,615 and $157,185 in the preceding example).

The *mean* average of income in top income groups can be *pulled up* by a few unusually high incomes at the top, as shown in the first chapter by the contrast between mean and median incomes of the top 10 percent. But the average can also be *pushed up* from below by rising numbers of people moving up—leaving what used to be considered a "middle class" income and "join-ing the ranks of the rich."

One of my favorite old *Wall Street Journal* editorials (for obvious reasons) explained on November 3, 1988, that "[t]he top fifth of the income distribution starts at $50,371. This line has been moving sharply upward as more people crowd it from below. To steal a line from Alan Reynolds . . . so many people have been getting rich there isn't room for them all in the top fifth."

Converting that old example into 2004 dollars, the top fifth (quintile) of the household income distribution started at $68,352 in 1980. Only eight years later, households needed a 14 percent increase in real income (to $77,625) to fit into the top fifth by 1988. And by 2004, the top fifth started at $88,029.[9]

Figure 3.1 shows how the minimum threshold defining the top fifth trended upward from 1973 to 2004, except around the time of recessions. The mean average of income above the thresholds generally moved up and

**FIGURE 3.1**

**Minimum Threshold for the Top 20 Percent and Mean Income above That Threshold**

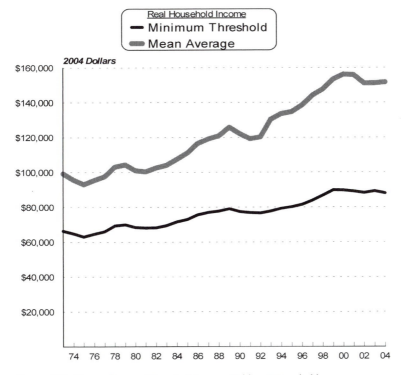

*Source:* U.S. Census Bureau, Historical Income Tables—Households.

down with the level of the threshold, though in a more dramatic way. Mean income in top income groups is more cyclcial than threshold or median income because some sources of the highest incomes are notoriously cyclical—such as small business profits, investment returns, commisions and bonuses.

Whenever the thresholds have been pushed up—by more people crowding the "top 20 percent" line from below—the average of incomes above the rising thresholds was almost certain to move up as matter of simple arithmetic. If you calculate a mean average of all the income above $88,029 in 2004, you are bound to come up with a larger figure than if you averaged all incomes above $68,352 (as we did in 1980). The average in 2004 *excluded* incomes between $68,352 and $88,029—incomes that were included in the average in 1980. Because the income in top groups is heavily skewed toward the lower end of the range, elminating incomes between $63,352 and $88,029 was bound to at least push the mean average up proportionately—by about 29 percent. Yet the reason the minimum needed to qualify for the top 20 percent increased by 50 percent from 1980 to 2004 was, as that old *Wall Street Journal* editorial put it, because "so many people have been getting rich there's room for them all in the top fifth." If only 20 percent earned more than $68,000 in 1980 but 25 percent earned more than $68,000 in 2004, for example, then by 2004 there was no longer nearly enough room for everyone earning more than $68,000 within the top 20 percent.

To be counted within the mean average of any *top* group, a household has to have an income above some "floor" or "threshold." The "threshold" defining membership in any *top* income group is not the same from one year to the next. On the contrary, that bar is raised whenever too many households join the ranks of the rich—by earning what was previously considered a relatively high income. That does not mean the rich are getting richer. It means *there are more of them.*

It has become commonplace to focus on the *percentage increase* in mean income among, say, the top 20 percent and then leap to the conclusion that those below the top 20 percent must not have shared in the rising prosperity. I call this "threshold illusion" because to the extent that the mean average at the top was pushed up by a rising threshold, the average incomes below the top quintile must also have increased. When thresholds rise, after all, the fourth quintile then includes incomes previously regarded as relatively rich (because they used to be in the top quintile). Because the mean average of income is much higher than the median for top income groups, and because incomes within top groups are clustered closer to the threshold than to the top, it is important to avoid threshold illusion. What lifts the floor beneath top income groups is a higher ceiling just below, caused by a greater number of people earning larger incomes.

Over a period of years, the mean average can rise because of more people "joining the ranks of the rich"—which raises the threshold. Or the mean average can rise because the typical (median) income of members of the top group has increased. Or the mean average can rise because of a possibly cyclical surge in a small number of very large incomes at the top. By itself, a mean average among top income groups cannot tell us which of these three possible explanations was the most important reason the mean went up or down. If mean income rose but the threshold did not, that would suggest that a relatively fixed number of households experienced the reported increase in mean incomes. But that rarely happens.

Because thresholds and means almost always rise together, at least part of the explanation of the rising mean is that greater numbers households had been "joining the ranks of the rich." The mean income in Figure 3.1 usually did rise more rapidly than the thresholds, particularly in the 1990s. From 1973 to 2004 the mean average rose by 52.7 percent while the threshold rose by 32.7 percent. But the rise in the mean was nonetheless significantly, though not exclusively, caused by the rise in the threshold defining the lower boundary of incomes included in that average.

References to long-term growth of "average" (mean) real income among top income groups, such as the top 1, 5, 10, or 20 percent, are inherently misleading because they fail to take into account of the movement of thresholds. Those thresholds *change*—in an upward direction when the economy is growing, and downward in recessions. When thresholds change, the mean average above those thresholds normally changes in the same direction. By itself, however, this just tells us that the range of incomes being included in the average has changed.

Threshold illusion would be minimized if we used a median average rather than a mean to describe average income of top income groups, as in the previous chapter. Because this is rarely done, however, it is prudent to at least examine what happened to thresholds when examining growth of average (mean) income among top income groups.

A rising percentage of households "joining the ranks of the rich" (and leaving the middle class) lifts the thresholds that define entry into each of the top income groups. Threshold illusion and claims the middle class is vanishing have much in common. They both involve failure to notice the critical distinction between a fixed number of rich becoming richer and a larger of percentage of households earning higher real incomes.

## NOTES

1. Griff Witte, "The Vanishing Middle-Class Job: As Income Gap Widens More U.S. Families Struggle to Stay on Track," *Washington Post*, September 20, 2004. http://www.washingtonpost.com/wp-dyn/articles/A34235-2004Sep19.html.

2. Bruce Bartlett, "Middle-Class Hooey," *National Review online*, September 27, 2004. http://www.nationalreview.com/nrof_bartlett/bartlett200409270808.asp.

3. U.S. Census Bureau, *Income, Poverty, and Health Insurance Coverage in the United States: 2004.*

4. Stephen Moore and Lincoln Anderson, "Great American Dream Machine," *Wall Street Journal*, December 21, 2005.

5. Mishel, Bernstein, and Allegretto, *The State of Working America, 2004–2005* (Economic Policy Institute, 2005), pp. 87–90.

6. Anthony P. Carnevale and Stephen J. Rose, "Low-Earners: Who Are They? Do They Have a Way Out?" in *Low-Wage Workers in the New Economy*, eds. Richard Kazis and Marc S. Miller (Washington, DC: Urban Institute Press, 2001), pp. 45, 63.

7. Sheldon Danziger, Peter Gottschalk, and Eugene Smolensky, "How the Rich Have Fared, 1973–87," *American Economic Review* (May 1989), pp. 310–14.

8. U.S. Census Bureau, "Historical Income Tables—Households," table H-2 (all races). http://www.census.gov/hhes/www/income/histinc/h01ar.html.

9. U.S. Census Bureau, "Historical Income Tables—Households," table H1. http://www.census.gov/hhes/www/income/histinc/H02ar.html.

# Four

## The Wage Stagnation Thesis

In the 25 years from 1980 to 2004 ... the wages of the typical worker actually fell slightly after accounting for inflation.
——"A Rising Tide?" *Washington Post* editorial
(March 12, 2006)

The major concern with income inequality in the United States today is the lack of growth of real wages for all but the top of the distribution, not the increase in inequality *per se*.
——Angus Deaton in F. Welch, *Causes and Consequences of Increasing Inequality* (2001)

---

The frequently repeated claim that real average wages have fallen since 1973 is based on a mean average that mixes part-time and full-time jobs together into a "weekly wages." Even that dubious average has been rising since 1992, and median wages have risen since 1980. Average real wages and benefits have risen by nearly 40 percent since 1973, after adjusting for inflation. Sensational claims that 80–90 percent of Americans have experienced low and stagnant real incomes since 1973 are also shown to be incorrect. The broadest measures of living standards are what consumers own (housing and consumer durables) and what they spend. Real consumption per person increased 74 percent from 1980 to 2004—a rate of improvement that far exceeded the trend from 1950 to 1979.

---

The long-term growth of real wages is a different topic than the distribution of income, although both topics involve equally thorny measurement problems. The two topics are frequently mingled together, however, to suggest there has been virtually no improvement in living standards for 80–90 percent of "working Americans" for 25 or 30 years.

Many of the most persistently gloomy reports about the U.S. living standards have long been based on the most misleading measure of labor income— namely, "average earnings of production and nonsupervisory workers" from the Bureau of Labor Statistics (BLS). On the basis of this dubious data, the initial essay in the 2005 *New York Times* series, *Class Matters*, concluded that "For most workers, the only time in the last three decades when the rise in hourly pay beat inflation was during the speculative bubble of the 90's."[1]

The claim that real wages have fallen almost continually since 1973 is one of those persistent stories (like the vanishing middle class) that has been endlessly repeated since the mid-1980s:

- In their 1988 book *The Great U-Turn*, Bennett Harrison and Barry Bluestone wrote, "We already know that real average weekly earnings have been falling since 1973. This is bad news in itself but what has been happening to the distribution of earnings could make the situation even worse."[2]
- In his 1990 book, *The Politics of Rich and Poor*, Kevin Phillips wrote, "For all workers, white collar as well as blue collar, their real average weekly wage—calculated in constant 1977 dollars—fell from $191.41 a week in 1972 to $171.07 in 1986."
- In his 1992 book, *Head to Head*, Lester Thurow wrote, "Between 1973 and 1990 America's real per capita GNP rose 28 percent, yet real hourly wages for nonsupervisory workers (about two thirds of the total work force) fell 12 percent, and real weekly wages fell 18 percent."[3]
- In their 1994 article in *Scientific American*, Paul Krugman and Robert Z. Lawrence began by saying, "The real wage of the average American worker more than doubled between the end of World War II and 1973. Since then, however, those wages have risen only 6 percent. Furthermore, only highly educated workers have seen their compensation rise; the real earnings of blue collar workers have fallen in most years since 1973. Why have wages stagnated?"[4]
- In a 1998 article in *American Prospect*, Jeffrey Madrick called the United States a "treadmill economy" largely because "the average wages of production and nonsupervisory workers, who basically comprise the lower 80 percent of earners, are still 10 or 15 percent below their 1973 highs."[5]
- In August 2005, a *Washington Times* editorial said, "The absence of any growth over the last five years in real average weekly earnings for 80 percent of workers is particularly striking given the fact that . . . nonfarm business productivity (output per hour of labor) has increased nearly 17 percent during the past five years."[6]

The statistics referred to in all of the above comments were always identified differently and incorrectly. Average earnings do *not* measure average hourly or weekly wages of "blue-collar" workers or "all workers" or the "lower 80 percent." On the contrary, nonsupervisory workers include "physicians, lawyers, accountants, nurses, social workers, research aides, teachers, drafters, photographers, beauticians, [and] musicians."[7]

The figures on average *weekly* earnings cannot be compared with output per *hour* (productivity) for many reasons. First, the earnings figures exclude all benefits and, second, hours worked per week among payroll workers have long been declining with the rise of part-time work in retailing and services. There is another BLS series on real hourly compensation, which is more comparable to productivity data (which is not to suggest that labor should capture all of the rewards from productivity-enhancing investment).

Average earnings estimates are a byproduct of a monthly BLS survey of employers, which is mainly used to estimate private nonfarm payroll employment. That survey does *not* attempt to represent 80 percent of the *entire* workforce, but 80 percent of the *private* nonfarm workforce. Since that excludes everyone who works for the federal, state, and local government, that means it covers only 62 percent of nonfarm civilian employees. Since it also excludes millions of self-employed people, those who work in agriculture and private household workers, it leaves out nearly half of all workers.

Average earnings are an arithmetic average—a *mean* not a median—derived from a voluntary survey of payroll employment at 155,000 businesses. The BLS adds up most of the dollars spent on payrolls (but not bonuses, stock options, and the like) and divides by paid hours (including vacations) but hours must sometimes be estimated. This "differs from wage rates," the BLS warns, and is "not the earnings average of 'typical' jobs or jobs held by 'typical' workers."

Average earnings *per week* combines part-time and full-time workers, and therefore does not even approximate the average earnings of either group. Table 4.1, by contrast, shows *median* weekly earnings for *full-time* wages and salary workers for broad occupational groups (excluding only farming, forestry, and fishing). Median earnings in 2004 were lowest for the 13.6 percent of full-time workers in miscellaneous service occupations, such as food services and janitorial services. But most professional, financial, sales, and office jobs are also services, and they generally pay well, as do skilled jobs in installation, maintenance, and repair. Production workers in manufacturing do not typically earn more than comparably skilled employees in service industries, nor was that true in the past.

Because average weekly earnings are a *mean* average (unlike Table 4.1) and because they mix part-time and full-time employees together, mass layoffs of part-timers and low-income workers would have the paradoxical effect of *raising* average earnings. Average weekly earnings can rise in hard times

**TABLE 4.1**
**Full-Time Wage and Salary Workers, 2004**

| Occupation | Number of Workers | Median Weekly Earnings ($) |
|---|---|---|
| Sales & Office | 24,950 | 558 |
| Professional | 21,371 | 883 |
| Service occupations | 13,763 | 411 |
| Management | 10,221 | 1052 |
| Production | 8,478 | 526 |
| Transportation | 6,604 | 520 |
| Construction & extraction | 6,232 | 604 |
| Business & financial | 4,558 | 847 |
| Installation & repair | 4,330 | 704 |
| All full-time workers | 101,224 | 638 |

*Source: Statistical Abstract of the United States* (2006), table 632.

because many part-time and/or low-wage workers lose their jobs. And average weekly earnings can fall in recoveries because previously unemployed low-wage workers—or a flood of unskilled immigrants—find jobs.

To grasp what is fundamentally wrong with using average earnings to measure typical living standards, imagine what would happen if the government could somehow enact and strictly enforce a $100-an-hour minimum wage. If that happened, then everyone incapable of adding at least $100 an hour to an employer's revenue would be permanently jobless. Since the average of those who still had jobs would include only people capable of earning at least $100 an hour, the "average earnings" figures among those still employed would look terrific (and so would average productivity).

Average earnings are *not* called "average wages" for good reasons. "Averages of hourly earnings differ from wage rates," explains the BLS, which never suggested that this series was an estimate of typical wage rates (much less of wages and benefits) on either an hourly or weekly basis.

In fact, this data series is so misleading that it is being phased-out by the Bureau of Labor Statistics (BLS). For one thing, as the BLS explains, "the production and non-supervisory worker hours and payroll data have become increasingly difficult to collect, because these categorizations are not meaningful to survey respondents. Many survey respondents report that it is not possible to tabulate their payroll records based on the production/non-supervisory definitions."[8]

An accountant in a manufacturing company should *not* be counted as a production worker, for example, but an accountant in a bank *should* be counted as a nonsupervisory worker.[9] Nonsupervisory is defined to exclude supervisors yet include "supervisory workers." Such arbitrary distinctions make responses "increasingly difficult to collect," suggesting the estimates depend on an increasingly dubious sample. Since the list of sampled firms is infrequently changed, the payroll survey is also notoriously weak in keeping track of what is happening to jobs or pay within relatively new firms.

There are other serious problems involved in trying to adjust any income figures for inflation over a period of years stretching back to 1973 (which is a uniquely bad year to begin with, because price controls in 1973 briefly suppressed and concealed inflation). No price index, least of all the fixed-weight consumer price index (CPI-W) normally used for this purpose, can actually provide a completely credible comparison of real incomes across three decades. Attempting to compare today's price index with one from 1973 would require comparing computers with typewriters, digital TIVO with rooftop antennas, and contemporary cars with Chevy Vegas and Ford Pintos.

Figure 4.1 adjusts average weekly earnings with the best available price index, the chain-weighted index for personal consumption expenditures (PCE). Yet real weekly earnings nonetheless appear to fall from a cyclical peak of $496 in 1973 (an illusory blip, because price controls understated inflation) to *cyclical* lows of $459 in 1982 and $429 in 1992 (in 2000 dollars).

By 2004, this flawed statistic was almost back to the 1973 level. Yet that still makes it look as though those who say "real average weekly earnings have been falling since 1973" may be technically correct (but misleading about *when* the decline occurred). To accept that conclusion, however, requires ignoring *all* other measures demonstrating substantial increases in U.S. living standards—such as the Census Bureau surveys, Commerce Department figures on real income or consumption per capita, and the real compensation series from the BLS.

Even aside from the many good reasons why the BLS is scrapping the average earnings figures, however, there is one overwhelming reason why the weekly figures cannot be taken seriously as a measure of typical living standards. As the BLS explains, there have been "persistent long-term increases in the proportion of part-time workers in retail trade and many of the service industries have reduced average workweeks in these industries." Millions of previously nonworking spouses and students sought and found part-time work, which diluted average earnings, particularly on a weekly basis. Substituting a low-wage job for no job (or an unpaid job at home) makes average earnings *appear* lower, yet results in *higher* family incomes.

Figure 4.2 shows that *hours worked per week* fell dramatically in retailing and in leisure and hospitality, while the number employed in those sectors

**FIGURE 4.1**
**Real Average Weekly Earnings of Private Nonfarm Production and Nonsupervisory Workers**

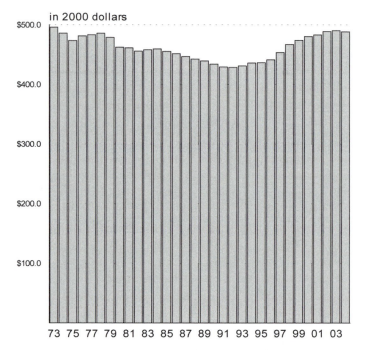

Private Nonfarm Production & Nonsupervisory Workers

*Note:* Adjusted for Inflation with the PCE Deflator.
*Source:* U.S. Bureau of Labor Statistics.

increased by millions. Because millions more "payroll employees" work fewer hours per week than was true in the past, any comparison of what happened to average *weekly* wages over time is dishonest.

As we discuss in Chapter 6, in the context of comparing corporate CEO pay with that of "average workers," some studies have actually taken these *weekly* earnings figures (regardless of hours worked per week) and multiplied them times 52 weeks, claiming the resulting figure is what average full-time workers earn per year. To call that disingenuous would be too kind.

## MEDIAN MAY NOT BE TYPICAL

A *Washington Post* editorial on May 12, 2006, launched an "occasional series about inequality" by reviving the wage stagnation thesis. "In the 25 years

**FIGURE 4.2**
**Average Weekly Wages Mislead When Weekly**
**Hours Decline**

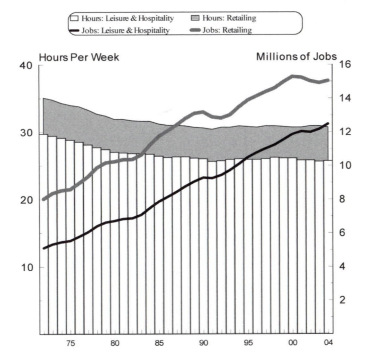

*Source:* http://www.bls.gov/webapps/legacy/cesbtab2.htm.

from 1980 from 2004," the editorial asserted, "the wages of typical workers fell slightly after accounting for inflation. So, too, did wages for the 50 percent of the work force that earned less than the typical, or median, employee."

Unlike past efforts, which talked about a mean average and included part-time workers, this editorial appeared to allude to a different BLS series from a different survey (of households rather than employers)—namely, the "usual median earnings of full-time wage and salary workers." Such median wages amounted to $262 in 1980 and $638 in 2004.

Translated into 2000 dollars, by using the PCE deflator, the median weekly wage rose to $589.40 in 2004 from $503.09 in 1980—an increase of 17.2 percent. Even using the less trustworthy consumer price index (CPI-U-RS) would still show a 12.6 percent real increase.

There were three recessions between 1980 and 2004, so comparing figures for the start and end of that period does not show what happened when. The real median wage in 1991 was $510.68, for example, so the increase by

2004 was 15.4 percent or 1.2 percent a year. We cannot compare that rate of increase with the past, to say it is either weaker or stronger than usual, because this data series began in 1979.

Because of major demographic changes, movements in the median wage do not necessarily describe what happened to "typical" workers over a decade or more. The median was mathematically diluted by the addition of millions of low-wage immigrants. Adding so many more people at the bottom of the income ladder redefined the mid-point (median). Yet it probably had little or no effect on those previously considered "typical" (middle-income) except to hold down their cost of fast food or home and lawn care.

Any measure of wages alone understates increases in living standards by excluding health and retirement benefits. The BLS index of real compensation includes benefits; it rose to 118.7 in 2004 from 89.5 in 1980—a gain of 32.6 percent. Even total compensation excludes income from investments, including the statistically invisible returns inside IRA and 401(k) plans. All measures of earned income likewise exclude the underground economy and transfer payments, including the Earned Income Tax Credit and Social Security.

The broadest measure of living standards is what consumers spend. Real consumption per person rose from $14,816 in 1980 (in 2000 dollars) to $25,816 in 2004—an unprecedented gain of 74.2 percent.

## EMPLOYEE BENEFITS ARE NOT WORTHLESS

The most obvious of many flaws in either the mean or median earnings figures is that they ignore employee benefits that have generally become more varied and more generous over time—not just health insurance but also life insurance, dental insurance, employer contributions to 401(k) retirement plans, etc. Such benefits *are* included in other BLS statistics, such as real compensation per hour (which is part of the productivity series).

Figure 4.3 shows *cumulative* increases in the BLS index for total compensation since 1973, including health insurance, retirement, and other benefits. This shows that compensation per hour rose by nearly 40 percent from 1973 to 2005, after adjusting for inflation, which was scarcely stagnant.

Talking about what happened "since 1973" conceals what happened when. The prosperous 1960s were followed by three increasingly severe inflationary recessions between 1970 and 1982, which certainly took their toll on real incomes. The consumer price index rose by 11.3 percent in 1979 and 13.5 percent in 1980; very few workers received wage increases nearly that large.

**FIGURE 4.3**
**Cumulative Annual Increases in Real Compensation
per Hour, Since 1973**

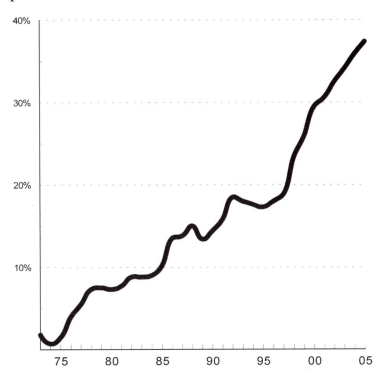

*Source: Economic Report of The President* (2005), table B-50. 2005 is third
quarter year-to-year; Economic Indicators 12-05.

Even aside from inflation, weakness of real *output* per worker was bound
to translate into weakness of real *income* per worker. As Martin Neil Baily,
Gary Burtless, and Robert Litan explained, "The slowdown in productivity
growth began in the late 1960s and early 1970s and was at its worst between
1973 and 1979."[10] Yet chronic complaints about declining real earnings
from 1988 to 2005 made it sound as though the problem was at its worst
long *after* 1980.

As can be seen in Figure 4.3, real hourly compensation fell 1.1 percent in
1974, which is why the wage stagnation thesis begins with 1973. It fell again
in 1980, when consumer prices rose by 11.6 percent. Gains from 1985 to
1992 were relatively strong, except in 1989. Real compensation fell for three
years in a row in 1993–95, even without accounting for the 1993 tax
increase. But real compensation grew briskly from 1997 to 2004 despite a
terrorist attack and recession in 2001 and a big spike in international oil

prices in 2004–2005 (we cannot realistically expect U.S. employers to compensate workers for imported oil prices, which are a big drag on profits for most firms).

The substantial cumulative increase in real compensation per hour from 1973 to 2004 is just one of many statistics that make it difficult to imagine why so many of economists claim to have not noticed that typical living standards were rising in those years.

## CONSUMPTION WITHOUT CONSUMERS?

The overwhelming bulk of income comes from work or transfer payments (which come from somebody else's work). Wages, salaries, and benefits accounted for 68.8 percent of personal income in 2004, for example, and transfer payments for 14.6 percent.[11] The Bureau of Economic Analysis adjusts total consumer spending for inflation and divides by the nation's population to arrive at real per capita consumption. In constant 2000 dollars, U.S. consumers spent $25,816 per person in 2004—nearly double the $13,371 figure for real per capita consumption in 1973.[12]

The March 2006 *Washington Post* editorial that claimed real median wages had fallen for 25 years also concluded that "the rising tide helped only workers at the top [10 percent]." In 2003, a *New York Times* journalist likewise wrote, "[T]he bottom 80 percent of Americans have seen their incomes stagnate for three decades."[13] But if all but the top 10–20 percent had experienced no real income gains for 25–30 years, how could real consumption per capita possibly have doubled since 1973? Although some would have us believe that most U.S. consumers simply got deeper and deeper in debt, year after year, such a claim implies that household net worth fell continually for decades. Yet, as Chapter 7 demonstrates, median household net worth (assets minus debts) has increased steadily and substantially.

Unless the top 10–20 percent could somehow consume unlimited numbers of houses, cars, shirts, and steaks, it is difficult to imagine how each American's real consumption could have doubled if real wages and salaries had really been unchanged. The average size of new homes rose from 1,500 square feet in 1970 to 2,349 square feet in 2004, and the national home ownership rate rose from 62.9 percent in 1970 to 69.2 percent by the end of 2004.[14] How could so many people be living in so much larger houses if only 10–20 percent had significant increases in income?

Could anyone believe that all those shopping malls that have sprung up since 1973, and all the new homes and restaurants, are really catering to just a fortunate few? How many cars and appliances could the top 10–20 percent have purchased?

**TABLE 4.2**
**Ownership of Consumer Goods**

|  | All Households 1971 (%) | Poor Households 2001 (%) |
|---|---|---|
| Car or truck (one or more) | 79.5 | 72.8 |
| Air conditioner | 31.8 | 75.6 |
| Color TV (one or more) | 43.3 | 97.3 |
| Refrigerator | 83.3 | 98.9 |
| Clothes Dryer | 44.5 | 55.6 |
| Microwave | >1.0 | 73.3 |
| DVD or VCR | 0 | 98.0 |
| Personal computer | 0 | 24.6 |
| Cell phone | 0 | 26.6 |

*Source:* W. Michael Cox and Richard Alm, *Myths of Rich & Poor*; Robert E. Rector and Kirk A. Johnson, "Understanding Poverty."

Table 4.2 compares the percentage of *poor* households owning such things as a car, color TV, or air conditioner in 2001 with the percentage of *all* U.S. households who owned such goods in 1971. The 1971 figures are from *Myths of Rich & Poor* by W. Michael Cox and Richard Alm; the 2001 figures are from a paper by Robert E. Rector and Kirk A. Johnson.[15] What this shows is that a larger percentage of poor households owned these goods in 2001 than average households did thirty years earlier (with the sole exception of cars). Scarcely anyone owned a microwave oven in 1971, and nobody owned a personal computer or cellular phone because they had not been invented—nor had DVDs, calculators, cordless phones, answering machines, digital cameras, iPods, and many other marvelous devices (including amazing medicines) that even most poor Americans now take for granted.

Figure 4.4 takes a really long look at the trend in U.S. living standards, as measured by real per capita consumption—what consumers could buy, per person, adjusted for inflation. The straight line is a trend line from 1929 through 2004, which includes just two infamous three-year declines in 1930–33 and 1979–82.

With a ruler and a sharp eye, it is easy to identify a *below-average* secular expansion from 1933 to 1961 during which the line did *not* rise as steeply as the 1929–2004 average (indicating relatively slow growth in real consumption per capita). That was followed by a dozen years of improvement from 1961 to 1973. But 1973 was an outlier—a single year in which inflation-adjusted measures of income, wages, and consumption appeared artificially strong because President Nixon's price controls temporarily suppressed and disguised actual inflation. There were widespread shortages,

**FIGURE 4.4**
**Real Per Capita Consumption in 2000 Dollars, 1929–2004**

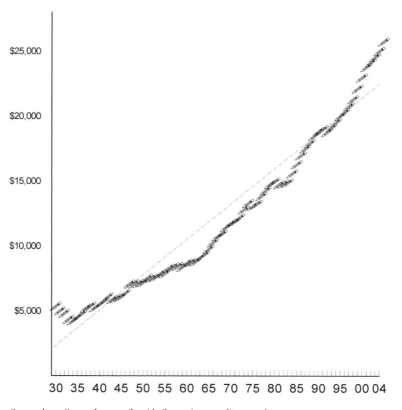

*Source*: http://www.bea.gov/bea/dn/home/personalincome.htm.

shrinking packages, and quality deterioration in 1973. After a dreadful inflationary recession in 1974–75, there were just four years of catch-up before another inflationary recession that lasted from 1980 to 1982.

Since 1982 there were two *unusually prosperous* periods during which the line rose much more steeply than the long-term average—namely, 1983–90 and 1992–2004. For some reason, however, many economists and economic journalists bemoan the unprecedented progress after 1982 and romanticize the sluggish progress of 1951 to 1973, which did not even manage to get the growth of living standards back up to the long-term trend.

According to Robert Pollin and Stephanie Luce, "The golden age, lasting roughly from the end of World War II through the 1960s, was characterized by . . . rising living standards, especially for the white male sector of the working class. By contrast, the leaden age has been distinguished by slow growth, high unemployment, more severe business cycles, and stagnating or de-clining living standards for the majority."[16]

Economists who depict 1951–1973 as a "golden age" invariably claim there has been virtual *stagnation* in typical living standards during the 1983–2005 period when real consumption per capita grew at an unprecedented pace. This amounts to reverse alchemy—turning gold into lead. It requires enormous statistical creativity among economists who fabricate numbers to facilitate this historical fiction. And it requires enormous credulity among economic journalists who often echo such statistics with inadequate skepticism and excessive rhetorical indignation.

## HIDING REALITY IN A FOOTNOTE

The improbable idea that real incomes (and therefore real consumption) have stagnated since 1973 for all but the top 10 or 20 percent has been outdone by an even more preposterous claim that real incomes stagnated for all but the top 1 percent. A page on the AFL-CIO Web site titled "What Is Wrong with CEO Pay—And What Union Funds Are Doing About It" reprinted a graph from the Piketty-Saez paper (where it is labeled Figure A1) ostensibly showing average real income soaring for the top 1 percent but stagnating "for everybody else."[17] These figures, culled from individual tax returns, have been widely reported but narrowly understood.

We cannot possibly know what *share* the *top* income groups receive unless we know how much money is earned by the *bottom* 90–99 percent. If the Piketty-Saez estimates grossly *understate* the level and growth of incomes among the bottom 90–99 percent of Americans, they must likewise *overstate* the relative share and growth of incomes among the top "tax units," which are almost always mistakenly referred to as *families* (although, as the next chapter shows, many of the top tax units are Subchapter-S and limited liability corporations).

According to the unique Piketty-Saez measure and definition of income for the year 2000, writes Emmanuel Saez, "the median income, as well as the average [mean] income for the bottom 90% of tax units is quite low, around $25,000."[18] Specifically, Table 1 from Piketty-Saez would have us believe the median income of the bottom 90 percent was $25,076 in 2000. That number is too low to be believed.

To say that 90 percent of all "tax units" had a *median* income "around $25,000" in 2000 is to say that *45 percent earned less than $25,000 a year.* Yet the Census Bureau estimates that only 19.2 percent of U.S. *families* (or 27.5 percent of households) earned less than $25,000 in 2000.[19] To say the bottom 90 percent had a *mean* income of around $25,000 is to say that if we could gather up all the salaries, interest and dividends of *90 percent* of American "tax units" and distribute the money equally that would have resulted in each taxpayer receiving only $25,000.

Mr. Saez spent enough years in the United States to realize his $25,000 figure is unbelievably low (as is his related estimate that everyone with an income above $87,334 was in the top 10 percent in 2000). Yet he offers only two inadequate explanations: "First, our income definition does not include any government transfers. Second, CPS income is reported at the household level which is larger than the tax unit we consider."

Transfer payments are critically important to the bottom 20 percent but they are much too small in total to even begin to explain an estimated median income of just $25,000 among the bottom 90 percent. The Piketty-Saez income definition is adjusted gross income (AGI) minus transfer payments and realized capital gains but adding back the adjustments. Adjusted gross income exceeded $6.2 trillion in 2003, or nearly $6.3 trillion after adding back the adjustments ($87.6 billion). The portion of Social Security income reported on tax returns was $97.8 billion, unemployment benefits $44 billion, and Earned Income Tax Credit refunds $34 billion. Including all three major transfer payments (as measured by tax returns) would have increased adjusted gross income by only 2.8 percent.

Mr. Saez's second explanation for the $25,000 figure relies on the distinction between a tax unit and a household. Two employed singles living together constitute one household but two tax units, so their combined household income could be twice as large as their income as measured per tax unit. Treating tax units as if they were families or households can indeed by misleading. Yet those who cite these Piketty-Saez figures *never* make that distinction. Paul Krugman, for example, wrote that "According to Piketty and Saez . . . in 1998 the top 0.01 percent received more than 3 percent of all income. That meant that the 13,000 richest *families* in America had almost as much income as the 20 million poorest *households*" [emphasis added].[20]

When Mr. Saez suggests that 90 percent of Americans had a median income of about $25,000 in the year 2000, such a low figure cannot be reconciled with household or family data from the Census Bureau, whether or not transfer payments are included. Median *family* income in the year 2000 was $50,732, without counting realized capital gains. Since half earned more than $50,732, it would have been impossible for 45 percent (half of 90 percent) to have earned less than $25,000. A *mean* average of income was $65,773 for families, $57,135 for households. Yet the tax-based estimates of Mr. Saez result in both mean and median averages for 90 percent of U.S. "tax units" that were not even half as large as the mean and median for *all* households or families.

Part of the problem is that not everyone reports all of their income to the tax collector. The IRS notes that reported AGI in 2002 was $961 billion smaller than a *comparable* measure of personal income (with the same adjustment), thus leaving 13.7 percent of personal income unaccounted for.[21]

Whatever the explanation, the fact that the Piketty-Saez estimates suggest that 90 percent of Americans have an average income near $25,000 and that 45 percent earn even less than $25,000 does not reflect a failure of the U.S. economy but a failure of those estimates.

When it comes to measuring long-term *trends* in these grossly understated incomes of the bottom 90–99 percent, the result of measuring income from income tax data is even less believable. A footnote to the graph the AFL-CIO reprinted explains that the visual depiction of income stagnation was actually an artistic deception: "From 1973 to 2000, the average income of the bottom 99% would have grown by about 40% in real terms instead of stagnating (as displayed in the figure above) if we had included all transfers (+7% effect), used the CPI-U-RS (+13% effect), and especially defined income per capita (20% effect)."

Piketty and Saez added that real income among the top 1 percent would also have grown faster if those essential corrections were made, so "the finding that top 1% incomes have done so much better than the bottom 99% since 1973 is therefore largely independent of those assumptions." To say the top 1 percent "would have done much better" without those "assumptions" does not excuse the graphical illusion that real incomes among the other 99 percent were "stagnating." If the graph in Piketty Saez was not deliberately intended to convey the false impression that nearly all U.S. households had experienced *stagnating* incomes since 1973, it is difficult to imagine what other purpose it might have been intended to serve.

This was just one of many deceptions arising from this and other studies purporting to measure long-term income gains among the top 1 percent, as we discover in the following chapter.

## NOTES

1. Janny Scott and David Leonhardt, "Shadowy Lines That Still Divide," in *Class Matters* (New York: Times Books, 2005), p. 19.

2. Bennett Harrison and Barry Bluestone, *The Great U-Turn: Corporate Restructuring and the Polarizing of America* (New York: Basic Books, 1988), p. 117.

3. Lester C. Thurow, *Head to Head* (New York: William Morrow and Co., 1992), p. 53.

4. Paul R. Krugman and Robert Z. Lawrence, "Trade, Jobs and Wages," *Scientific American*, vol. 270(1) (April 1994).

5. Jeffrey Madrick, "The Treadmill Economy," *American Prospect*, vol. 9 (11) (November 1, 1998). http://www.prospect.org/web/page.ww?section=rootandname=ViewPrintandarticleId =4575.

6. Editorial, "The Facts on Wage Trends," *Washington Times*, August 15, 2005.

7. U.S. Bureau of Labor Statistics, "Technical Notes to Establishment Survey Data Published in Employment and Earnings" (May 6, 2005). http://www.bls.gov/web/cestn1 .htm.

8. U.S. Bureau of Labor Statistics, "Recent and Planned Changes to the Current Employment Statistics Survey" (August 29, 2005). http://www.bls.gov/ces/cesww.htm.

9. Paul Ryscavage, *Income Inequality in America: An Analysis of Trends* (Armonk, NY: M.E. Sharpe, 1999), p. 91.

10. Martin Neil Baily, Gary Burtless, and Robert E. Litan, *Growth with Equity* (Washington, DC: Brookings Institution, 1993).

11. "Sources of Personal Income," *Economic Indicators* (December 2005). http://www .gpoaccess.gov/indicators/.

12. Bureau of Economic Analysis, "National Income and Product Accounts Tables," table 7.1 (Selected Per Capita Product and Income Series in Current and Chained Dollars). http://www.bea.gov/bea/dn/nipaweb/index.asp.

13. David Cay Johnston, *Perfectly Legal* (New York: Penguin Books, 2003), p. 307.

14. The square footage of homes in 1970 is from Cox and Alm, cited in the following note, and figures for 2004 are from the *Statistical Abstract of the United States* (2006). Homeownership in 1970 is taken from http://www.census.gov/hhes/www/housing/census/ historic/owner.html.

15. W. Michael Cox and Richard Alm, *Myths of Rich and Poor: Why We're Better Off Than We Think* (New York: Basic Books, 1999), p. 15. Robert E. Rector and Kirk A. Johnson, "Understanding Poverty in America," *Executive Summary Backgrounder 1713* (Heritage Foundation, January 14, 2004), p. 3. http://www.heritage.org/Research/welfare/ bg1713.cfm.

16. Robert Pollin and Stephanie Luce, *The Living Wage: Building a Fair Economy* (New York: New Press, 1998), p. 23.

17. AFL-CIO website, http://www.aflcio.org/corporatewatch/paywatch/retirementsecurity/ index.cfm.

18. Saez, "Reported Incomes and Marginal Tax Rates," *NBER Working Paper* 10273 p. 17.

19. *Statistical Abstract of the United States* (2006), tables 673 and 678. To put Mr. Saez's $25,000 estimate in perspective, an income below $17,603 for a family of four was officially poor in 2000.

20. Krugman, "For Richer."

21. U.S. Department of the Treasury. *SOI Tax Stats—SOI Bulletin—Historical Tables and Appendix*, "Table 6: Total Adjusted Gross Income Estimated from National Income and Product Accounts (NIPA) and as Reported on Individual Income Tax Returns per Statistics of Income, Tax Years 1950–2002." http://www.irs.gov/taxstats/article/0,,id=115033,00 .html.

# Five

# The Top 1 Percent

The after-tax income of the top 1 percent of American households jumped 139 percent, to more than $700,000, from 1979 to 2001, according to the Congressional Budget Office.
>    —Janny Scott and David Leonhardt, *Class Matters* (2005)

[Emmanuel Saez and Thomas Piketty] calculated a long-run distribution of income in America from information on tax returns. Their latest study shows that the top 1% of Americans now receive 15% of all income, up from about 8% in the 1960s and 1970s.
>    —"Dividing The Pie," *The Economist* (February 2, 2006)

---

Estimates of the share of income earned by the top 1 percent are assembled from a sample of individual income tax returns. Such estimates are problematic because the 1986 tax reform changed what is reported as income to the IRS. Lower tax rates on individual income induced thousands of businesses to switch to filing under the individual tax rather than the corporate tax. Corporate executives switched from accepting stock options taxed as capital gains to "nonqualified" options taxed as W-2 salaries. New tax-deferred savings plans resulted in much of the dividends, interest income and capital gains of middle-income taxpayers disappearing from the tax rolls. Studies estimating the income share of the top 1 percent often include capital gains received by that group simply because those gains are taxable, yet exclude Social Security and other transfer payments from their measure of lower incomes.

---

Dramatic news reports about seemingly huge increases in income going to the top 1 percent did not begin to appear until 1992, because the Census Bureau does not publish estimates for groups smaller than the top 5 percent. Ever since 1992, however, there have been dozens of reports, editorials, and columns expressing anxiety and outrage about the apparently large and rising share of personal income received by the top 1 percent (about 1.3 million), top 0.1 percent (130,000), and even the top 0.01 percent (13,000) of taxpayers.

All of these widely publicized estimates arrive at different numbers in different ways, but they all depend on a sample of about 100,000 individual income tax returns. Tax-based studies of income distribution come from three main sources. The only official estimates were first created by the Congressional Budget Office (CBO), because Congress requested estimates of which income group bears what share of various federal taxes.[1] An entirely different set of estimates of *before-tax* income among the top 10 percent of taxpayers, going back to 1913, first appeared in the fall of 2001 in a historical study by two French economists: Thomas Piketty of Ecole Normale Superieure in Paris and Emmanuel Saez of U.C. Berkeley.[2] Tax-based estimates for a unique measure of "retrospective income" were also prepared for academic conferences by Michael Strudler and Tom Petska of the Statistics of Income (SOI) division of the Internal Revenue Service (IRS) and Ryan Petska of Ernst and Young.[3] In 2005, a paper by Ian Dew-Baker and Robert J. Gordon used money income reported on W-2 forms (wages, salaries, and stock options) as a proxy for real wage rates by income group for 1966–2001.[4]

Not everyone believes such income tax data can provide a reasonably accurate picture of the level of relative earnings among U.S. households in any particular year, much less of the change in that distribution of income over decades. Daniel Feenberg and James Poterba have argued that "for studying the distribution of incomes below the top tier, tax returns are not the best source of information. Not all low-income taxpayers file tax returns, and even for those who do, tax returns do not include information on most transfer payments."[5]

In this chapter, we find that tax returns are also not the best source of information for middle incomes either, because most dividends, interest, and capital gains from the savings of middle-income families used to be taxable (and therefore recorded on tax returns) while more and more of their investment income has recently been accumulating inside tax-deferred savings plans for retirement and college.

Because tax returns fail to include most transfer payments to those with lower incomes and most investment income of those with middle incomes, this automatically increases the apparent share of income going to top income groups.

Princeton economist and *New York Times* columnist Paul Krugman once criticized a Treasury Department study for *using income tax data* to gauge people's mobility between lower and higher income groups. "Since only about half the working population actually paid taxes over the entire period," he wrote, "this meant that the study was already biased toward tracking the relatively successful."[6] This chapter confirms that tax statistics are indeed increasingly "biased toward tracking the relatively successful."

Income-tax data could be a better way to estimate incomes than Census Bureau and Federal Reserve polls only if people were more likely to tell the truth about their income to the IRS than to pollsters. Yet people have much less to gain from lying to pollsters.

Aside from legal tax avoidance and illegal tax evasion, a far more serious problem with using tax data to measure income is that what is *defined* as income on tax returns was radically changed by, among other things, the Tax Reform of 1986. The Statistics of Income Division of the IRS explicitly warns that, "Data for years 1987 and after *are not comparable* to pre-1987 data because of major changes in the definition of 'adjusted gross income' (AGI)."[7]

There was no requirement to report income from tax-exempt municipal bonds until 1987, for example, so such income (which is highly concentrated among those with the highest incomes) was simply invisible on previous tax returns. Yet tax-exempt interest is now included in some studies that use an "expanded" definition of income, such as the CBO. Lower individual tax rates and relaxed financial regulations after 1987 also made it much more attractive for publicly traded corporations (with shares traded on stock exchanges) to go private—to file their income under the individual income tax as Subchapter-S corporations, partnerships or limited liability companies (LLCs). There was a rush to move income from the corporate income tax form to the individual tax after 1986 that has continued ever since.

In April 2006, *Washington Post* columnist Steven Pearlstein noted that "such prominent private brands as Neiman Marcus, Sears, Kmart, Toys "R" Us, Dunkin' Donuts, J. Crew, Georgia-Pacific and Hertz are now in private hands." Whenever Subchapter-C corporate income was transformed into the income of Subchapter-S corporations or limited liability companies, income that used to appear only on *corporate* tax forms began to show up as millions of dollars of new income in the *individual* tax data. Tax-based income distribution studies then misinterpret that switching of income from corporate to individual tax as if rich "individuals" were earning much more money. Profits of America Online appeared only on the corporate income tax returns so far, but may eventually show up as individual income because that firm is now a limited liability company, AOL LLC, which often portends private ownership.

When income is switched from corporate to private, individual income tax returns wrongly record that as an increase of the highest incomes. This is called "income switching." Similarly, when new companies that would have been set up as Subchapter-C corporations under previous rules decide to instead remain under the individual tax, that too is income switching. The costly accounting rules of the Sarbanes-Oxley Act of 2002, which only apply to public firms, are thought to have encouraged more firms to go private and fewer to go public.

When tax return data is used to compare average income among the top 1 percent before and after 1987, the "individual" incomes after 1987 now include billions that were previously recorded as corporate income or (in the case of interest on tax-exempt bonds) not recorded at all. This is not to deny that a few hundred top celebrities, entrepreneurs, hedge fund managers, and corporate bosses are not making millions more than they used to. They are. Yet the way that corporate executives are paid also changed after 1986, with a new type of stock options that are taxed as ordinary income displacingthe previously favored "incentive" stock options taxed as capital gains (and therefore excluded from tax-based estimates of top salaries in the1970s).

Estimates of the top 1 percent's income gathered from individual tax returns are seriously compromised by huge changes in the way both businesses and individuals report their income. This is not just true of top income groups, but also of tax return data about low and middle incomes.

The lowest incomes have become increasingly understated by excluding transfer payments that have accounted for a *rising* share of actual income. All but one of the tax-based studies excludes checks from Social Security and the Earned Income Tax Credit (EITC). And the incomes of those in the middle have become increasingly understated because a *rising* share of their investment income is now tax-deferred and therefore no longer visible in tax return data. All of these statistical problems come together in estimated shares of loosely defined "income" supposedly received by the top 1 percent, so that the *increasingly overstated* income of that tiny group was certain to rise as share of the *increasingly understated* income reported to the IRS by everyone else.

This chapter explains in greater detail why income tax data provides extraordinarily misleading information about income distribution, particularly when comparing income shares over a long period of time (a "time series") during which there were massive changes in the income tax law.

## POLITICS AND THE PRESS

In 1992, Sylvia Nasar of the *New York Times* was the first to make a big news story out of tax-based estimates suggesting rapid growth of incomes among the top 1 percent. In an essay in *Commentary* in 2005, Bruce Bartlett, who was deputy assistant secretary of the U.S. Treasury from 1988 to 1993, revisited the controversy that old article stirred up.[8]

The *New York Times* revised its first edition of this story without any explanation in its final edition. The first edition said, "An outsized 60 percent of the growth in after-tax income of all American families between 1977 and 1989—and an even heftier three-fourths of the gain in pretax income—went to the wealthiest 660,000 families, each of which had an annual income of at least $310,000 a year, for a household of four. . . . While total income for all 66 million American families expanded by about $740 billion in inflation-adjusted dollars during the Carter-Reagan years, the [$190 billion] slice belonging to the top 1 percent grew to 13 percent of all family income, up from 9 percent."[9]

Those figures came from an analysis of CBO estimates by Paul Krugman. Since Ms. Nasar said the slice belonging to the top 1 percent was $190 billion, that figure amounted to just 25.7 percent of the $740 billion total gain—not 60 percent (or 70 percent as Mr. Krugman later wrote). The revised edition spoke of the growth of "average income" rather than "total income." Yet that late revision did not appear to be noticed or understood. Instead, the mistaken view that the top 1 percent had captured 60–70 percent of the nation's entire increase in income during the 1980s gained wide currency.

In their campaign book, *Putting People First*, candidates Bill Clinton and Al Gore wrote, "During the 1980s, the wealthiest 1 percent of Americans got 70 percent of income gains."[10] In an April 23, 1992, letter to *The Wall Street Journal*, J. Bradford DeLong of U.C. Berkeley wrote, "Since World War II the top 1% has earned about 8% of national income, so we would expect it to receive 8% of real income gains. . . . But over the past 15 years the top 1% has not received 8% of real income gains. It has received 60%."

What Ms. Nasar meant, however, was *not* that the top 1 percent received 60 percent of all income gains in the economy—which her figures proved impossible—but rather that 60 percent was the change in size of that particular group's "slice"—from 9 percent to 13 percent. Yet even that unusual comparison would have been 44 percent (four divided by nine), if the figures were right.

As the CBO later struggled to explain, "about one-fourth [of all income gains] went to families [actually, taxpayers] in the top 1 percent." The CBO claimed that if those figures were adjusted for family size, the "slice" going to the top 1 percent increased by 44 percent from 1977 to 1989, or 33 percent if realized capital gains were left out.[11]

When asked by the *Wall Street Journal* in 1992 to respond quickly to Ms. Nasar's piece, I offered a few ancillary points about one-time capital gains from the stock market recovery, and about the rising amount of income needed to be included within the top 1 percent.[12] I also complained about the political gimmick of defining 1977 rather than 1980 as the start of the 1980s.[13] In a 1993 Clinton Administration report, the 1981–1989 term of the Reagan Administration was stretched to include the entire Carter term and the first Iraq War: "Throughout the 1980s, slow growth in living standards was accompanied by growing inequality. . . . People at the bottom of the income scale actually lost ground: measured in inflation-adjusted dollars, their incomes fell between 1977 and 1991."[14]

A lively exchange about the Nasar-Krugman data came to involve Clayton Yeutter, the president's counselor for domestic policy, writing in the *New York Times*, former assistant treasury secretary Paul Craig Roberts in *Business Week*, Paul Krugman in the *American Prospect*, and myself.[15]

Looking back on those entertaining debates of 1992, it now seems clear that *all* of us (including the CBO itself) completely missed the most important reasons why these tax-based income figures simply did not mean what everyone assumed they meant.

Figures from individual tax returns should never be used for this purpose because *what is counted as income* on tax returns depends on the contemporary tax laws, which changed spectacularly in the 1980s.[16]

When Piketty and Saez first published their own tax-based income estimates in 2001, those estimates showed the share earned by the top 1 percent falling from 12.2 percent in 1940–1949 to 9.6 percent in 1950–1959, 8.2 percent in 1960–1969, and 7.9 percent in 1970–1979. The 1960–1979 estimates seemed to vindicate Mr. DeLong's comment (the source of which was a mystery in 1992) that "Since World War II the top 1% has earned about 8% of national income." Yet it did not follow that "we would expect it [the top 1%] to receive 8% of real income gains." Too much had changed.

Unprecedented changes in marginal tax rates, capital gains tax rates, tax-deferred savings plans, executive stock options, welfare, and the relationship between individual and corporate tax systems altered the historical relationships between actual income earned and the *types* of income that end up being reported on individual tax returns.

Meanwhile, what was previously described as "threshold illusion" also made long-term comparisons misleading. The top 1 percent received 9.3 percent of household income in 1979, according to the CBO, but that included all income above $147,800 (in 2003 dollars). The top 1 percent received 14.3 percent in 2003 (or 12.2 percent after taxes), but that included only those incomes above $237,500.[17] A mean average of all income above

$237,500 was sure to be larger than an average of all income above $147,800, of course, but that threshold was raised because many more people earned more than $147,800 in 2003 than in 1973—too many to still fit within the top 1 percent.

Table 5.1 shows that the CBO's estimate of the top 1 percent's share of pretax household income fell with the stock market crash of October 1987 and surged with the stock market boom in 1996–2000, but otherwise showed no significant and sustained upward trend. The Piketty-Saez estimates are nearly as high as the CBO figures in most years despite excluding capital gains because they are not actually shares of *total* income at all; income from Social Security and other transfer payments is excluded. The Piketty-Saez estimates rise and fall with the stock market from 1996 to 2002 because most capital gains from stock options of executives and nonexecutives were taxed as ordinary income by the 1990s (unlike the 1970s and 1980s).

In a massive understatement, Piketty and Saez note that "a significant part of the gain [in top income shares] is concentrated in two years, 1987 and 1988, just after the Tax Reform Act of 1986."[18] Because the CBO estimates include capital gains, the top 1 percent's share appears shifted

**TABLE 5.1**
**Estimated Income Share of Top 1 Percent**

| Years | CBO (%) | Piketty-Saez (%) |
|-------|---------|------------------|
| 1986 | 14.0 | 9.1 |
| 1987 | 11.2 | 10.8 |
| 1988 | 13.3 | 13.2 |
| 1989 | 12.5 | 12.6 |
| 1990 | 12.1 | 13.0 |
| 1991 | 11.2 | 12.2 |
| 1992 | 12.3 | 13.5 |
| 1993 | 11.9 | 12.8 |
| 1994 | 12.1 | 12.9 |
| 1995 | 12.5 | 13.3 |
| 1996 | 13.8 | 14.1 |
| 1997 | 14.9 | 14.8 |
| 1998 | 15.7 | 15.3 |
| 1999 | 16.7 | 15.9 |
| 2000 | 17.8 | 16.9 |
| 2001 | 14.8 | 15.5 |
| 2002 | 13.5 | 14.7 |
| 2003 | 14.3 | NA |

*Note:* CBO includes taxable capital gains; Piketty-Saez excludes transfer payments.

forward to 1986 as investors rushed to sell stocks before the capital gains tax rose from 20 percent to 28 percent.[19] And the stock market crash of October 1987 presumably left stockholders with fewer net capital gains.

With capital gains excluded, as they are from this set of Piketty-Saez estimates, the top 1 percent's share suddenly jumped from 9.2 percent in 1985–1986, when the top tax rate was 50 percent, to 13.3 percent in 1988 when the top tax rate dropped to 28 percent. Much more pretax income was reported at the much lower tax rate, but that was not a sudden "increase in inequality." It was a sudden increase in the amount of high income reported on individual income tax returns.

Aside from the unprecedented stock market euphoria of 1996–2000, which was scarcely a long-term trend, neither the estimates of the CBO nor that of Piketty-Saez show any significant and sustained upward trend except for the dramatic changes before and after the Tax Reform Act of 1986. This is merely one reason among many as to why it is extremely deceptive to compare tax-based estimates of income distribution from 1970 to 1979 with any year after 1986—particularly with a year such as 2000–2001 when stock prices were unusually high (stock prices bottomed in the second quarter of 2003).

In 2006, Piketty and Saez complained that "the top 0.1% income share [one-tenth of 1 percent] was around 2.5% in the 1970s and reached a peak above 9% in 2000."[20] As this chapter demonstrates, such comparisons of recent peak estimates with those of 1970s are *completely* invalid because of massive changes in what is or is not recorded as income under the individual income tax.

Piketty and Saez claimed, without explanation, that income gains "concentrated within the top 1% (and especially the top 0.1%) . . . have come at the expense of the bottom and the middle class." There is no reason why anyone's income gains need be at the expense of anyone else. Besides, we later show that executive and nonexecutive stock option windfalls, which accounted for many of the 1996–2000 gains among the top 0.1 percent, were entirely "at the expense of" stockholders.

The increasingly common abuse of individual income-tax data to estimate changes in the top 1 percent's share of income between the 1970s and any year after 1986 is probably the single biggest error in the entire error-prone topic of income distribution.

## SHIFTING FROM CORPORATE TO INDIVIDUAL TAX

The most glaring problem with comparing income tax data before and after the 1986 tax reform is that a rapidly rising share of high-income "individual" taxpayers has consisted of *Subchapter-S corporations, limited liability companies (LLCs), partnerships,* and *proprietorships* that previously would have chosen to file as Subchapter-C corporations. As IRS economist Kelly Luttrell explained:

The long-term growth of S-corporation returns was encouraged by four legislative acts: the Tax Reform Act of 1986, the Revenue Reconciliation Act of 1990, the Revenue Reconciliation Act of 1993, and the Small Business Protection Act of 1996. Filings of S-corporation returns have increased at an annual rate of nearly 9.0 percent since the enactment of the Tax Reform Act of 1986. During the same period, taxable [Subchapter-C] corporations have experienced an average annual decline of 1.3 percent.[21]

The number of S-corporation returns was nearly 3.2 million by 2002, Ms. Luttrell found, including 90,700 in that year alone that "elected to make the conversion from a taxable corporation to an S-Corporation."

Business profits and losses were far less likely to show up on individual tax returns back in 1977–1980 than in subsequent years mainly because corporate tax rates were then much lower than individual tax rates. By contrast, individual tax rates have been little higher than corporate tax rates (and sometimes lower) since 1987. That is why a large amount of highest income on individual tax returns used to be reported as corporate profits.

In 1980, individual income tax rates were 64 percent on taxable income above $50,000 and 70 percent above $100,000. The corporate tax rates were much lower—30 percent on income above $50,000 and 46 percent above $100,000.[22] In 1977–1980, the much *higher* tax rates on businesses filing under the individual tax code provided a strong incentive for professionals, farmers, and closely held businesses to file as Subchapter-C corporations. Even before 1986, there was a phased-in reduction in individual tax rates from 1981 to 1984 that narrowed the wide gap between high individual tax rates and lower corporate tax rates.

"ERTA 1981 produced a sudden burst of S-corporation income (which was negligible up to 1981)," noted Emmanuel Saez; "This is most likely due to a shift from C-corporations to S-corporations. It is interesting to note that the increase in S-corporation income is concentrated mostly in the top .01%." Before 1981, he added, "S-corporation income was extremely small, as indeed the standard C-corporation form was more advantageous for high income individual owners because the top individual tax rate was much higher than the corporate tax rate and taxes on capital gains were relatively low. S-corporation income increases sharply from 1986 to 1988 and increases slowly afterwards."[23]

Rules governing Subchapter-S originally allowed only thirty-five stockholders but that number was expanded in stages to 100. The Small Business

Protection Act of 1996 allowed *banks* to file as Subchapter-S corporations.[24] "Surprisingly, a large number of banks do not pay corporate income tax because they have converted to a Subchapter-S corporation. As of December 2003, there were over 2000 Sub-S banks, with the largest at $9 billion."[25] Before 1996, the profits of those banks could not have appeared in taxable income of "individuals," but now they do.

In contrast with 1977–1980, big reductions in the highest individual tax rates that were phased-in 1982–1984 and 1987–1988 provided a strong incentive for professionals, farmers, and small-tomid-sized businesses to file as partnerships, proprietorships, LLCs, or Subchapter-S corporations with up to 100 shareholders (whose owners are taxed at individual rates).

"As of 1986," notes Alan Auerbach of U.C. Berkeley, "about one-fourth of all U.S. corporations were S-corporations; by 1997, this share had risen to more than half. In 2001, S-corporations accounted for almost a quarter of before-tax corporate profits."[26]

"The large reduction in individual tax rates under the Tax Reform Act of 1986," wrote Treasury Department economists Robert Carroll and Warren Hrung, "was followed by a large increase of the pass-through form, such as S corporations. S-corporation assets increased from 1.6 percent of total corporate assets in 1985 to 4.1 percent by 1990. The net income of S Corporations as a share of total corporate net income rose from 5.8 percent in 1985 to 9.3 percent in 1990."[27]

Another IRS study found that the Tax Reform Act of 1986 "had a large effect on how certain corporations chose to be taxed. Certain C Corporations took advantage of the lower maximum individual tax rate and converted to S status in 1987... Converted companies were generally larger than... established S Corporations."[28]

Figure 5.1 uses tax-based figures from Piketty and Saez to show business income from Subchapter-S Corporations, LLCs, partnerships, and proprietorships as a share of all income reported by the top 1 percent and the top 0.1 percent. Among the top 0.1 percent (about 130,000 taxpayers by 2001), business profits accounted for 29.6 percent of total income—up from only 6.6 percent in 1981. Subchapter-S corporations, LLCs, and partnerships have accounted for an increasingly large portion of the income attributed to the top 0.1 percent and top 1 percent.

Tax shifting—the movement of business income from corporate to individual tax returns—clearly accounted for a very substantial share of the post-1980 growth of income attributed to the top 0.1 percent and the top 1 percent.

Shifting profits from the corporate to the individual income tax form was simply a bookkeeping change, having nothing to do with the actual

**FIGURE 5.1**
**Business Income's Share of Total Income of Top 1 Percent
and Top 0.1 Percent**

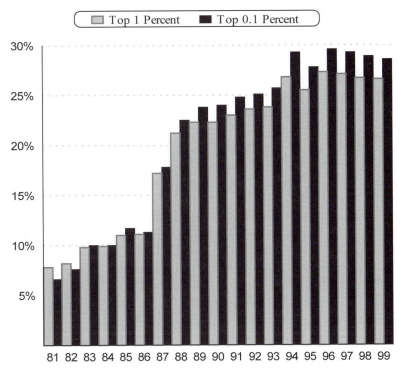

*Note:* Caculated from Individual Income Tax Data.
*Source:* Thomas Piketty & Emmanuel Saez (2004), table A.7.

distribution of income. That fact alone makes it illegitimate to use individual income tax data to gauge shares of income over time. It also makes it illegitimate to describe taxpaying units as "households" or "families."[29]

## INCOMES BELOW ZERO?

Ironically, using tax data to measure mean income could also *understate* typical money income in the *bottom* quintile. That is because business losses are subtracted from individual income, leaving an apparent income that is very low—sometimes below zero.

The degree of understatement of the lowest "individual" income due to business losses is most severe during recessions. That is why Gramlich, Kasten, and Sammartino had to explain away their unwanted finding that real income in the lowest decile grew by 7.5 percent between 1985 and 1990. They correctly noted that "growth rates can be misleading" in the lowest decile because "much of the growth is attributable to a reduction in business losses."[30] The tax-based income *share* of the lowest decile (10 percent) and quintile (20 percent) is also misleading for the same reason. What looks like a very low income "household" in the tax return data can include many normally profitable businesses having a tough year.

In the CBO's unusually broad measure of expanded income, "households with negative income are excluded from the lowest income category but are in the totals." Households with negative income? Because of this statistical oddity, the combined income shares of all five quintiles add up to 102 percent of the total, which implies that "households" with incomes *below zero* account for 2 percent of total income.

Negative income is one of several conceptual confusions that arise from wrongly assuming the individual income tax is actually just a tax on individuals.

Excluding negative income from the lowest income category does not solve this problem. For the same reason some firms report a negative income in bad years, others report a positive yet dismally low income. Many normally profitable small businesses barely turn a profit from time to time. They do not necessarily report *negative* income but may nonetheless show up in the lowest income category at times, and then in the top 10 percent at other times.

Tax returns with negative incomes cannot be assumed to represent "households in the lowest income category" for the same reason tax returns in the top 1 percent cannot be assumed to represent "households" in the highest income category. Neither statistic is necessarily about households at all, but is often greatly affected by fluctuating *business income* that has been increasingly reported under the individual income tax rather than the corporate profits tax.

Ian Dew-Becker and Robert J. Gordon "assume that losses are not economically significant, but rather are a result of give-aways in the tax code. . . . By ignoring losses, we make the assumption that year-after-year losses are not economically meaningful but rather reflect opportunities provided by the tax system for middle-income and upper-income people to shelter income from taxes. These losses are not what we mean by 'poverty' and are economically different from the situation of those who earn only wage income and are in the bottom 20 percent of the distribution."[31]

Dew-Becker and Gordon assume all business losses (not just those that occur year-after-year) are fictional, the result of unexplained tax shelters. But businesses *do* lose money—their costs sometimes exceed revenues. To disregard such business losses in the individual income tax data (while retaining incomes of profitable firms) simply exposes the fact that income distribution estimates based on such data are not really about the incomes of households at all, but about the incomes of a changing mixture of households and businesses.

Business losses are not what anyone means by poverty, but business profits are likewise not what most of us mean by personal affluence. As Dew-Becker and Gordon point out, "The top 1 and 0.1 percent have a far higher share of new non-labor income than wage income." Yet that new nonlabor income includes, as Emmanuel Saez noted, "a surge in business income reported by high income individual taxpayers due to a shift away from the corporate sector."[32]

The growing importance of business profits and losses within the individual income tax data explains why studies based on tax return data have had to define "family income" in ways we would not ordinarily associate with the income of families—such as the Strudler-Petska adjustments for "depreciation in excess of straight-line depreciation."[33] Small businesses rarely make much use of accelerated depreciation, partly because they have been able to write-off most costs of business equipment immediately in recent years (up to $108,000 in 2006). The fact that IRS economists Strudler and Petska believe the individual income tax data need to be adjusted for accelerated depreciation suggests that profits of larger businesses present a pervasive problem for those interpreting individual income tax data as household rather than business income.

The fact that tax-based income studies attempt to cope with accelerated depreciation and negative income simply confirms that the commingling of business and personal income makes such data increasingly untrustworthy.

## TAX RATES AFFECT TAX AVOIDANCE

The difference between reported and actual income also poses a big problem when it comes to the ways in which high-income people respond to big changes in *marginal* tax rates—the tax on each additional (marginal) dollar of *taxable* income (gross income minus adjustments, exemptions, and deductions).

There is, first of all, considerable evidence that lower tax rates on capital gains result in previously undisclosed additions to wealth (unrealized capital gains) showing up as income on tax returns. I surveyed a dozen U.S. studies on that subject for an Australian tax reform commission.[34] They all show that whenever the capital gains tax rate was reduced, investors held more assets in forms subject to this tax and traded those assets more frequently and therefore reported more capital gains income than otherwise (aside from whether the stock market did well or poorly).[35]

Such increased *reporting* of capital gains on tax returns resulted in a very large increase in top incomes in studies such as those of CBO and Strudler-Petska that count such *taxable* gains as income. Yet the fact that a larger fraction of capital gains were realized rather than unrealized each year did not necessarily represent an actual increase in wealth or income.

Even aside from capital gains, the amount of income *reported* in the highest tax bracket has proven to be highly responsive to just how high those tax rates are on marginal (added) income. The highest *marginal* tax rate on individual incomes—the tax rate on an extra dollar of income—fell from 50 percent in 1986 to 37.5 percent in 1987 and 28 percent in 1988. Feenberg and Poterba subsequently observed that if you left out capital gains realizations (which spurted in 1986), then the top 0.1 percent of returns reported *5.1 percent* of total income in 1988—nearly double their 2.8 percent share in 1986. Actual pretax income of the top 0.1 percent could not possibly have doubled in two years, so Feenberg and Poterba concluded that big cut in marginal tax rates "raised the incentive for high-income households to report current taxable income rather than engage in tax avoidance activities."[36]

The responsiveness of reported income to each 1 percent change in tax rates is called the "taxable income elasticity." Emmanuel Saez estimated such elasticity using gross rather than taxable income, which conceals any response to higher tax rates involving more aggressive use of deductions (a bigger mortgage) or adjustments (a bigger contribution to a Keogh account). He nonetheless concluded, "The data strongly suggests that those taxpayers with very high incomes are much more responsive to taxation than taxpayers in the middle or upper middle class."[37]

Income reported on tax returns by the top 1 percent should be expected to rise in a period of falling tax rates such as 1986–1988 partly because of the greater incentive to work harder—entrepreneurs start more businesses, spouses of high-bracket taxpayers rejoin the labor force, retirements are delayed, those previously working abroad or in the underground cash economy take jobs that require taxes to be paid, etc.[38]

As Feenberg and Poterba found, however, high-income people also report more income because there is less incentive to avoid taxes (by investing in tax-exempt bonds, for example) and more incentive for managers to prefer being paid in taxable cash rather than tax-exempt perks and tax-deferred future income.

In a 2005 survey of such research by Saez and others, Treasury economists Robert Carroll and Warren Hrung found "the more recent studies suggesting a taxable income elasticity of about 0.4." Such an estimate, they explained, "suggests that over 50 percent of the static revenue gain [from increasing the two highest marginal tax rates] might be offset through the taxable income response.[39]

Yet that figure is near the bottom of the range of estimates they surveyed. The two studies reporting a lower 0.40 estimate found the response much higher at higher incomes. Jon Gruber and Emmanuel Saez estimated the elasticity rose to 0.56 at incomes above $100,000. Saez has an estimate of 0.63 among the top 1 percent of taxpayers. Feldstein's estimate is higher still, at 1.0.

Even the lowest of these estimates predict that raising the top two tax rates would shrink *reported* income so much that any expected revenue gain would be more than cut in half. If that happened, the top 1 percent would report much less before-tax income than previously, which would not necessarily mean they had lower incomes. Yet tax-based studies would nonetheless misconstrue that as an actual reduction in before-tax incomes among the top 1 percent rather than simply an increase in tax avoidance.

Taxable income elasticity is another reason why the top 1 percent's share of income reported on tax returns in 2003 (when the top marginal tax rate was 15 percent on dividends and capital gains and 35 percent on salaries) cannot be sensibly compared with the share reported before 1981, when top marginal tax rates were twice that high.

Those who rely on tax returns to estimate income shares are compelled to assume reported income is the same as actual income. That means they have to disregard all evidence of substantial taxable income elasticity among high-income taxpayers.

## CANADA, BRITAIN, AND CEOs

In a 2005 paper with Michael Veal, Emmanuel Saez argued that the apparent gain in the share of income going to the top 1 percent and top 0.1 percent could not have been due to shifting businesses income from corporate to individual tax returns because the share going to the top 1 percent also rose in Canada where such shifting did not occur. This argument is partly contradicted by the data from Piketty and Saez in Figure 5.1. It is also contradicted by the evidence just discussed, which found the top 1 percent *report more income* when marginal tax rates are greatly reduced. As Saez observed, "top income shares within the top 1% show striking evidence of large and immediate responses to the tax cuts of the 1980s."[40] Why would that not also be true in other countries? Is it surprising that many more Russians earn and report high incomes under the recent top tax rate of 13 percent than they did when the top tax rate was 90 percent?

According to the Organization for Economic Cooperation and Development (OECD), "Tax-based data for 4 OECD countries on the share of the equivalised [comparable] disposable income accruing to the top 1% of the population (as a share of the income of the top decile) . . . suggest large increases in this share in all countries except France."[41]

Those four countries included the U.K. as well as the United States, Canada, and France. Saez and Veal offer a theory that covers only two of the four. They conjecture that the top 1 percent's rising share incomes in Canada was *not* because rich people report more income when tax rates fall (taxable income elasticity), but was instead because competition with the United States for top corporate executives raised the compensation of Canadian executives.[42]

Unless we assume CEOs only travel by land, the global competition for executives is no different between the United States and Britain than between the United States and Canada. Yet the OECD graphs show that the income share of the top 1 percent rose much more dramatically in the U.K. than it did in Canada. Moreover, the *Wall Street Journal* echoes a common claim that "the typical British CEO earns a little more than half of what his or her U.S. counterpart makes."[43] That comparison is between apples and oranges, or even between grapes and watermelons. It makes British CEOs look overpaid, actually, since typical British corporations surely do not have anything close to half the market value (capitalization) or earnings of typical U.S. corporations.

In any case, the comparative compensation of a few hundred top CEOs in four countries cannot begin to explain why income tax data show the top 1 percent's share of reported income rising most rapidly in the United States and U.K., less so in Canada and not at all in France. Yet those facts are entirely consistent with the literature on taxable income elasticity.

In the United States, the top marginal rate was cut from 70 percent in 1980 to 50 percent in 1982 and to 28 percent in 1988. In the U.K., the top marginal tax rate was cut from 83 percent to 60 percent in 1981, and 40 percent in 1990. In 2006, tax rates in the United States and U.K. were still only half as high as they had been in 1980. Meanwhile, France marched off in the opposite direction—reintroducing a 1.8 percent wealth tax in 1989, *increasing* the top marginal tax rate on incomes from 51.8 percent to 56.8 percent in 1992, and adding an extra 0.5 percent tax on all income "for reimbursement of social debt" (Piketty and Saez incorrectly report the top tax rate in France as 48 percent, ignoring two surtaxes).[44]

In Canada, the 1988 cut in the federal tax rate tells only half the story because some high Provincial tax rates were also reduced after 2000. By 2005, Canada's combined federal-provincial rate had been reduced from 60.4 percent to 48.2 percent in Quebec, from 50.5 percent to 43.7 percent in British Columbia, and from 48.8 percent to 39 percent in Alberta.[45]

Reported income of the top 1 percent rose most dramatically in the two countries that cut top tax rates in half, rose much less in Canada where top tax rates were not so drastically reduced, and did not rise at all in France— the only country that increased the highest marginal tax rates while the others were lowering theirs. That is exactly what the research on taxable income elasticity predicts would have happened.

"While progressivity has unambiguously declined in the United States and in the United Kingdom," note Piketty and Saez, "it has increased somewhat in France." As the research on taxable income elasticity predicts, France has been having much more trouble finding many rich people to tax. Piketty and Saez estimate that average tax rates in France were 37.8 percent in 2005, and the bottom 90 percent faced a similar average tax of 36.7 percent. In other words, taxes collected from top 10 percent in France barely made a dent in the average tax burden of everyone else. In the United States, by contrast, the average tax rate was 23.4 percent but the bottom 90 percent paid an average rate of just 18.5 percent, with most of that going for Social Security and Medicare benefits.[46] Piketty and Saez (who happen to be French) appear to view the French system as superior simply because it resulted in so few high-income taxpayers.

The effect of tax rates on reported income at the top is also suggested by a Towers and Perrin report finding CEOs in France receive 19 percent of their pay in the form of tax-favored benefits and perquisites and only 41 percent as "variable" (risky) pay that depends on performance. Their U.S. and Canadian counterparts received only 11 percent of pay as benefit and perks, with 62 percent of the total pay package being variable in the U.S. and 51 percent in Canada.[47] This shows why international comparisons of *cash* compensation mislead. And it also shows one way that high marginal tax rates (as in France) reduce reported incomes among the top 1 percent: Over-taxed executives can react by refusing to accept much risk and by negotiating to receive less of their pay in taxable cash and more as benefits and perks.

Much of the apparent increase in the top 1 percent's income share in the United States after the 1986 tax reform was due to the fact that high-income taxpayers everywhere respond to lower tax rate in ways that increase the amount of income they report as individual income. When that happens (unlike France), it lightens the tax burden on everyone else. Far from in-creases in *reported* income among the top 10 percent in the United States after 1986 having been "at the expense of" others, it has resulted in more than 43 million low-income U.S. taxpayers being relieved of any federal income tax bill by 2006 according to the Tax Foundation (and many of them instead receiving an EITC check). The relative tax burden borne by middle-income taxpayers was greatly lightened after the highest U.S. tax rates fell far below those in France, where tax rates on the bottom 90 percent are now literally twice as high as they are in the United States If income distribution is measured by the amounts reported on tax returns, then France's greater equality of *before-tax* income at the top appears very expensive in terms of much lower *after-tax* incomes for the middle.

## HOW STOCK OPTIONS BECAME VISIBLE

In the next chapter we discover that the largest differences among many estimates of CEO pay arise from the different ways they try to put a value on stock options "granted" (given) to executives and other employees. Stock options confer the right to buy a specific number of shares of stock after a "vesting" period (usually three to five years) but before the options "expire" (usually ten years). If the stock price at the time the options are "exercised" (cashed-in) is higher than the price at the time they were granted, the difference is either taxed as a capital gain or as ordinary income depending on the variety of stock option used. Tax-based income estimates measure the value of stock options when exercised, because that is when they show up on tax returns as either salary income or as capital gains. Many surveys of CEO compensation instead attempt to estimate the future value of such options when they were first granted.

Millions of people, not just executives, received large windfalls in 1997–2001 from exercising stock options granted three to ten years before. But those gains did not come from other workers—they came from stockholders who did not complain too much because options are only worth something if the stock price has gone up. When stock options are exercised the company must cover the cost by either spending cash that would otherwise have been invested (thus reducing future earnings for shareholders) or by issuing new stock and thereby "diluting" the value of older stock (because future earnings are shared among more stockholders). The zero-sum notion that stock option gains are received "at the expense of" workers is wrong.

Executive stock options are nothing new (I even received stock options as a lowly bank economist in 1976–1980). What is new is the fact that they now are mainly of the "nonqualified" type that show up on W-2 tax return data if they are exercised. Because that did not use to be the case, comparisons of labor income among the top 1 percent with such figures from the 1970s must exaggerate the increase because the older tax returns of corporate executives recorded their income from stock options as capital gains rather than as salaries. "Because gains from stock options prior to the 1970s were not generally taxed as personal income and consequently not recorded on personal income tax returns, tax returns may provide a biased estimated of the incomes of top earners," noted Carola Frydman and Raven E. Saks.[48]

"The practice of granting stock options was started in the 1950s," according to Pricewaterhouse Coopers; "High technology companies started granting broad-based options in the 1960s, and by 1970 many more employees were receiving regular option grants.[49] What changed, particularly after 1988, was the *type* of stock options granted and the way any income from such options was or was not reported as ordinary income on income tax returns.

Before 1972, the top tax rate on ordinary income was 70–77 percent, so sensible executives only negotiated for incentive stock options (ISOs) taxed at much lower capital gains tax rates of 25–34 percent.

Suppose a chief executive officer (CEO) was granted one million ISOs in 1971 at the market price of $10 a share and later exercised the right to buy shares at that price in 1979 when the strike price had increased to $11. The potential $1 million capital gain would *not* have been reported as income because the executive had to hold on to those shares long enough to qualify for the lower tax on long-term capital gains (which was risky; the stock might fall). The currently much more popular options are "nonqualified" for capital gains treatment because the shares are sold soon after the option is exercised.

Capital gains resulting from *nonqualified* options—unlike those from the earlier ISOs—are now reported on W-2 forms and therefore appear as salary income in studies that estimate the distribution of incomes (or wage rates) from income tax returns. Changes in the tax law in 1972, and particularly in 1988, made nonqualified options much more attractive and incentive stock options much less so. And that makes it illegitimate to compare recent tax return data on high "wages" with those of 1966–1987, when most exercised stock options were *not* reported as ordinary income.

Executive incomes from stock options *were* reported as capital gains in the 1970s and early 1980s, but Dew-Becker and Gordon, and Piketty and Saez, do not include capital gains. A later section of this chapter agrees with them that taxable gains should not be included. Yet their tax-based comparisons of top incomes over time are nonetheless badly contaminated by income shifting between the capital gains tax and the ordinary income tax— just as they are also degraded by shifting between the corporate and individual tax.

Under 1969 tax law, any gains from *nonqualified* stock options *granted* in 1972 or later could eventually be taxed at a lower 50 percent rate on "earned income" after about three to ten years when they were vested and exercised. That is why virtually all gains resulting from exercising executive stock options before 1975 (and most such gains before 1990) are totally invisible in tax-based studies purporting to show huge gains in salaries among the top 1 percent since 1966 or 1973.

Although the tax on interest and dividends remained at 70 percent from 1972 to 1981, the maximum tax on earned income was 50 percent. Meanwhile, the tax on capital gains was increased to 36.5 percent in 1972 and 40 percent from 1976 to 1978, making even incentive stock options (and therefore options in general) relatively unattractive by the late 1970s. An inflationary recession from 1980 through 1982 made any sort of stock-based compensation look downright frightening. But lower tax rates in 1983–1984, and particularly after 1987, changed that completely—and not just for executives.

Executive stock options usually do not expire for ten years. When the top tax rate was reduced from 50 percent in 1986 to 28 percent in 1988 that provided a huge incentive for executives to *delay* cashing-in nonqualified options until 1988 or later. Because the tax on capital gains was simultaneously increased to 28 percent, that also provided a huge incentive for even faster income switching between incentive stock options (taxed as capital gains) and nonqualified stock options (then taxed at the same rate).

Lower tax rates on ordinary income also contributed to the proliferation of nonexecutive stock options, widely distributed among millions of lower-level employees during the 1990s. By 2002, the Pricewaterhouse Coopers report estimated that "between seven and ten million employees (approximately 7% of the total workforce) in the U.S. currently receive stock options." If the employee stock options of *millions* people were considered, rather than just those of a few hundred CEOs, then stock options in general may explain quite a lot of the 1997–2001 surge (and subsequent fall) in W-2 income reported by the top 1.3 million taxpayers.

## W-2 INCOME AND THE TOP 13,000

In 2005 another tax-based study of incomes was written by Ian Dew-Becker and Robert J. Gordon of Northwestern University.[50] They presented estimates for only six years—1966, 1972, 1979, 1987, 1997, and 2001—and their figures for total incomes face the same problems as the other studies. Their separate figures for what they call "wage income" avoid many of those problems, however, while highlighting the problem of stock option income switching.

The Dew-Becker and Gordon study purported to compare growth of wages and salaries (and *nonqualified* stock options) between higher and lower income groups from 1966 to 2001 by converting total "wage income" into hourly wage rates. They made that heroic leap from total income to hourly income by assuming (implicitly) that there has been no increase since 1966 in the number of two-earner households in the top 10–20 percent of tax returns, and also no reduction in the percentage of workers putting in 40 hours a week among the bottom 20 percent (and also no new under-reporting of tips and other cash income in order to qualify for the EITC).

Continuing the recent trend of slicing the top 1 percent into smaller and smaller bits, the top group was narrowed all the way down to the top one-hundredth of 1 percent (the 99.99th percentile). In 1972, that meant just 7, 760 taxpayers. By 2001, the 99.99th percentile had grown to about 13,000 taxpayers whose combined salaries and stock options added up to $83 bil-lion *before taxes*—less than 1 percent of all personal income (which was $8.7 trillion).

Reporting on this study, columnist Paul Krugman seemed predictably displeased that "between 1972 and 2001 the wage and salary income... at the 99.99th percentile rose 497 percent. No, that's not a misprint.... It's time to face up to the fact that rising inequality is driven by the giant income gains of a tiny elite."[51]

How could the incomes of the remaining 99.99 percent of taxpayers be driven by a tiny elite who received less than 1 percent of personal income? When Larry Page and Sergey Brin became overnight billionaires by selling Google shares in April 2004, for example, that did not make anyone a dollar poorer. On the contrary, it made new shareholders richer too. The Google founders did not take a bigger *share* of income; they created whole new sources of income (and knowledge) for themselves and others.

Some imagine the government could have simply taxed away an even bigger share of the top 13,000 taxpayers' reported earnings (the $83 billion is a before-tax figure) while still expecting the 13,000 to keep earning and reporting as much income as before. Research on taxable income elasticity reminds us that such a policy can backfire, leaving much less income re-ported and therefore less available to tax.

Dew-Becker and Gordon estimated that in 2001 the top one-hundredth of 1 percent of taxpayers received 1.8 percent of labor income alone, up from 0.3 percent in 1972. The increase from 0.3 to 1.8 percent was 497 percent. So what? Even if definition of W-2 income had remained the same between 1972 and 2001 (it did not), there is no reason to believe that if those 13,000 taxpayers had reported less pretax income in 2001 (and paid less in taxes) then the other 99.99 percent of taxpayers would have had more.

Much of the apparent "salary" income among the top 13,000 was ac-tually executive stock options that were rapidly exercised in early 2001 before the stock market totally collapsed. Stock options are fundamentally different from salaries because they are *financed entirely by stockholders*, not from an employer's operating budget. When such options are exercised the company has to supply the shares at a price lower than the current market price. To do so it must either issue new shares (which "dilutes" earnings per share for other shareholders) or use cash to buy back shares (which also shrinks future earnings because that cash would otherwise have been invested).

CEO stock options are never earned at the expense of other employees; they are earned only at the expense of stockholders if and when those stockholders also benefited from a higher stock price.

The executive stock options exercised in 2001 differed from those exercised by the top 7,760 in 1972 because (1) executive stock options in 1972 were typically counted as capital gains rather than as salaries, and (2) 13,000 is a larger number of tax returns than 7,760. There were undoubtedly more and bigger stock option gains in 2001 than in 1972, but we cannot tell *how much* bigger by looking at W-2 income tax data. The old gains are not there.

The comparison of 1972 and 2001 tax return data was no misprint, but it was invalid. Income tax data about top incomes from 1972 are simply not comparable with those of 2001 because of critical changes in the tax laws enacted from 1969 to 1986. Executive stock options cashed-in during 2001 were counted as salaries while executive stock options in 1972 were of a different variety that did not appear in the salary data. There were also many new popular fringe benefits in 2001 that did not have to be reported on W-2 forms, but that is a comparatively small problem.

Table 5.2 shows the Dew-Becker and Gordon inflation-adjusted estimates of total wages, salaries, and stock options for various percentiles of

**TABLE 5.2**
**Dew-Becker and Gordon Estimates of Labor Income (Billions in 2000 Dollars)**

|  | 1972 | 1997 | 2001 | Nonlabor Income Share of 2001 Total (%) |
|---|---|---|---|---|
| 0–20 | 54.2 | 78.0 | 91.9 | 21.0 |
| 20–50 | 360.1 | 488.6 | 569.1 | 23.7 |
| 50–80 | 770.3 | 1156.4 | 1330.2 | 23.3 |
| 80–90 | 382.9 | 661.5 | 771.3 | 18.2 |
| 90–95 | 237.2 | 448.6 | 530.0 | 15.3 |
| 95–99 | 248.0 | 533.5 | 640.0 | 16.4 |
| 99–99.9 | 98.4 | 218.6 | 339.4 | 25.7 |
| 99.9–100 | 27.0 | 152.5 | 210.1 | 42.8 |
| Millions of Tax Returns | 77.6 | 122.4 | 130.3 | |

*Note:* Table includes nonqualified stock options when exercised.
*Source:* Dew-Becker & Gordon (2005), tables 7 & 9.

taxpayers. It starts with 1972 because that is closest among their sample years to 1973, which is the customary starting date (nirvana) among proponents of the wage stagnation thesis. In Chapter 4, the table excludes 1979 and 1987 for simplicity and because most executive stock options were not included in these figures before 1988, but now are.

In this table, "0–20" in the first row means the bottom quintile of tax returns rather than households. The second row (20–50) means those between the bottom fifth and the middle (median). The third row (50–80) includes those from the mid-point up to the threshold of the top 20 percent. The top 20 percent is split into five slices, with 80–90 being the bottom half of the top quintile, 90–95 the next highest 5 percent, 95–99 the next 4 percent and the top two rows together adding up to the top 1 percent. The top 1 percent is estimated to have received 12.2 percent of pretax labor income in 2001, which differs from other tax-based estimates just as each of those differs from the rest. The differences permit zealous journalists to pick their favorites, but also serve to remind us that estimates are estimates and that income is not easy to define much less measure.

Aside from the recession in 2001, the data from 1997 and 2001 are comparable. Prior years are not comparable because demography and tax rates were greatly changed. From 1997 to 2001 Dew-Becker and Gordon estimate that real "wage rates" rose by 2.5 percent a year among median taxpayers, 2.9 percent in the bottom fifth (0–20) and top tenth—all faster than their 2.2 percent estimated growth of productivity (real output per hour of work). And, yes, their measure of real labor income grew at nearly a 4.4 percent rate for the top 0.1 percent, thanks in large part to stock options in the high-tech industries being exercised just before the stock market turned truly ugly.

The dollar figures in the table are converted to 2000 dollars, but not adjusted for population growth. The bottom row was added to show a big reason why *every* group's real earnings increased between 1972 and 2001— every income group contained 68 percent more tax returns in 2001 than in 1972.

The last column of Table 5.2 shows that labor income alone excludes 21–24 percent of the income that shows up on tax returns of all but the top 20 percent, and nearly 43 percent of total income among the top 0.1 percent (where shifting of business income has been particularly important). These dollar figures (unlike some others) also exclude all capital gains, both taxable and tax-deferred.

Comparing the 1972 and 2001 estimates in Table 5.2, reported wages and salaries per tax return increased in every income group from the median to top(that is, total income grew faster than the 68 percent increase in the number of returns). Tax returns are not at all the same as households, however. What is even more important is that total labor incomes in each income group are critically dependent on *how many in each income are working and how many hours they work*. To assume that differences in incomes between the top and bottom fifths simply reflect differences in their hourly wage rates is to assume much too much.

In Chapter 2 we found that there are nearly six times as many full-time workers in the top fifth as in the bottom fifth. But that was not always the case. In 1966–1972, being a full-time worker meant at least 40 hours (as a department store floor manager, my time clock was set for 48–54 hours). Today, full-time often means 9-to-5, or 35 hours. Dew-Becker and Gordon make across-the-board adjustments for hours, but there are reasons to believe typical hours may have fallen for bottom income groups and increased at the top.

Since 1972 there has been a huge increase in the demand for and supply of part-time jobs among those below median income and an even more dramatic increase in the percentage of working women in the top 20 percent.

Dew-Becker and Gordon are compelled to "make no assumptions about the distribution of the changes in hours over time" in order to describe percentage changes in total W-2 income as if they were equivalent to changes in wage rates in, say, the bottom quintile or top decile.[52] But "making no assumption" amounts to making an untenable assumption that there have been no significant demographic changes since 1966 or 1972. Yet there were *millions* more college-educated working wives in the top income groups in 2001 than in 1972, and fewer full-time workers in the bottom fifth.

The bottom fifth in 2001 contained a much larger proportion of senior widows and single mothers than in 1972. But many seniors and single mothers did a little part-time work (because retail and food service offered many more part-time opportunities) and therefore reported a small amount of W-2 income to supplement Social Security, welfare, or child support. The percentage of two-earner families in the top quintile or decile was *much* larger in 2001 than in 1972, and many more of them had college degrees, so their joint tax returns naturally reported much more salary income at the top. Does the *combined* W-2 income of the top 10–20 percent of taxpayers prove their hourly wage rates rose very rapidly? Obviously not; where there was often just one paycheck in 1972, by 2001 there were usually two.

Sorting shares of W-2 income according to taxpayers' ranking by various percentiles does not provide any credible information about the distribution of hourly wage rates in years so different as 1972 and 2001.

Recent W-2 salary data for the top 1 percent or top one-hundredth of 1 percent cannot be compared with data from 1975–1990 because such data now includes nearly all income from executive stock options while in the past it included little or none.

The Dew-Becker and Gordon study provided one more reason among many why it is simply incorrect to compare income reported on tax returns by top income groups in 1972–1973 with amounts reported in 2000–2001. Their sample of W-2 income cannot be used to describe relative growth rates in real wages among various income groups because the proportion of full-time workers in top and bottom groups has changed. And tax shifting made executive stock options invisible in their past data but atypically huge during the 2001 scramble to cash-in before stocks fell further. Windfalls from that rush to exercise stock options in 2001 were not a type of income "shared" with other employees but with other stockholders.

Putting together previous sections with this one, this chapter shows that income reported on tax returns by the top 1 percent in recent years is entirely different from what was reported as income by the much smaller number of top 1 percent returns in the 1970s.

## INVISIBLE INVESTMENT INCOME

Although recent tax returns therefore reveal a much larger portion of the incomes of top taxpayers than was true in the past, they also reveal a much *smaller* portion of the investment incomes of middle-income taxpayers. The share of income at the top is increasingly exaggerated because most of the investment income of middle-income taxpayers is rapidly being excluded from tax returns.

To calculate the top 1 percent's share of total income, it is not enough to carefully define and measure the incomes of everyone in that group. That would only provide 1/99th of the required information. We also need to have a *comparable* measure of income for the other 99 percent.

Piketty and Saez present their tax-based income estimates only for the top 10 percent. As they explain, "Our long-run series are generally confined to top income and wealth shares and contain little information about bottom segments of the distribution."[53] To compare their tax-based figures for 10 percent of tax units to total income of all households, they use personal income minus transfer payments as the denominator of that ratio. But personal income is a distinctly different measure of income than income as defined by the IRS (which is also different from amounts actually reported).[54] And what shows up as income on individual tax returns has changed quite dramatically since the 1970s, for *all* income groups.

As we have seen, tax returns of the top 1 percent in the 1970s did not reveal (1) windfalls from executive stock options or (2) tax-exempt interest income or (3) most of their business income (which was usually accumulated as retained corporate earnings). But that is not all.

The ratio of top incomes to middle incomes has also increased because recent tax data reveal a much *smaller* fraction of middle incomes than they used to. Data collected from income tax returns cannot cope with *the proliferation of tax-deferred savings accounts* for retirement and college. Contributions excluded from individual or corporate income in 2005 alone amounted to $45.9 billion for 401(k) plans, $9.4 billion for Keogh plans, and $7.3 billion for IRAs.[55] Assets of 401(k) plans soared from $385 billion in 1990 to more than $2.1 trillion by 2004.[56]

The overwhelming problem this poses for tax-based income distribution studies is that "inside build-up"—from accumulated capital gains, dividends, and interest income in tax-deferred savings plans—is just as much income as are *taxable* capital gains, dividends, and interest. But this income is no longer visible on tax returns, as it was in the 1970s. By contrast, nearly all investment income of the highest income earners *does* appear on tax returns. That is because people with high incomes are not permitted to contribute to some tax-sheltered retirement accounts (such as an IRA or Roth 401-k) and the amount of contributions is tightly limited for accounts they are allowed to use.

Piketty and Saez correctly observe that "the ratio of dividends reported on individual tax returns to personal dividends in the National Accounts has declined continuously . . . to less than 40% in 1995. But the point is that this decline is due mostly to the growth of funded pension plans and retirement savings accounts through which individuals receive dividends that are never reported as dividends on income tax returns. For the highest income earners, this additional source of dividends is likely to be very small relative to dividends reported on tax returns."[57] Yet such invisible dividends—and also capital gains and interest earnings—are *not small* for those who are *not* the highest income earners. They are huge.

All tax-based income distribution studies count dividends and interest earnings as annual income. The CBO, Strudler-Petska, and some of the Piketty-Saez tables also treat *taxable* capital gains as income in the year in which assets are sold. For all but the most affluent nonbusiness taxpayers, however, most dividends, interest income, and capital gains have been increasingly concentrated inside tax-deferred or tax-exempt savings plans.

Because the bulk of investment income among top income groups remains *taxable*, while tax-deferred investment income of those with more modest incomes is not, tax-based income distribution studies create the false impression of a large and growing share of investment income going only to the top income groups.

"At the end of 2002," notes the CBO, $10.1 trillion was in tax-deferred retirement plans, or which $9 trillion was taxable upon withdrawal."[58]

If that $10.1 trillion earned a middling 7 percent return, the investment income alone would be $707 billion in the first year—$707 billion of capital gains, dividends, and interest income that could *not* appear in tax-based studies of income being earned by those who own these accounts. Much of it should eventually show up as taxable income "upon withdrawal," but mostly in the distant future.

The Social Security Administration reports that new contributions to deferred compensation plans amounted to $172.5 billion in 2004 alone while taxable distributions from such plans were only $1.2 billion.[59]

The *real* value of the oldest types of private tax-deferred accounts (IRA, Keogh and 401-k plans) tripled in the 1990s, rising from about $1.9 trillion in 1990 to $5.8 trillion in 1999, measured in constant 2000 dollars.[60] Soaring stock prices produced enormous *capital gains* (both realized and unrealized) inside tax-deferred savings accounts and therefore excluded from the income tax data used by the CBO and others to estimate income distribution. The top 1 percent also experienced big capital gains, but nearly all of those gains were *taxable* and therefore *uniquely visible* in tax return data. And capital gains from exercising executive stock options in the 1990s were rarely recorded as capital gains in the 1990s, because lower tax rates had encouraged switching to nonqualified stock options that show up as "wage income" on W-2 forms.

Contributions to Roth 401(k) after 2005, or a Roth-IRA after 1998, or a 529 college savings plan after 2001 do *not* reduce adjusted gross income (AGI), as other tax-deferred accounts do. But the "inside build-up" in a Roth or 529 plan is *completely tax-exempt*, not just tax-deferred, so all of that investment income will *never* appear in the tax data used to estimate income distribution.

Before these tax-favored savings plans became commonplace, virtually every dollar of investment income from the savings of middle-income taxpayers *was* reported as taxable income and therefore counted as income in studies that use those older tax returns to estimate income distribution. Today, by contrast, most investment returns from the savings of middle-income taxpayers are rarely or never taxed. This makes it singularly inappropriate to use tax data to compare income shares *before and after* the explosion of tax-deferred accounts. Doing so makes it *appear* that middle-income investors in the 1970s had far more capital gains, dividends, and interest income than they did in the 1990s, simply because those investments used to be fully taxable and now are not. Growth of middle incomes *since* the 1970s is therefore grossly *understated* because an increasingly huge portion of middle-class investment income is no longer reported on tax returns.

By understating the growth of actual investment income of middle-income taxpayers—including income hidden within tax-deferred and tax-exempt savings plans—income tax data must also overstate the *relative* growth of income among the top 1 percent, and therefore the top 1 percent's *share* of the poorly measured total.

Allocating capital gains, dividends, and interest income among income groups on the basis of the share that shows up on income tax returns must exaggerate the share of income among top income groups by understating *invisible* capital gains in middle-income savings plans. The result has been to create a *statistical illusion* that those who were not part of top 10 percent benefited very little from the rising value of stocks and bonds from 1982 through early 2000.

The facts show otherwise. Edward Wolff of New York University found that pension accounts of all sorts (mostly tax-deferred) amounted to only 17.7 percent of all the assets held by the top 1 percent in 1995, but pension accounts accounted for *37.7 percent* of the assets of those in the bottom 90 percent.[61]

Federal Reserve Board economist Arthur Kennickel reported that by 2001 the top 1 percent of wealth holders had just 5.5 percent of their assets in tax-favored retirement accounts. By contrast, the 50th through 95th percentiles (from the median up to the top 5 percent) had 14.5 percent of their assets in tax-deferred retirement accounts—up from 7.6 percent in 1989. The average for all families likewise rose from 6.5 percent in 1989 to 11.9 percent in 2001.[62]

Table 5.3, from James Poterba of M.I.T., illustrates the relative importance of tax-deferred accounts among those who were and were not in the top income tax brackets in 1998 (when the top statutory rate was 39.6 percent, but phase-outs of deductions and exemptions could push the marginal rate above 41 percent).[63]

The first three rows are taxpayers with relatively low taxable income (after deductions and exemptions), with most of that income taxed at the lowest 15 percent tax rate. The fourth and fifth rows (tax rates between 28 and 38 percent) correspond to a middle or upper-middle level of taxable income. The last rows are taxpayers with incomes that were high, but not necessarily extremely high—more comparable to the top 5 percent than the top 1 percent (whose percentage of assets held in tax-deferred accounts would be much smaller than shown here).

**TABLE 5.3**
**Distribution of Tax-Deferred Account Holders by Marginal Tax Rates, 1998**

| Marginal Tax Rate on Interest Income (%) | Percentage of Tax-Deferred Account Holders (%) | Percentage of Assets Held in Tax-Deferred Accounts (%) |
|---|---|---|
| <15 | 10.0 | 6.8 |
| 15 | 33.9 | 8.3 |
| 15–27 | 9.1 | 14.2 |
| 28–30 | 35.7 | 32.1 |
| 31–38 | 6.2 | 14.5 |
| 39–41 | 3.1 | 11.1 |
| >41 | 2.1 | 12.9 |

*Source:* James M. Poterba, "Valuing Assets in Retirement Savings Accounts," Boston College, 2004.

The second column shows that even in 1998, when 401(k) was not as widespread as it later became, nearly 89 percent of all tax-deferred accounts were held by those in the lowest two tax brackets. Those in the top tax bracket—the last two rows—generally had much larger accounts, but those accounts were nonetheless a much smaller fraction of their total assets. The third column shows that *tax-deferred accounts amounted to a third of all assets for those in the middling 28 percent tax bracket, but only about 12 percent for those in the top tax bracket.*

A similar but relatively minor problem arose after 1997, when a new tax law allowed couples to realize tax-free capital gains of up to half a million dollars ($250,000 apiece) on the sale of homes every two years. Taxpayers only have to report the sale of their primary home if they have a gain larger than the exempt amount. Before 1997 the tax on capital gains from home sales could often be *deferred* by buying a home of higher value, but that was not always feasible for those who suffered a pay cut and/or moved to an area where real estate prices were lower. Capital gains on real estate sales accounted for only 10 percent of all taxable capital gains in 1998, down from 26 percent of all taxable capital gains in 1985, and the generous 1997 exclusion presumably explains most of that difference.[64] Estimates of income distribution that include taxable capital gain include a much larger share of capital gains from home sales before 1997, thereby missing the increase in capital gains of many middle-income homeowners during the 1997–2005 boom in housing prices.

The appearance of top-heavy growth of investment income since the 1970s (particularly from capital gains) largely reflects the fact that most of the top 1 percent's investment income has remained taxable in recent years while most comparable gains for middle-income taxpayers are no longer recorded in tax returns.

## WHY INCLUDE ONLY REALIZED AND TAXABLE GAINS?

Piketty and Saez argue that "capital gains are typically very lumpy (they are realized once every few years), so that ranking tax returns by income including capital gains lead to artificially overestimate very top income levels."[65] Yet they nonetheless provided estimates that included those capital gains that are reported on Schedule D of tax returns. And because those estimates increase the apparent share of income for the top 1 percent, they are often cited by reporters seeking the largest possible number (such as the comment from the *Economist* at the beginning of the chapter that the top 1 percent receives 15 percent of pretax income).

Despite all of the previously mentioned ambiguities in all tax-based income distribution estimates, those inclined to publicize and promote these estimates find one argument particularly compelling. "Unlike much of the Census data," says the Economic Policy Institute, "the Piketty-Saez data include realized capital gains." The same group adds that, "Inequality data from the Census Bureau lack the comprehensiveness of the CBO data (i.e., the Census data exclude realized capital gains)."[66]

The rationale for including only realized, taxable capital gains is supposedly based on "Haig-Simons" principles, named for two economists who came up with the idea, Robert Haig (1921) and Henry Simons (1938). Due to the influence of Haig and Simons, many economists in the English-speaking countries came to believe that taxable income "should" consist of consumption plus annual additions to wealth (defined as marketable assets minus debts, or "net worth").

The IRS, like the CBO, remains devoted to the old Haig-Simons ideal, explaining it as follows:

The H-S [Haig-Simons] income of a household that consumed $25,000 and saved $2,000 in a year would be $27,000. Alternatively, the H-S income of a household that consumed $25,000 and had no additions to savings, but had assets that declined in value by $1,000 in a year, would be $24,000.[67]

Many economists outside the government disagree with the idea of treating savings as taxable income. In any case, the Haig-Simons concept of income is clearly *immeasurable*. It would require adding all capital gains to annual income, regardless of whether or not they are realized or taxed (including gains now inside tax-deferred savings plans), and subtracting all capital losses. Such a measure would have shown gargantuan *declines* in top incomes while the stock market crashed from March 2000 to March 2003. And a Haig-Simons measure would likewise have shown sizable increases in middle incomes during the subsequent "housing bubble."

In explaining one of several "expanded" measures of income in 1993, an economist with the Statistics of Income division of the IRS wrote, "Expanded income is meant to be a measure of income that is conceptually closer to H-S [Haig-Simons] than AGI [adjusted gross income], but which is derived entirely from items already reported on income tax returns."[68] Yet it is literally impossible to come remotely close to a Haig-Simons measure of income by using "items already reported on income tax returns."

A Haig-Simons definition of income would have to include the accrual of dividends, interest, and capital gains that are now hidden inside tax-deferred pension accounts. Yet that information is not available from tax returns. On the other hand, a Haig-Simons definition would *not* include "income" from drawing-down pensions in old age, which *is* counted as income in tax returns.[69]

A Haig-Simons definition of income would include appreciation in the value of all assets owned, including homes—*whether sold or not*. A Haig-Simons definition would *not* include as income those realized and taxable capital gains which arise only because the asset is (1) sold that year, and (2) not concealed inside tax-deferred pension funds or tax-exempt housing.

In short, the Haig-Simons concept of income does *not* justify the common practice of adding realized, *taxable* capital gains to incomes. Doing so amounts to partly applying a Haig-Simons measure to taxable gains among top income groups but not to gains that are tax-deferred, tax-exempt, or unrealized (because the asset was not sold).

## MISALLOCATING THE CORPORATE TAX

The fact that a rising share of middle-income investment income is no longer taxable, as it was in 1977–1980, creates a puzzle for the Congressional Budget Office. The agency's assignment was to figure out what share of *taxes* are paid by, say, the top 1 percent. And that includes the *corporate* income tax.

In CBO studies, the profits and taxes of publicly traded Subchapter-C corporations are allocated to top taxpayers on the basis of what individual tax returns say about which income groups appear to earn the most income from investments. "CBO assumes that corporate income taxes are borne by owners of capital in proportion to their income from interest, dividends, rents and capital gains."[70] The actual incidence of the corporate tax is far more complicated than the CBO assumes.[71] But the biggest problem with this CBO procedure arises from all the *invisible investment income* accumulating within tax-deferred and tax-exempt savings plans.

Since billions of dollars of middle-income dividends, interest income, and capital gains are no longer taxable, as they were in the 1970s, the CBO's *tax-based* data make it appear as though the middle class has been abandoning the stock market in droves. Yet Chapter 7 shows that a far larger percentage of middle-income Americans are stockholders than was true even in the early 1990s, but most of their stock is now held in tax-deferred savings plans.

CBO estimates nonetheless imply that the top 1 percent's share of corporate wealth rose from 38.7 percent in 1991 to 57.5 percent in 2003. But that is only because "income from securities owned by retirement plans . . . was excluded."[72] Because increasing shares of income from middle-income investments disappeared into tax-deferred plans, the CBO estimates that the bottom 80 percent of "households" received only 15.2 percent of all (taxable) investment income in 2002—down from 23.1 percent in 1979. With only the investment income of high-income taxpayers remaining visible in tax data, the CBO assigned the top 1 percent 57.5 percent of the corporate tax burden in 2002, up from just 37.8 percent in 1979.

One ironic effect of exaggerating the top 1 percent's share of investment income—and therefore the top 1 percent's share of the *corporate* tax—is that this is the only reason the top 1 percent have been said to have received the biggest tax cut. Because of lower *corporate* tax rates and periods of accelerated depreciation (quick write-off of new equipment), the CBO figures the top 1 percent's *effective* corporate income tax rate (*not* the marginal rate) fell from 13.8 percent in 1979 to a record low of 6.2 percent in 2001—the span of years selected in the *New York Times* quotation at the start of this chapter. By contrast, the CBO estimated that the top 1 percent's effective *individual* income tax rate *rose* from 21.8 percent in 1979 to 24.1 percent in 2001.[73] The dubious allocation of 57.5 percent of the reduced *corporate* tax to the top 1 percent is the reason why *after-tax* income among the top 1 percent appeared to increase more from 1979 to 2001 than *before-tax* income.

The CBO's flawed method allocated over half of that corporate tax cut to the top 1 percent, which made the *combined* corporate plus individual tax burden on the top 1 percent look as though it had declined even though the effective individual tax rate did not. And that, in turn, is why egalitarian journalists typically use the CBO figures only when talking about shares of *after-tax* income before and after the *corporate* tax cuts, then switch to Piketty-Saez or SOI figures when making different debating points about the top 1 percent's allegedly rising share of *before-tax* income.

Despite the questionable assignment of corporate tax cuts, the CBO estimates show no sustained increase in the top 1 percent's share of *after-tax* income since the 1986 tax reform. *The top 1 percent received 13.2 percent of after-tax income in 1986, according to the CBO, 12.6 percent in 2001 and 12.2 percent in 2003.* As we saw in Table 5.1, above, even the CBO's *pretax* figures (which ignore the rising share of individual income taxes paid by the top 1 percent) also show no *sustained* increase in the share of income earned by the top 1 percent after 1986. That may explain why the *New York Times* writers have ceased mentioning CBO estimates except when talking about *percentage growth* of after-tax income for 1979 to 2001 (without explaining that such a figure partly reflects the increase in number of taxpayers since 1979). *New York Times* writers such as Paul Krugman and David Cay Johnston have recently switched from citing CBO estimates to using those of Piketty-Saez or Dew-Becker and Gordon when claiming the top 1 percent have experienced a continually rising *share* of *pretax* income, because CBO estimates show the top 1 percent's share of *after-tax* income falling from 1986 to 2003.

Hundreds of billions of dollars of annual dividends, interest, and capital gains that accrue to households with relatively modest incomes are *invisible* to the CBO and IRS, however, because such investment earnings accrue within tax-deferred or tax-exempt savings plans. That simple fact, in turn, makes it fallacious to allocate corporate income or corporate taxes on the basis of that dwindling portion of investment income that remains visible on tax returns. It also makes it fallacious to use individual income tax data to estimate what share of total income (including investment income) accrues to top, middle, and bottom income groups.

## PAD THE TOP, SHRINK THE MIDDLE, SKIP THE BOTTOM

Tax-based studies of income distribution exaggerate top incomes by including business income and (in most cases) realized and taxable capital gains. In one case, just mentioned, they also count accelerated depreciation as income.

Tax-based studies of income distribution greatly understate comparable earnings of middle-income households by excluding capital gains, dividends, and interest income accruing in *tax-deferred* retirement plans or as *tax-exempt* investment returns (from home sales, Roth retirement plans and 529 college savings plans).

Most tax-based studies (the CBO is an exception) *exclude most or all transfer payments*, thus virtually ignoring about three-fourths of the cash and in-kind income of the lowest quintile. The Piketty-Saez definition of income, for example, "excludes all transfers such as Social Security benefits, unemployment insurance, welfare assistance, etc. The importance of transfers has grown over time. They represent in 2000 about 15% of personal income and around 10% in 1973."[74]

Table 5.4 confirms that transfer payments have indeed accounted for a rising share of personal income over time. The flip side of that trend, however, is that *private wages and salaries* have accounted for a *shrinking* share of personal income, even before subtracting the taxes needed to pay for those rising transfer payments. Yet those ostensibly concerned about "inequality" invariably focus on income from work in the private sector (such as worrying about low minimum wage and high CEO pay) and do not even bother to count rising transfer payments intended to supplement lower incomes.

Piketty and Saez always "ignore entirely transfer programs, which accrue disproportionately to the bottom of the income distribution."[75] But that means their widely publicized estimates of the top 1 percent's share of income were unquestionably exaggerated even for 1960, and became more and more exaggerated with each passing decade. Because transfer payments have been a *rising* share of income, to exclude transfers payments automatically exaggerates both level of the top 1 percent's share of undercounted total income and also the *rate of growth* of that mismeasured share over time. The ratio of top income to total income has been artificially increased by the fact that the denominator of that ratio (total income) has been *increasingly* understated by the exclusion of transfers. This is one reason why studies that exclude most or all transfer payments appear to show the top 1 percent receiving a rising share of "total" income from 1988 to 2000 while Congressional Budget Office estimates (which do count some transfer payments) show no such trend, particularly in after-tax income.

**TABLE 5.4**
**Shares of Pretax Personal Income**

|  | Private Wages and Salaries (%) | Transfer Payments (%) |
|---|---|---|
| 1960 | 54.4 | 5.9 |
| 1970 | 51.8 | 8.5 |
| 1980 | 48.4 | 11.7 |
| 1990 | 45.8 | 11.7 |
| 2000 | 47.3 | 13.1 |
| 2004 | 45.7 | 14.2 |

*Source: Economic Report of the President* (2005), table B-29.

When it comes to estimating how personal income is distributed, excluding transfer payments is not a matter of excluding 14 percent from the bottom, middle, and top of the income distribution. On the contrary, as shown in Chapter 2, transfer payments account for 73–78 percent of all income among the bottom quintile, depending on whether or not in-kind transfers are included.

Studies such as Piketty-Saez, which exclude transfer payments from their measure of income have automatically forfeited any credibility when it comes to estimating income shares among income groups. In Strudler, Petska, and Petska, "Social Security benefits were omitted because they were not reported on tax returns until 1984."[76] But income cannot be defined on the basis of statistical convenience. Social Security provides 85 percent of all the income of seniors in the bottom two quintiles, where retirees are disproportionately represented.[77] Unless the authors would argue that Social Security checks are not income, any conclusions they arrived at after excluding such an enormous source of income among low- and middle-income households are necessarily incorrect and irrelevant.

Excluding Social Security benefits seriously *understates* the share of income received by the bottom half of households, and therefore *overstates* income shares at the top. Nearly every measure of income shares excludes the Earned Income Tax Credit—which paid $37 billion to more than 21 million families in 2003.[78] Also, to exclude all means-tested antipoverty programs means *most* real income of the bottom quintile (and much income of the second highest quintile). The Piketty-Saez paper *completely excludes at least three-fourths of the income of the poorest fifth of the population.*

This is ironic, since these flawed statistics are commonly cited as justification for greatly enlarging the same programs that are not even counted as income. Doubling the Earned Income Tax Credit, TANF, SSI and all in-kind benefits would have no effect at all on the "distribution of income" as income is defined in most tax-based studies.

If statisticians do not bother to count three-fourths of the income of those with low incomes, the result must exaggerate the income shares of everyone else—notably, of high-income taxpayers whose taxes finance many transfer payments to the poor.

In a paper presented at the annual meeting of the Western Economics Association in July 2006, I estimated that including transfer payments in the denominator of the Piketty-Saez data would reduce the top percentile's income share in 2002 from 14.7 percent to 12.1 percent. Increasing the denominator to account for underreporting ("the AGI gap") would further reduce the top percentile's share to 10.9 percent that same year. I also estimated that "income shifting" from corporate to individual tax returns since 1981 added 2.1 percentage points to the share reported by the top 1 percent by 2002 (so that 10.9 percent in 2002 would have been comparable to about 8.8 percent in 1981, if the business share of top 1 percent incomes had remained the same).[79] Yet those three adjustments fail to account for several other dramatic changes in the way income was reported on tax returns before and after the 1980s—particularly the many billions of dollars of investment income that was shifted from taxable to tax-deferred savings accounts.

This chapter demonstrated beyond reasonable doubt that what is counted as income on tax returns has changed dramatically since 1981–1986 because of massive changes in U.S. tax laws.

Studies that use individual income tax data to estimate relative income shares before and after 1986 are irreparably disfigured by the fact that

1. many businesses shifted from filing under the corporate tax code to filing under the individual code after 1986;

2. most middle-income investment earnings are no longer reported on tax returns but are instead accumulated within tax-deferred and tax-exempt savings plans;

3. income reported to the IRS is highly sensitive to top tax rates on capital gains and other income;

4. executive stock options did not use to be reported as salaries but now are;

5. income from tax-exempt bonds did not use to be reported as income but now it often is; and

6. most or all income from transfer payments is usually excluded.

For these and other reasons, the practice of using individual tax return data to measure long-term changes in income shares is inexcusably deceptive. The use of dubious definitions of income and the variable commingling of personal and business income make all tax-based "top 1 percent" figures essentially meaningless.

## NOTES

1. Congressional Budget Office, *Historical Effective Federal Tax Rates: 1979 to 2003* (December 2005). http.//www.cbo.gov/ftpdocs/70xx/doc7000/12-29-FedTaxRates.pdf.

2. Thomas Piketty and Emmanuel Saez, "Income Inequality in the United States, 1913–1998," *NBER Working Paper* 8467 (September 2001), published in *Quarterly Journal of Economics* (February 2003). Unless identified as the *NBER* (2001) version, all subsequent references refer to an updated online draft of November 2004, which extends the estimates through 2002. http://emlab.berkeley.edu/users/saez/pikettysaezOUP04US.pdf.

3. Michael Strudler, Tom Petska, and Ryan Petska, "Further Analysis of the Distribution of Income and Taxes, 1979–2002," (Statistics of Income Division, IRS, November 2004). http://ftp.irs.gov/pub/irs-soi/04asastr.pdf.

4. Ian Dew-Becker and Robert J. Gordon, "Where Did the Productivity Growth Go? Inflation Dynamics and the Distribution of Income," *NBER Working Paper* 11842 (December 2005).

5. Daniel R. Feenberg and James M. Poterba, "Income Inequality and the Incomes of Very High-Income Taxpayers: Evidence from Tax Returns," in *Tax Policy and the Economy*, ed. James M. Poterba, vol. 7 (Cambridge, MA: NBER/MIT Press, 1993), p. 147.

6. "An Unequal Exchange," in Paul Krugman, *Accidental Theorist* (New York: W.W. Norton, 1998). http://www.j-bradford-delong.net/Economists/favorite_krugman.html.

7. U.S. Department of the Treasury. *SOI Tax Stats—SOI Bulletin—Historical Tables and Appendix*, table 6, footnote 3. http://www.irs.gov/taxstats/article/0,,id=115033,00.html.

8. Bruce Bartlett, "Class Struggle in America?" *Commentary* (July–August 2005).

9. Sylvia Nasar, "The 1980's: A Very Good Time for the Very Rich," *New York Times*, March 5, 1992, Late Edition—Final.

10. Bill Clinton and Al Gore, *Putting People First* (New York: Times Books, 1992), p. 5.

11. CBO Staff Memorandum, "Measuring the Distribution of Income Gains" (March 1992).

12. Alan Reynolds, "The Middle Class Boom of the 1980s," *Wall Street Journal*, March 12, 1992.

13. On page 111 of *Peddling Prosperity* (New York: W.W. Norton, 1994), Paul Krugman claimed that I had spoken of "the whole decade of the 1980's—from 1982 to 1990." What I said was *1980* to 1990. That becomes clear on page 117 of the same book where I was criticized for alluding to *1980* to 1989 data to describe the Reagan years. See Alan Reynolds, "Peddling Pomposity," reprinted from *The International Economy* (1994) at http://www.pkarchive.org/others/krugman3.html.

14. Office of Management and Budget, *A Vision of Change for America* (February 17, 1993), p. 7.

15. Alan Reynolds, "Upstarts and Downstarts," *National Review*, August 31, 1992, http://www.nationalreview.com/reagan/reynolds200406101357.asp; Paul Krugman, "The Rich, The Right, and The Facts," *American Prospect* (Fall 1992). http://www.pkarchive.org/economy/therich.html; Paul Craig Roberts, "The Congressional Budget Office's Skewed Numbers," *Business Week*, March 23, 1992; Clayton Yeutter, "When 'Fairness' Isn't Fair," *New York Times*, March 24, 1992.

16. The issue we all missed is roughly similar to what came to be known as the "Lucas Critique." Nobel Laureate Robert Lucas argued that predictions based on historical data would be invalid if *policy changes* altered the relationships between the relevant variables. Robert E. Lucas, Jr., "Econometric Policy Evaluation: A Critique," in *Theory, Policy, Institutions: Papers from the Carnegie-Rochester Conferences on Public Policy*, eds. Karl Brunner and Alan Meltzer (Amsterdam: North Holland, 1983), pp. 257–84.

17. Congressional Budget Office, *Historical Effective Federal Tax Rates: 1979 to 2003* (December 2005), table 1C. The top 1 percent's share of income plus capital gains was unusually high only in 1986 (22.6 percent) and 1999 (21.2 percent)—the first reflecting asset sales to avoid higher capital gains taxes in 1987 and the second reflecting the tech stock "bubble."

18. Piketty and Saez, "Income Inequality in the United States, 1913–1998," *NBER* (2001), p. 8.

19. Feenberg and Poterba estimate that if capital gains are included, then the top 0.5 percent (half of 1 percent) of taxpayers accounted for 12.2 percent of adjusted gross income in 1986 but only 9.3 percent in the following year, 1987. Excluding capital gains reverses that timing, with the top 0.5 percent accounting for less than 6.4 percent of AGI in 1986 but for nearly 7.7 percent in 1987. Daniel Feenberg and James M. Poterba, "Income and Tax Share of Very High-Income Households, 1960–1995," *American Economic Review*, vol. 90(5) (May 2000), table 1.

20. Thomas Piketty and Emmanuel Saez, "How Progressive Is the U.S. Federal Tax System? A Historical and International Perspective" (March 2006), pp. 11–12. Forthcoming in the *Journal of Economic Perspectives*, http:/elsa.berkeley.edu/~saez/.

21. Kelly Luttrell, "S Corporation Returns, 2002," IRS, *SOI Bulletin* (Spring 2005). http://www.irs.gov/pub/irs-soi/02scorp.pdf.

22. Tax Foundation, *Facts and Figures on Government Finance* (1995), tables C-37 and C-40.

23. Saez, "Reported Incomes and Marginal Tax Rates," *NBER Working Paper* 10273, p. 27.

24. Ken B. Cyree, Scott E. Hein, and Timothy W. Koch, "Avoiding Double Taxation: The Case of Commercial Banks," (presentation to the Financial Management Association, October 2005). http://wintersd.ba.ttu.edu/Seminar%20Papers/avoiding%20double%20 taxation%20CHW%20Feb%205%202005a.pdf.

25. National Association of Federal Credit Unions. http://www.ssfcu.org/MythvsRealityand FactSheet.pdf.

26. Alan J. Auerbach, "Who Bears the Corporate Tax?" *NBER Working Paper* 11686 (October 2005), p. 4.

27. Robert Carroll and Warren Hrung, "What Does the Taxable Income Elasticity Say About Dynamic Responses to Tax Changes?" *American Economic Review*, vol. 95(5) (May 2005), p. 429.

28. Susan M. Wittman and Amy Gill, "S-Corporation Elections after the Tax Reform Act of 1986," *SOI Bulletin* (Spring 1998), IRS Publication 1136.

29. Paul Krugman, for example, describes tax units as households and households as families. "According to Piketty and Saez . . . in 1998 the top 0.01 percent received more than 3 percent of all income. That meant that the 13,000 richest families in America had almost as much income as the 20 million poorest households." Krugman, "For Richer."

30. Edward M. Gramlich, Richard Kasten, and Frank Sammartino, "Growing Inequality in the 1980s: The Role of Federal Taxes and Cash Transfers," in *Uneven Tides: Rising Inequality in America*, eds. Sheldon Danziger and Peter Gottschalk (New York: Russell Sage Foundation, 1994), p. 233.

31. Dew-Becker and Gordon, "Where Did the Productivity Growth Go?" p. 41.

32. Saez, "Reported Incomes and Marginal Tax Rates," *NBERWorking Paper* 10273, abstract and p. 29.

33. Strudler, Petska, and Petska, "Further Analysis of the Distribution of Income and Taxes," p. 1. Statistics of Income division, IRS. Tables updated to 2003 on October 2005. http://www.irs.gov/pub/irs-soi/04asastr.pdf.

34. Alan Reynolds, "Estimating Realizations and Revenue at Lower Tax Rates," in *Capital Gains Tax: Analysis of Reform Options for Australia, A study commissioned by the Australian Stock Exchange Ltd for the Review of Business Taxation* (chapter 4, July 1999), http://www.asx.com .au-about-pdf-cgt.pdf.url; see also Alan J. Auerbach and Jonathan M. Siegel, "Capital Gains Realizations of the Rich and Sophisticated" *NBER Working Paper* 7532 (2000).

35. The 2003 reduction in tax rates on dividends and capital gains (to 15 percent) seems to increase reported income from those sources: "For 2003, income items that increased appreciably included net capital gains and dividends, which increased 23.3 percent and 11.5 percent, respectively." Michael Parisi and Susan Hollenbeck, "Individual Tax Returns, 2003," *SOI Bulletin* (Fall 2005).

36. Feenberg and Poterba, "Income Inequality and the Incomes of Very High-Income Taxpayers," p. ix, table 4.

37. Saez, "Reported Incomes and Marginal Tax Rates" (*NBER working paper* 10273), p. 7.

38. Edward C. Prescott, "Why Do Americans Work So Much and Europeans So Little?" (Federal Reserve Bank of Minneapolis, July 2004). http://minneapolisfed.org/research/common/pub_detail.cfm?pb_autonum_id=905; Steven J. Davis and Magnus Henrekson, "Tax Effects on Work Activity, Industry Mix and Shadow Economy Size: Evidence from Rich Country Comparisons" (Working Paper 560, Stockholm School of Economics, June 2004). http://ideas.repec.org/p/hhs/hastef/0560.html.

39. Carroll and Hrung, "What Does the Taxable Income Elasticity Say?" p. 430.

40. Saez, "Reported Incomes and Marginal Tax Rates" (*NBER Working Paper* 10273), p. 4.

41. Michael Förster and Marco Mira d'Ercole, *Income Distribution and Poverty in OECD Countries in the Second Half of the 1990s* (Paris: OECD, 2005) box 1, p. 16.

42. Emmanuel Saez and Michael R. Veal, "The Evolution of High Incomes in Northern America: Lessons from Canadian Evidence," *American Economic Review*, vol. 95(6) (June 2005).

43. Joanna L. Ossinger, "Poorer Relations: When It Comes to CEO Pay, Why Are the British So Different?" *Wall Street Journal*, April 10, 2006.

44. University of Michigan World Tax Base. http://www.bus.umich.edu/OTPR/otpr/OTPRdataV3.asp.

45. Pricewaterhouse Coopers, *Individual Taxes: Worldwide Summaries*, various issues.

46. Piketty and Saez, "How Progressive is the U.S. Federal Tax System?" Table 2.

47. Towers Perrin, *2005–2006 Worldwide Total Remuneration—Selected Charts*, January 11, 2006, p. 3. http://www.towersperrin.com/tp/jsp/search.jsp.

48. Carola Frydman and Raven E. Saks, "Historical Trends in Executive Compensation 1936–2003" University of Chicago Graduate School of Business (November 15, 2005), p. 5. http://gsbwww.uchicago.edu/research/workshops/wae/FrydmanSecondPaper.pdf.

49. Pricewaterhouse Coopers, "Employee Stock Options in the EU and the USA" (Final Report, August 2002). http://europa.eu.int/comm/enterprise/entrepreneurship/support_measures/stock_options/usa.pdf.

50. Dew-Becker and Gordon, "Where Did the Productivity Growth Go?"

51. Showing he had not read the study, Krugman guessed the 99.99th percentile began at "well over $6 million," although Dew-Becker and Gordon said it began at $3.2 million. Paul Krugman, "Graduates Versus Oligarchs," *New York Times*, February 27, 2006.

52. Dew-Becker and Gordon, "Where Did the Productivity Growth Go?" p. 38, table 8.

53. Thomas Piketty and Emmanuel Saez, "The Evolution of Top Incomes: A Historical and International Perspective," *NBER Working Paper* 11055 (January 2006).

54. Advocates of tax-based income distribution estimates claim personal income grossly underestimate the highest incomes because "top coding" in Census Bureau data conceals detailed information about the highest incomes. If true, then personal income data must also undercount *total* income. Whatever sum is added to the top incomes by using tax return data

should also be added to the total, or the resulting ratio of top incomes to total incomes inflates the top group's share.

55. U.S. Budget 2005, *Analytical Perspectives*, table 19-1, p. 319.

56. Investment Company Institute. http://www.ici.org/home/faqs_401k.html.

57. Piketty and Saez, "Income Inequality in the United States, 1913–1998," *NBER* (2001), p. 16.

58. Congressional Budget Office, Tax-Deferred Retirement Savings in Long-Term Revenue Projections (May 2004), p. 8. http://www.cbo.gov/showdoc.cfm?index=5418andsequence=0.

59. Social Security Administration, "Wage Statistics for 2004" (January 16, 2006). http://www.ssa.gov/cgi-bin/netcomp.cgi?year=2004.

60. From 1990 to 1999 IRA and Keogh accounts rose from $791 billion to $2.7 trillion, in 2000 dollars, and plans of the 401(k) variety increased from $1.1 trillion to well over $3 trillion, measured in 2000 dollars using the PCE deflator. The nominal figures for defined contribution plans are from the Investment Company Institute, Fundamentals (August 2005). IRA and Keogh data are from the Federal Reserve Board. http://www.federalreserve.gov/releases/z1/Current/data.htm.

61. Edward N. Wolff, "Recent Trends in the Size Distribution of Household Wealth," *Journal of Economic Perspectives* (Summer 1998), table 6, p. 140.

62. Arthur B. Kennickell, "A Rolling Tide: Changes in the Distribution of Wealth in the U.S., 1989–2001" (Federal Reserve Board, September 2003), tables 10 and 11. http://www.federalreserve.gov/pubs/oss/oss2/method.html.

63. James M. Poterba, "Valuing Assets in Retirement Savings Accounts" (working paper 2004-11, Center for Retirement Research at Boston College, April 2004). http://www.bc.edu/centers/crr/papers/wp_2004-11.pdf.

64. Congressional Budget Office, "Capital Gains and Federal Revenues" (October 9, 2002), figure 1.

65. Piketty and Saez, "Income Inequality in the United States, 1913–1998," *NBER* (2001), p. 38.

66. Mishel, Bernstein, and Allegretto, *The State of Working America, 2004–2005* (Economic Policy Institute, 2005), pp. 58, 64.

67. Brian Balkovic, "High Income Tax Returns for 2002," *Statistics of Income Bulletin* (Spring 2005). http://www.irs.gov/pub/irs-soi/02hiinco.pdf.

68. John Latzy, "High Income Tax Returns for 1993," *SI Tax Stats—Individual High Income Returns.* http://www.irs.gov/pub/irs-soi/hicome.pdf.

69. "The Haig-Simons definition would require that pension contributions and accruals be included in FEI, but not pension benefits." Julie-Anne Cronin, "U.S. Treasury Distributional Analysis Methodology" (U.S. Treasury, Office of Tax Analysis Paper 85, September 1999).

70. Congressional Budget Office, *Historical Effective Federal Tax Rates* (March 2005), p. 2.

71. Auerbach, "Who Bears the Corporate Tax?"

72. David Cay Johnston, "Corporate Wealth Share Rises for Top-Income Americans," *New York Times*, January 29, 2006.

73. Congressional Budget Office, *Historical Effective Federal Tax Rates: 1979 to 2003* (December 2005), table 3A.

74. Congressional Budget Office, *Historical Effective Federal Tax Rates* (March 2005), footnote to figure A-1.

75. Piketty and Saez, "How Progressive is the U.S. Federal Tax System?" (March 2006), p. 4.

76. Strudler, Petska, and Petska, "Further Analysis of the Distribution of Income and Taxes."

77. AARP, "Sources of Income for Older Persons in 2003" (October 2005), table 3. http://assets.aarp.org/rgcenter/econ/dd125_income.pdf.

78. Nada Eissa and Austin Nichols, "Tax-Transfer Policy and Labor-Market Outcomes," *American Economic Review*, vol. 95(5) (May 2005), p. 88.

79. Alan Reynolds, "The Misuse of Tax Data to Estimate Income Distribution," paper presented to the Western Economics Association International 81st Annual Conference, San Diego, CA, July 1, 2006.

# Six

# CEOs and Celebrities

CEOs together with sports and entertainment stars explain what is going on in the top 1 percent of the income distribution.
—Ian Dew-Becker and Robert J. Gordon, "Where Did the Productivity Gains Go?" (2005)

The number of top chief executive officers (CEOs) is far too small to explain average incomes of the top 1 percent even if top celebrities are added. Claims that average CEO pay is 500–1000 times as much as that of average workers are based on faulty estimates, not facts. The incomes of the top 100–500 CEOs rose unexpectedly with the stock market boom of 1997–2000, then fell by an estimated 48–53 percent through 2003. Such ups and downs of CEO pay cannot be explained by the theory that managers dominate their boards. Activist efforts in 1993 to curb CEO pay by limiting the tax deduction for large salaries backfired by fostering substitution of stock options for salaries before a stock market boom. Activist efforts to substitute restricted stock for stock options after 2003 mainly shifted risk from CEOs to stockholders.

Those who write most excitably about a rising share of income received by the top 1 percent often attempt to link such tax-based estimates to a surge in compensation among the top 100–500 corporate chief executive officers (CEOs). And those who write most excitably about the compensation of CEOs often link that narrow issue to the broader issue of income inequality in general.

"The explosion in CEO pay over the past 30 years is an amazing story in its own right," wrote Paul Krugman in October 2002; "But it is only the most spectacular indicator of a broader story, the reconcentration of income and wealth in the U.S."[1] He then segued from *Fortune* magazine's 1999 estimate of the compensation of 100 best-paid CEOs to the Piketty-Saez estimates of incomes among the top 1 percent—as though the incomes of 100 might somehow explain the incomes of 1.3 million. Because such a connection is so unlikely, subsequent media stories have instead attempted to link CEO pay to the incomes of the top one-tenth of one percent (0.1 percent) in 2005, and even to the top one-hundredth of one percent (0.01 percent) in 2006.

In 2005, a *New York Times* article stated that income reported on tax returns had risen in 2003 (for the first time in three years) among the top 0.1 percent—one in a thousand—described as "129,000 taxpayers with reported incomes of $1.3 million or more."[2] Edward Wolff of New York University was called upon to offer up the obligatory ritualistic explanation that "the data could be tied to . . . a sharp rise in the pay of chief executives." How could average incomes among 129,000 taxpayers possibly be explained by the pay of just a few hundred chief executives?

A few months earlier the same *New York Times* writer had used a different source to report that in 2002 there were 145,000 taxpayers among the top 0.1 percent with incomes that averaged $3 million each. But the number of such taxpayers could not have shrunk from 145,000 in 2002 to 129,000 in 2003, so it seems wiser, and more accurate, to keep their number at about 130,000 for both years. At $3 million each, the total income of those 130,000 taxpayers would add up to $390 billion in 2002.[3] Yet all the CEOs of all the big S&P 500 firms together earned only $5 billion in 2002, according to an estimate from Bebchuk and Grinstein, which will be discussed later. Subtracting $5 billion for the 500 top CEOs would still leave, totally unaccounted for, the remaining $385 billion of top 0.1 percent incomes.

Trying to use CEO pay to explain the incomes of 130,000 was not much more successful than using CEO pay to explain the incomes of 1.3 million. So, Ian Dew-Becker and Robert J. Gordon felt compelled to narrow the subject even further to "the 13,000 IRS tax returns in the 99.99th percentile, which in 2001 accounted for $83 billion of income with an entry threshold of $3.2 million [and an average income of $6.4 million each]."[4] That is just 1 percent of the top 1 percent, or one-hundredth of one percent of the total. Unfortunately, the pay of a few hundred top CEOs still does not get us very far in explaining the incomes of even 13,000.

The widespread proliferation of stock options among several million nonexecutive employees in the 1990s undoubtedly did have quite a lot to do with the big increase in reported "salaries" among the top 1–10 percent in 1996–2001, and with the rarely mentioned *decline* of top income shares in 2002 and 2003. Hundreds of thousands of nonexecutive employees gained *one-time* windfalls during the tech stock boom that still left some large gains on the table in early 2001. But to admit that stock option windfalls temporarily enriched so many workers would require admitting the fashionable efforts to demonize a small number of CEOs are simply beside the point.

Trendy comparisons of top CEO pay to that of "average employees" are also beside the point because many thousands of *ordinary employees* who worked for the same companies whose stock options soared also gained ephemeral windfalls by exercising stock options, and thereby landed in the top 1–10 percent *for a single year.* Since those euphoric days of 5000 on the NASDAQ stock index were gone with the wind by 2006, it is difficult to understand why journalists nonetheless remained entranced by tax-based income studies, such as Dew-Becker and Gordon, which stop the clock in 2001.

What makes the Dew-Becker and Gordon paper uniquely relevant to this chapter about elite incomes is that they alone attempted to justify the claim made by Piketty and Saez, Krugman, and others that stock-based compensation of the top 100 corporate CEO's has been by far the most important development to "explain what is going on in the top 1 percent of the income distribution."

The Piketty-Saez-Krugman efforts to explain incomes of the top 1.3 million as driven by 100 CEOs came up short by 1,299,900. So Dew-Becker and Gordon changed the subject by shrinking their target to only 13,000 taxpayers and by expanding the definition of "CEO" to mean the *top five* executives at 1500 firms, from the study by Bebchuk and Grinstein. Their "inference is that most of these [7500] executives are in the IRS 99.99th percentile." Unfortunately, that inference is unjustified.

The total of salaries and stock options had to exceed $3.2 in 2001 to be counted within even the 99.99th percentile. Yet average pay of the top five executives, which includes the CEO, was $1.1 million among 600 smaller firms in 2001, and $2.1 million among 400 mid-sized firms. Even when the mean average of incomes of these groups of 2000–3000 executives were above $3.2 million (which was only true of CEOs of 900 firms) that does not mean everyone in the group earned that much. Mean averages of executive pay are typically much higher than median averages, because of a few very high pay packages, so fewer than half were apt to have earned the Bebchuk-Grinstein mean averages. Unlike Dew-Becker and Gordon, who measure stock options when exercised, Bebchuk and Grinstein estimate the value of options when they were first granted. It was not possible for those receiving stock option grants in 2001 to exercise them during that same year, when Dew-Becker and Gordon are trying to explain income from exercised options among the top 13,000 taxpayers. And the relatively high *estimated* value of stock options granted in 2001 soon turned out to be much too high as stock prices kept falling.

The Bebchuk-Grinstein estimates suggests that several hundred CEOs earned more than $3.2 million in 2001, if we take seriously the estimates of the value of options granted that year, and that a few hundred other top-five executives may have passed that mark on paper (but probably not in reality). Whether several hundred ephemeral windfalls from *exercised* executive stock options were excessive in the year 2001 (many were, but not intentionally), the sums involved never added up to enough money to have any significant impact on income distribution among broad groups, such as deciles or quintiles or Gini coefficients. Before 1992, the focus of income distribution debates was on relatively *large numbers of people with low incomes*, rather than on increasingly tiny numbers of very rich. The use and abuse of income tax data has completely changed the subject, and not in a constructive direction.

Little tails do not wag big dogs. We are never going to learn anything useful about the incomes of the top 1.3 million taxpayers, or even the top 13,000, by obsessing over the salaries and stock options of 100–500 corporate CEOs. And we are never going to learn anything useful about income distribution in general by obsessing over 13,000 taxpayers who together earned $83 billion during a year when personal income exceeded $8.7 trillion.


## ONLY ONE SOURCE OF RICHES?

To prove their claim that top executive compensation (rather than limited liability companies and Subchapter-S corporations) accounted for most of the increase in income shares among the top 1 percent, Thomas Piketty and Emmanuel Saez combed through *Forbes'* magazine's surveys of 800 CEOs to estimate average incomes among just *100* best-paid CEOs from 1970 to 2003.

The *New York Times'* survey of executive pay in 2005 (which is one of many) featured a large graph showing "in 2004 the top 10 percent of executives earned at least 350 times the average worker's pay." But the source of that data (an interesting historical study by Carola Frydman and Raven Saks) covered only sixty-two of the largest U.S. firms, so the top 10 percent referred to a nonrepresentative sample of only six people.

The same graph also showed, however, that *median* CEO pay for the whole sample was "104 times the average worker's pay." Keep that 104 figure in mind later, when we will encounter a bizarre array of estimates claiming that average CEOs earned 500–1,000 times the average worker's pay. Whether such income comparisons describe six executives or a hundred, they always involve comparing *above-average* executives with below-average employees.

There are 44,000 CEOs receiving *Chief Executive* magazine, and even that number does not count them all. To describe handpicked samples of 100–500 CEOs as average is nonsensical. Even the relatively large Bebchuk-Grinstein sample of CEO pay at 1,500 firms is an above-average elite.

The *Forbes* survey chosen by Piketty and Saez includes the value of *exercised* stock options, which they say accounted for as much as 79 percent of total compensation of the top 100 in the late 1990s. But that means their 100 best-paid CEOs were *different people* each year depending on which CEOs happened to cash-in vested stock options.

In the context of discussing income growth among the top *1 percent* (1.3 million), Mr. Saez later expanded the list beyond one hundred CEOs to include "other top executives, sports, movies, and television stars."[5] Dew-Becker and Gordon likewise claim, "CEOs together with sports and entertainment stars explain what is going on in the top 1 percent of the income distribution."[6]

Adding a few hundred top celebrities and athletes to the Piketty-Saez list of 100 top executives cannot get us much closer to explaining average incomes for 1.3 million. It may, however, help put CEO pay in perspective.

*Forbes* also produces lists of best-paid celebrities and athletes. The top ten celebrities earned an *average* of $118.6 million each in 2004, compared with $58.6 million for top ten corporate CEOs. Golfer Tiger Woods earned $80.3 million in 2004 and athletes Peyton Manning, Michael Jordan, and Shaquille O'Neal earned between $32 million and $42 million. No CEO came close to matching Oprah Winfrey's $225 million. Only one CEO in the top ten in 2004 had also made the list in 2001.

U.S. journalists, economists, and political figures rarely express indignation about the super-high incomes of anyone *except* corporate executives. Scarcely anyone professes outrage about *Forbes* list of the twenty best-paid actors, who averaged $23 million apiece in 2005. U.S. business magazines and newspapers do not even bother with annual surveys of the incomes of the best-paid trial lawyers, TV news anchors, executives of private companies, investment bankers, or portfolio managers.

*New York* magazine's 2004 survey of local talent managed to turn up three famous hedge-fund managers who earned between $550 million and $1.02 billion in 2004. Those huge incomes were in no sense "distributed" at the expense of ordinary workers. They were earned from fees willingly paid by affluent and sophisticated investors (hedge-fund managers usually keep 20 percent of profits they earn for their investors). The Irish rock group U-2 grossed $260 million from concerts alone in 2005, but that was from tickets willingly paid by Bono fans.[7] Readers of *Parade* magazine were expected to be amused rather than outraged that rapper Sean "P. Diddy" Combs earned

$36 million in 2005 while radio talker Howard Stern got by on a mere $31 million.[8] Once again, however, there is no reason to believe that if Combs and Stern had been paid millions less their loss would have somehow benefited those with lower incomes (including most of their fans).

Many people share a voyeuristic fascination with what other people earn yet regard it as none of their business—*except* when discussing corporate executives.

In a rare exception, the *National Journal* took note of the fact that forty-eight "trade associations, think tanks, professional societies, and labor unions . . . awarded their chief executives with salary and benefits of $1 million or more in 2003 and 2004."[9] The *Wall Street Journal* also seemed critical of the fact that the conductors of the New York Philharmonic, Chicago Symphony, and Metropolitan Opera were paid more than $1.9 million in 2004 (which amounted to 10 percent of annual ticket sales for the New York Philharmonic).[10] The publisher of the *New York Times,* Arthur Sulzberger, Jr., also earned more than $1.9 million—more than enough to qualify for his own paper's "hyper-rich" description of the top 0.1 percent.[11] Former *Today* show host Katie Couric took a pay cut to only $15 million a year to appear on the CBS nightly news for twenty-two minutes each night, yet she is described as "perky" rather than "hyper-rich."

The endless public scolding about certain individuals being "grossly overpaid" or receiving "outrageous" or "obscene" incomes is almost exclusively reserved to top executives of the world's largest publicly traded corporations. That suggests these complaints about CEO pay are *not* about being too rich per se, but about *how* a person gets rich. Running a huge corporation does not seem to be considered quite as legitimate or honorable a way of making millions as, say, playing an excellent game of golf, being a TV news anchor or newspaper publisher, acting, singing, or producing popular books and movies.

The reason for resenting affluent businessmen rather than affluent celebrities is psychological rather than logical. In some cases it appears to reflect social snobbery and the ancient Anglo-American tradition of regarding commerce as too commercial and businessmen (or the "bourgeoisie" in Karl Marx's lexicon) as unwelcome social climbers—a class without much class.

Some of the most vocal critics of CEO pay make a revealing distinction between old money of high society and the nouveau riche businessmen. "The influential dynasties of the twentieth century, like the Kennedys, the Rockefellers and, yes, the Sulzbergers," wrote Paul Krugman, demonstrated "a strong sense of noblesse oblige, justifying their existence by standing for high principles."[12] The $3.4 billion that Bill and Melinda Gates donated to their foundation in 2004 alone is apparently not considered in the same league.[13]

Geraldine Fabrikant's chapter in the *New York Times* book *Class Matters* added the later generations of Vanderbilts, Mellons, and duPonts as other influential dynasties of "American high society" with "a signature style of living based on understatement and old-fashioned patrician values." The purpose of Ms. Fabrikant's article was to draw a class distinction between such high society on Massachusetts' Nantucket Island and the tacky, low-brow "new money" (businessmen and celebrities) who "tend to be brash, confident and unapologetic."[14] Such patronizing disdain for commercial success dates back to an era when the "landed gentry" were regarded as so-cially much nobler than the *bourgeoisie* because businessmen *work* while true gentlemen were men of leisure chasing foxes on horseback.

Another likely explanation of the hostility uniquely reserved for corporate CEOs reflects the zero-sum fallacy—the unexamined opinion that one person's gain must be someone else's loss.

One reason the millions sporadically earned by corporate CEOs are viewed so differently from larger millions routinely earned by celebrities and old dynasties is because many people can too easily be persuaded that if companies paid their executives less then they would pay their other employees more. Yet there is no economic theory or evidence to suggest that could be true.

First of all, executive gains from stock options or restricted stock are *entirely* at the expense of stockholders, not employees. Exercised options are a cost to other shareholders because the difference between the grant price and the exercise price has to be financed by issuing more shares (which dilutes earnings per share) or by using cash that could otherwise have been invested. Grants of restricted stock to executives are also entirely at the expense of other shareholders, because they dilute the value of other shares. *Stock-based compensation* of executives—which account for nearly all of the periodic big windfalls that make the headlines—is not at the expense of that company's other workers or of workers in general.

If I do *not* own shares in a company, then how many shares that company gives or promises to executives (with strings attached) is literally none of my business. When it comes to companies that I do own shares in, then the fact that I invested in those companies suggests I do not really mind sharing my shares with those executives. After all, I know there is no better way to ensure that executives act in the shareholders' interest rather than their own (which is called the "agency problem," because CEOs are just agents of the owners).

Some of the world's best (and wealthiest) corporate executives are paid almost entirely according to what happens to the company's stock, including

Warren Buffett, who owns 43 percent of all shares in Berkshire Hathaway, and Bill Gates, who owns nearly 10 percent of all 10.3 billion shares in Microsoft. Apple CEO and cofounder Steve Jobs is paid one dollar a year, and so are Google founders Larry Page and Sergey Brin. Wise stockholders understand that the only way these top executives can gain wealth is if other stockholders do too.

Secondly, the job market for executives is entirely separate from the markets for assembly-line workers or clerks. Any company that routinely paid more than the going rate for routine job skills would soon lose out in the global competition for investor capital and be forced to downsize and/or go bankrupt. Any company that routinely paid too little for needed workers, however, would lose out in the competition for skilled and motivated employees because the best workers would gravitate to rival firms.

This chapter later documents a very large drop in CEO pay in 2001–2003. That certainly did *not* result in an increase in average worker pay as the zero-sum theory predicts. The pay of CEOs and ordinary workers normally rise together when the economy is doing well. But CEO pay is as volatile as the stock market, and that makes it disingenuous to compare *percentage increases* in CEO pay with that of workers during the good years unless one also compares the declines in hard times.

Whatever the explanation for all the popular attention uniquely focused on the high incomes of a few hundred top business executives, it does not explain how *economists* could possibly imagine that this has much to do with income inequality. The more people one adds to these lists of top CEOs (or celebrities) the smaller and more diluted any average of their incomes must become, because CEOs at smaller firms earn much less than the elite and so do less-popular actors and athletes.[15] But even if you were to increase the size of such a list to one thousand more-or-less prominent executives and also added a thousand more-or-less famous celebrities, that list would still not begin to explain average incomes of the top 0.1 percent of taxpayers (130,000), much less the top 1 percent (1.3 million).

## MEASUREMENT PROBLEMS

Many contradictory statistics have been published that claim to measure average CEO compensation among the above-average companies in the S&P 500 index, the *Fortune* 500, or some annually changed list of those who happened to reach the top 100 each year by selling restricted stock or cashing-in stock options.

There are at least a dozen annual surveys of executive compensation from major newspapers, business magazines, and compensation companies. No two of them come up with roughly the same figures, even when they happen to sample the same firms. The resulting contradictory and wildly varying estimates of "average" compensation among above-average CEOs are nonetheless reported as if they were established facts. They are actually just heroic *estimates* involving various questionable methods of estimating the past and/or future value of stock options.

Stock options are *contingent* compensation for work over several years in the future. The contingencies are (1) that the executive or employee is not fired and does not resign before the vesting period is over, and (2) that the stock price is higher after vesting than it was when the employee received the stock options.

Stock options are usually sporadic, *nonrecurring* income. With customary vesting and expiration dates, any executive or nonexecutive employee who exercised stock options in 1999 would have been granted those options between 1989 and 1996. Since stock options are often valued during the year in which the employee/executive exercised them (this is *always* the case with tax-based income studies), the incomes of CEOs who *exercised* options in 1999 would appear much larger than their income in other years even though the options were actually earned (granted) in one or more of the previous 3–7 years. Although 100 CEOs therefore appear to have exceptionally high incomes in any particular year such as 1999 that definitely does not mean *the same* 100 CEOs have such high incomes year after year. Nor does it mean that any executive earned this income during *the same year* he or she exercised the options.

Stock options are *never* payment for a single year of work, yet all surveys of executive compensation treat them as if they were. Some try to estimate the "fair value" or "potential value" of options to executives on the day those options are granted, using various simple or sophisticated estimating techniques. Other surveys use the actual cost to corporate shareholders of stock options several years later, when the options were actually exercised.

A few surveys incorrectly double-count the value of stock options when granted and again when exercised.

Those surveys that use the *estimated* value of options exaggerated the value of options granted shortly before early 2000 when stock prices (particularly in Internet and telecommunications companies) began a steep three-year decline. Surveys that use the actual cash received from exercising stock options also show CEO pay rising and falling with the stock market, but the amount and timing is different than it is with surveys that estimated the value of options when granted. Older options exercised in early 2001 could still be very lucrative, yet new options *granted* later that year would have had a much, much lower *estimated* value than options on the same stock issued back in 1999 or early 2000 when stock prices were much higher.

*Forbes,* the Corporate Library, and the *Wall Street Journal* add to each executive's income the actual cost of stock options to the company in the year in which they are *exercised. Fortune* has long used various short cuts to *estimate* the "fair value" of stock options to employees in the year in which they are *granted. Business Week* switched teams: "Instead of counting the windfalls from option exercises as part of the annual pay package, as we have in the past, we're counting [estimating] the value of annual option grants."[16]

Unfortunately, as John Bryne wisely observed in *Business Week,* "some observers now do both, double-counting the same goodies so that the numbers look much larger than they actually are."[17] Austan Goolsbee of the University of Chicago, for example, defines executive income to include both an estimate of the potential value of options when they are granted and the executives' actual gains if those options are later exercised.[18] That *counts the same options twice* if they are exercised, and it also includes as income a preliminary estimate of the value of options that are *never* exercised (because the stock price fell or the company fired the executive). *USA Today* also combines both "stock-option gains [from exercising old options] and potential returns from fresh option grants."[19] There is no excuse for such double-counting of options except that it makes "the numbers look much larger than they actually are," as Bryne put it.

## PAY FOR PERFORMANCE?

Exercised stock options are the pay-off for a risky form of stock-based compensation received three to ten years in the *past* (because of vesting requirements and expiration dates). Newly granted stock options are incentives for *future* performance. Yet every survey of CEO pay miscounts stock options as if they were pay for *a single year*—the year in which they were granted *or* the year they were exercised. That has inspired an almost universal misunderstanding of what "pay for performance" means. A corporate Board's decision to grant new stock options as a *future* incentive (after three to five years of vesting) has nothing to do with what happened to the company's stock *last year*, before the grant was made. An executive's decision to exercise long-held options after the stock has fallen has nothing to do with the Board's decisions about how much he should be paid that year.

The Corporate Library survey for fiscal year 2004 was based on an admirably broad survey of the largest companies. But the allegedly dramatic *increases* from one year to the next are driven by the fact that stock options and restricted stock accumulated in past years are counted as compensation during the year in which they are exercised. For those with modest salaries in normal years, this creates huge *percentage* gains in total income whenever stock is sold. Steve Jobs is normally paid $1 a year at Apple, so that if he sold some Apple stock for $100,000 following a year in which he sold none, that would look like a ridiculously large percentage gain. To measure volatile compensation in terms of percentage increases is a trick designed to deceive, particularly since these averages omit percentage *decreases* the year *after* options are exercised.

A Corporate Library press release about the 2004 estimates thus focused on "27 CEOs who received increases that were over 1,000 percent....For example, Total Compensation for James Bagley, CEO of Lam Research Corporation, increased by 7,440 percent, triggered by over $31 million in stock option profits."[20] The Corporate Library (a for-profit "activist" publisher) then averaged such *percentage* gains and reported with great fanfare that the median *percentage gain* among people such as Mr. Bagley was 30 percent. That simply meant that among those whose total pay package went up rather than down (average CEO pay clearly *fell* in 2002–2003), half of the percentage increases were larger than 30 percent because executives chose that year to exercise older stock options. Even with exercised options included, the Corporate Library could not claim "the average CEO" received 30 percent more *dollars*. On the contrary, the same report said, "[T]otal Annual Compensation increased by a median of 11.77 percent." Many indignant journalists and editorial writers nonetheless imagined this was evidence that corporate boards had foolishly given average CEOs a 30 percent pay hike in 2004. Such statistical blunders have become the norm when reporting CEO pay. It is almost as though being politically correct is more important than being factually correct.

Since many companies' earnings or stock prices did not rise by 30 percent, journalists cited the alleged 30 percent gain in pay (ignoring the 11.77 percent figure from the same source) as evidence that corporate boards were handing out huge pay hikes for CEOs that were not connected to the previous year's performance. That evidence was hopelessly flawed, but the comparison would have been irrelevant in any case.

If the CEO is largely compensated in stock options or restricted stock, and if performance is defined as stockholders would (namely, as a higher stock price and/or dividend), then CEO pay is *automatically* linked to performance. The fact that executives may choose to exercise old stock options in one year rather than another provides no information about whether CEO pay is linked to performance.

When it comes to granting new stock options, the issue of "pay for performance" is almost as commonly garbled as in the case of exercising old stock options. In these cases, journalists and self-styled "shareholder activists" point to what happened to a company's earnings or share price during the previous year (which may have involved a recession or energy price shock) and use that year's past performance as a reason to object to granting stock options or restricted stock to enhance the CEO's *future* incentives.

If this year's shareholders only cared about *last year's* stock performance—the most common journalistic definition of "pay for performance"—then they would want 100 percent of CEO compensation to be in the form of January bonuses tied to last year's stock prices. Yet basing future pay on past performance would offer executives no incentive at all to do better in the future. That is why grants of stock options or restricted stock in any given year are not, and should not be, related to what happened to the company's earnings or stock price in any previous year.

## DOWN IS NOT UP

Figure 6.1 presents a broad measure of average (mean) CEO pay for big S&P 500 companies and for "Small-Cap 600" firms from 1993 to 2003. These figures, which use the *grant* value of stock options, were prepared by Lucian Bebchuk of the Harvard Law School and Yaniv Grinstein of Cornell University.[21] Mr. Bebchuk is a prominent *critic* of executive compensation, whose theories on that topic will be discussed later, so there is very little chance these numbers are too low.

According to the Bebchuk-Grinstein definition of CEO pay, chief executive officers of giant companies in the Standard and Poor's 500 stock index (S&P 500) were paid $9.1 million apiece in 2003. Since there are always a few large outliers, such *mean* averages of top CEO pay are exaggerated—not as representative as a median average. The *Wall Street Journal* reported that, "the median CEO of the Standard & Poor's 500 companies had a total compensation of $6 million in 2004."[22]

Using that atypical $9.1 million *mean* for 2003, however, the combined compensation of all 500 CEOs would have amounted to less than $4.6 billion—a drop in the bucket compared with the stock market value (market capitalization) of companies they manage, which was nearly $11.3 trillion by the end of 2005.[23]

A total compensation figure of $4.6 billion for top 500 CEOs was also a drop in the bucket compared to total incomes of about $390 billion reportedly earned by the top 0.1 percent of taxpayers (130,000).

The first thing to notice in Figure 6.1 is that CEO pay among the top 500 *fell* by nearly 48 percent from 2000 to 2003—from $17.4 million to $9.1 million. The $9.1 million figure for 2003 was no higher than it was in 1997. Among small-cap firms, CEO pay never rose much above $2 million,

**FIGURE 6.1**
**Average CEO Compensation and the S&P 500**
**Stock Index**

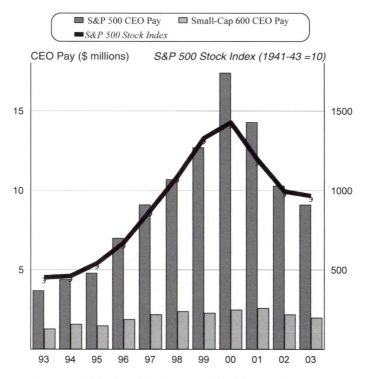

Source: L. Bebchuck and Y. Grinstein, *Oxford Review of Economic Policy* (2005).

where it was in 2003. Among CEOs of mid-cap firms (not shown), the mean average fell from $5.1 million in 1999 to $4 million in 2003.

The dark line in Figure 6.1 shows what happened to the S&P 500 *stock index*, which rose and fell in remarkably close conformity to the rise and fall of CEO pay for these same 500 firms. That is exactly what is *supposed* to happen with stock-based compensation. It is what "pay for performance" really means—CEOs benefit only if other stockholders do too.

Amazingly, press reports about CEO pay after the year 2000 left readers with the exact opposite impression—that CEO pay had risen sharply and steadily every year from 2000 to 2005. Writing in the *New York Times* in 2006, Ben Stein claimed that "the graph for the pay of CEOs is a vertical line in the last five years."[24] Even a *Wall Street Journal* column about the Bebchuk-Grinstein paper imagined that "[t]op-executive pay is . . . rising faster than earnings and faster than stock-market returns. And growth in pay has been accelerating."[25] Yet that columnist's own source (Bebchuk and Grinstein) clearly shows that top-executive pay rose and fell in lockstep with the stock market. A 48 percent decline in CEO pay over three years can hardly be described as "accelerating" or a "vertical line."

A second thing to notice in Figure 6.1 is that CEO pay at the biggest 500 companies was *much* larger than it was at the *relatively* smaller (but still quite large) "Small-Cap 600." Those who describe a mean average of CEO pay among 500 of the world's largest companies as "average" CEO pay are stretching the truth.

"Market capitalization" (as in the phrase "small-cap") refers to the total market value of a company's shares. The larger the firm, the larger the CEO's compensation is likely to be. And more valuable the company's shares become, the more valuable an executive's stock-based compensation will be. Risky businesses also tend to offer more stock-based compensation. These observable differences in CEO pay make economic sense, which suggests that CEO compensation is not as capricious as many assume.[26]

The fact that CEOs of large-cap corporations earned much more than CEOs of small-cap corporations is one reason why it makes no sense to compare executive pay among the largest U.S. corporations with executive pay in other countries. In a display of statistical whimsy common to this topic, one *Wall Street Journal* writer worried that U.S. CEOs earned $6 million in 2004 while British CEOs earned $4.9 million; another complained that top U.S. CEOs earned $2.3 million in 2004 "compared with $317,864 for the heads of 187 Japanese companies."[27] Even if we could figure out what such variable figures actually mean, or how they were translated into dollars, to compare pay among foreign companies with pay among U.S. companies is often like comparing pay among the "Small-Cap 600" with that among the "S&P 500." In the 2004 *Forbes* list of the fifty most valuable companies in the world, measured by market capitalization, twenty-nine were from the United States, but only one from Japan.[28] Unlike the United States, no sample of even as few as 100 companies in any other country contains more than a half dozen of significant size.

The Bebchuk-Grinstein sample covers 1,500 CEOs, although only 1,100 are shown in Figure 6.1. When that elite list is further narrowed to only the top 100 CEOs, their pay is clearly not an "average" at all but the cream of the crop.

Piketty and Saez, for example, compared *Forbes*' estimate of the mean average of salaries and exercised stock options among the 100 best-paid CEOs to mean salaries *for the population as a whole* (rather than at those same 100 top companies). Their estimated real compensation for the top 100 CEOs rose very rapidly in 1998–2000 because it includes *exercised* stock options, which were by then far more valuable than expected when they were granted three to ten years earlier.

Just as reporters who wrote about the Bebchuk-Grinstein study failed to notice the top 500 CEOs suffered a 48 percent pay cut from 2000 to 2003, reporters who repeatedly cited the Piketty-Saez figures never reported that their estimate of "top 100" CEO pay *fell* by 53 percent from 1999 to 2003. Meanwhile, leading newspaper writers continued to describe the 48–53 percent drop in CEO pay in those years as an "accelerating," or a "vertical line."

The Bebchuk-Grinstein measure of "compensation in any given year" includes an estimate of the value of stock options when they are granted, so it does *not* count stock options exercised in any give year. It does, however, include bonuses paid for the *previous* year and the estimated *future* value of stock options *granted* during any given year. Such a mélange of *past and future pay* cannot be intelligently compared with company earnings in "any given year." Yet the authors make that sort of comparison in order to claim that pay in any given year was not linked to "performance" (which they define as earnings rather than stock performance) in that same year.

The value of stock-related pay, as Bebchuk and Grinstein measure it, accounted for 78 percent of CEO compensation among the S&P 500 elite in the peak year of 2000. The figure was so large because it mostly consists of a Black-Scholes estimate of what stock options appeared to be worth at the time they were granted in 2000, before the stock market crashed. However, stock options granted "in any given year," like 2000, could not be exercised for at least three more years, after being vested. By that time very few owners of stock options were able to exercise them at all, much less at the lofty value they were estimated to have in 1999–2000, when stock prices peaked.

If performance is measured by what really matters to stockholders— namely, by what happened to S&P 500 *stocks*—both the rise of CEO pay in the late 1990s and the fall from 2000 to 2003 were obviously linked very closely to the rise and fall of the stock market. In the second half of the 1990s "the [S&P] 500 index gained 247.4 percent doubling the 118.7 percent payoff of the small-cap 600."[29] Most S&P 500 stockholders did very well at that time—*including* executives of the big-cap S&P 500 firms. That should hardly be a surprise, since the driving goal of those who complained the loudest about CEO pay in 1990–1993 was to make sure that in following years executives would be paid less in salary and more in stock options.

## A THOUSAND-TO-ONE SHOT

On January 21, 2006, a *Wall Street Journal* feature story said, "In 2004, the aggregate compensation of the chief executive officers of the S&P 500 companies...totaled about $5 billion, up 39% from 2003, according to Paul Hodgson of the Corporate Library." If you divide $5 billion among 500 CEOs, that is $10 million apiece. But the alleged 39 percent increase in 2004 implies that the 500 CEOs received just $7.2 million apiece in 2003. Meanwhile, a graph in the same *Wall Street Journal* story shows average CEO compensation as only $2.16 million in 2005.[30] At that point, most readers must have been as befuddled as the writer. But that was not the end of the confusion.

A sidebar to the same report claimed that "the average CEO's salary in the U.S. is 475 times greater than the average worker's salary."[31] If average CEO pay was $2.16 million, then a ratio of 475 : 1 implies average workers earn only $4,547 a year. If average CEO pay was $7.2 million in 2003 then a ratio of 475 : 1 implies "the average worker's salary" was only $15,158 (about $7.29 an hour), which is much less than half of any credible average.[32] If the wildly different estimates on CEO pay were even close to being "average," then the ratio of 475 1 makes no sense.

Where do all these numbers come from? Does anybody even care?

Other journalists cited the first page of a book by Lucian Bebchuk and Jesse Fried as the source for the otherwise elusive claim that average CEOs earned 500 times as much as the average worker. But Bebchuk and Fried, in turn, just cited another journalist—Janice Revell of *Fortune*—who asserted in the March 31, 2003, issue that "in 1991 the average large-company CEO earned about 140 times the pay of an average rank-and-file worker; today it's more like 500 times."[33] There was no source given and no explanation of what those "averages" were supposed to mean.

The Economic Policy Institute, which can scarcely be accused of a procorporate bias, estimated "the ratio of CEO to average worker pay" at 145 in 2002 and 185 in 2003.[34] The Fryden-Saks study mentioned earlier (the one cited by the *New York Times* on April 9, 2006) estimated that "in 2004 half of executives earned more than 104 times the average worker's pay."

To say that CEOs earn 104 times the average worker's pay, or even 145–185 times, does not sound so astonishing. After all, the fate of the company may be in the CEO's hands. So there has been a great deal of statistical creativity used to push such ratios all the way up to 475–500, or even beyond 1,000 : 1. To do so requires grossly exaggerating "average" CEO pay, of course, but also grossly *understating* a relevant average of "ordinary worker" pay.

Where did the *Wall Street Journal* and *Fortune* come up with the idea that the average CEO's salary is 475–500 times as large as the average worker's salary? Those mystery numbers most likely came from a periodic pamphlet called *Executive Excess*, which claimed the alleged "ratio of average CEO pay to the average pay of ordinary workers" was 525 in 2000, 281 in 2002, and 431 in 2004.[35] It is of passing interest that journalists writing after 2002 did not refer to that pamphlet's much lower estimate of 281 in 2002, and also did not reveal the source.

"The average CEO now takes home a paycheck 431 times that of their average worker," according to Chuck Collins and Felice Yeskel, who tried to use that figure to explain why "income inequality is now near all-time highs, with . . . the biggest gains going to the top 5 percent and 1 percent of households."[36]

Collins and Yeskel, the authors of *Economic Apartheid in America*, are cofounders of United for a Fair Economy, which got together with an old leftist group, the Institute for Policy Studies, and put out *Executive Excess*. The 2005 version was an antiwar tract subtitled *Defense Contractors Get More Buck for the Bang*.[37] The most novel thing about that "study" is not the way the authors pushed CEO pay up (by adding exercised options to a *Business Week* survey), but the way they pushed "average worker" pay down.

*Executive Excess* takes the discredited "average weekly earnings" figure and multiplies it times fifty-two weeks to conclude that "the average production worker made $27,460 in 2004." But that weekly average contains tens of millions of part-time workers, so multiplying weekly earnings times fifty-two results in a preposterous estimate of what average *full-time* workers earn in a year.

It is particularly misleading to compare incomes earned from working 20–25 hours per week with managers and professionals in the top 10 percent who often work twice that long. Peter Kuhn and Fernando Lozano found that between 1980 and 2001, "the share of employed 25-64-year-old men who usually work 50 or more hours per week on their main job rose . . . from 22.2 to 30.5 percent among college-educated men employed full-time."[38] Although many studies have remarked on the higher *annual* earnings of those with a college education, such studies rarely take account of the fact that more of the college-educated are also working *longer hours*. As a result, incomes *per hour* between the more and less educated do not differ so much as income *per year*. There are also more workers per household among the college-educated population (and in the top quintile).[39]

*Executive Excess* illustrates how the ratio of CEO pay to that of an "average worker" can be exaggerated by *underestimating employee incomes*. But a far more popular way of boosting that ratio is by adding phony *estimates* to CEO pay.

In October 2002, Paul Krugman wrote in the *New York Times Magazine* that average compensation among the 100 highest-paid CEOs in the *Fortune* 500 had risen to $37.5 million in 1999, which, he claimed, was "more than 1000 times the pay of ordinary workers." This was, he argued, "only the most spectacular indicator of a broader story, the reconcentration of income and wealth in the United States"[40]

At least three-fourths of the alleged $37.5 million, however, was a rough *estimate* of the expected value CEO stock options *granted* in 1999. *Fortune* guessed that prices of stocks behind those 1999 options would increase by a third, and valued 1999 stock options accordingly.

By October 2002, however, the tech-heavy NASDAQ stock index had collapsed—dropping from a peak of 5046.6 to 1329.8. Corning stock soared above $100 a share in the fall of 2000 on the fiber-optic wave, for example, and then fell below $2 in two years. Even the blue chip Dow-Jones index, which hit 11,722.97 in early 2000, had dropped to 7528.4 by October 4, 2002.

By the time Mr. Krugman published his 1000:1 ratio, it should have been painfully obvious that stock options granted in 1999 were no longer nearly as valuable as *Fortune* had estimated. Most high-tech options were worthless. By April of 2002, *Business Week* (which at that time counted options when exercised rather than when granted) had already reported that the drop in average CEO pay during 2001 alone "was nearly 31%."[41] *Fortune*'s hypothetical estimate of the value of CEO stock options granted in 1999 was also worthless by 2002, as was Mr. Krugman's equally hypothetical 1000: ratio.

*Fortune*'s estimate of the compensation of the top 100 CEOs in 2002 was 58 percent smaller than their inflated estimate for 1999.[42] Using 2002 rather than 1999 estimates would leave the pay of top 100 (not average) CEOs at roughly 420 times Krugman's noncomparable estimate of average wages.

Dozens of CEOs in 2002 saw their pay drop to zero. During the first five months of 2002 CEOs were being retired at the rate of two a day, eighty in May alone.[43] Another forty-four departed in the first eleven business days that June.[44] In the judgment of corporate boards, those CEOs had indeed been overpaid, in retrospect. But that risk of being fired is one reason why pay (including prenegotiated severance pay) is so high. A fired CEO cannot easily get a second chance.

Long after stock prices collapsed and dozens of CEOs had been sacked, Paul Krugman was still treating *Fortune*'s flawed estimate of 1999 stock options as if the top 100 CEOs had actually collected $37.5 million apiece and put the money in the bank. But most of those millions never amounted to anything more than illusory estimates. A CEO cannot even buy a cup of coffee with an estimate. Many journalists less trained in economics were also making the same mistake of *confusing estimates with reality*. Consider just three examples on three consecutives days:[45]

- On March 26, 2002, *Wall Street Journal* writers Gregg Hitt and Jacob M. Schlesinger exclaimed, "In 2000, Enron issued stock options worth $155 million, according to a common method of valuing options." In reality, stock options Enron issued in 2000 were completely worthless.
- On March 27, 2002, *Washington Post* writer Alec Klein wrote, "Despite a tough financial year, AOL Time Warner Inc's chairman and chief executive [Steve Case] was rewarded in 2001 with stock options worth an estimated $76 million." That $76 million relied on AOL Time Warner stock rising to $49–73 a share, so those options were also worthless.
- On March 28, 2002, *Washington Post* writer Charles R. Babcock wrote, "During the boom year of 2000, some highly successful companies issued so many stock options to their executives and employees that they paid little or no corporate tax because the options were deductible." On the contrary, there is a corporate deduction (as there is with *all* labor costs) only when options are exercised, *not* when granted. Most high-tech options granted "during the boom year of 2000" were worthless by 2002, producing no income and therefore no deductions.

By October 2002, it should have been obvious that any precrash estimates of the value of stock options granted in 1999 or 2000 were wildly exaggerated. Yet the rampant confusion of old estimates with current reality in 2002 inspired a political backlash against executive stock options that had no effect on how much CEOs were later paid, of course, but merely altered the mixture of pay packages to replace stock options with restricted stock. The political and media hostility to stock options appears to have had much more impact in reducing the availability of such options among lower-level employees.

The other side of Krugman's illusive 1000 : 1 ratio—the salaries of "ordinary workers"—did not even refer to average salaries within the same 100 super-successful firms, which typically pay unusually generous salaries and benefits to their unusually skilled "ordinary workers." During the stock market boom of 1996–2000, the most lucrative benefit for hundreds of thousands of nonexecutive employees during the stock market peak of 1999–2000 was exactly the same benefit that accounted for most of the pay of CEOs—stock options.

Companies such as Microsoft, Amazon, Intel, Sun Microsystems, AOL, Ford, and Southwest Airlines were granting *most* stock options to *nonexecutive* employees at the time. Microsoft never gave options to top executives, only to other employees (the famed "Microsoft millionaires" of that era). Quite a few companies still grant most stock options to ordinary employees, and that benefit was never confined to high-tech firms alone. Whole Foods Market's *Annual Report* for 2005 says, "Approximately 93% of the options...have been granted to Team Members who are not executive officers."

The National Center for Employee Ownership estimated that 10 million Americans held stock options by 2001. Joseph Blasi of Rutgers found that ninety-seven of the top 100 e-commerce companies offered options to most or all employees. A 2003 WorldatWork study showed that 15 percent of all public companies offered options to most or all employees.[46]

Estimates of the ratio of CEO pay to that of other employees always count stock options of executives as income but never count the stock options of other employees. This obviously distorts any comparison of broadly defined executive *compensation* (including options) to narrowly defined employee wages (excluding options). It is true that most employees in the whole U.S. economy did not have the opportunity for big windfalls that stock options can provide. But it is also true that average executives of the thousands of companies in the U.S. economy do not earn one million dollars a year, much less many millions.

Although the stock options of only 100–500 CEOs cannot possibly explain the large ups and down in mean income during 1996–2003 among 130,000–1,300,000 taxpayers (the top 0.1 percent and 1 percent, respectively), stock options exercised or not exercised by hundreds of thousands of *nonexecutive* employees offer a far more significant and believable explanation.

Another peculiar aspect of the academic economists' fixation on 100–500 corporate CEOs is that more and more businesses continue to switch from filing under the corporate income tax to filing under the individual income tax. Some private companies are huge but out of the limelight, such as Koch Industries, Bechtel, and Cargill. Many are well known, such as Pricewaterhouse Coopers, Ernst & Young, Gallo wine, MGM, Neiman Marcus, Hallmark cards, Kohler plumbing, Levi Strauss, and others. We do not hear any complaints about what their executives earn, however, because only publicly traded corporations have to report executive compensation to the Securities and Exchange Commission (SEC).

Since private companies have to compete for business skills and talent in the same job market as public companies, we can infer that they must be paying at least as much as comparable public corporations do. *Washington Post* columnist Steven Pearlstein observed, "Private equity firms...are attracting not only the top business school graduates these days, but also Corporate legends like General Electric's Jack Welch (Clayton Dubiler & Rice), Gap's Mickey Drexler (Texas Pacific Group) and International Business

Machines' Lou Gerstner (Carlyle Group)."[47] People who complained about the compensation of Jack Welch and Lou Gerstner while they were famously effective corporate CEOs can no longer complain about their pay in private business.

Private firms are not the only ones to raid U.S. corporations seeking the best managers. "Indian businesses have hired dozens of executives from [U.S.] companies," reports the *Wall Street Journal*, "especially with higher salaries."[48]

It seems unlikely that seasoned U.S. executives are suffering big pay cuts for the privilege of moving from a public to a private business, or moving to India. If anyone ever could actually succeed in limiting CEO pay among publicly traded firms then even larger numbers of the best executives and business school graduates would move to private or foreign firms, and even fewer firms would remain public. The resulting scarcity of first-rate managers among surviving public firms would, ironically, drive up CEO pay. The endless crusade against high CEO pay in general (as opposed to specific abuses, notably at retirement) is fundamentally quixotic.

We can learn from observation that some CEOs were overpaid after they are fired. But we can also learn from observation that some CEOs were *underpaid* after they are recruited by some other firm—perhaps a private company or one in another country.

## THE MARKET FOR EXECUTIVE TALENT

Any suggestion that *most* CEOs are routinely overpaid implies corporations could attract, retain, and motivate these executives with substantially cheaper pay packages. Economists describe being paid more than needed as "rent." If rent extraction were the rule rather than the exception, however, it would mean most U.S. companies behave inefficiently most of the time. Yet that would make it hard to explain how most U.S. companies (and their stocks) even survive, much less prosper, in an increasingly competitive world.

Studies of executive compensation have uncovered no evidence that American CEOs *in general* can systematically extract rent from compliant Boards of Directors.

- In a survey of numerous studies produced for the National Bureau of Economic Research in the early 1990s, Nancy Rose remarked, "We find no evidence for the popular view that boards typically fail to penalize CEOs for poor financial performance or reward them disproportionately well for good performance."[49]
- Michelle Hanlon, Shivaram Rajgopal, and Terry Shevlin studied the value of new stock option grants to the top five executives in 2000 firms from 1992–2000, and found "little evidence in support of rent extraction" by top managers.[50]

• A survey of evidence on executive compensation for the Federal Reserve Bank of New York concluded, "[E]mpirical evidence suggests that, on average, firms base their equity incentives on systematic and theoretically sensible factors."[51]

All such empirical evidence that the market for executives is reasonably *efficient* was dismissed on theoretical grounds in *Pay Without Performance* by law professors Lucian Bebchuk and Jesse Fried, which extended a previous article they coauthored with David Walker. Their theorizing required a subjective redefinition of the economists' concept of rent "to refer to the additional value that managers obtain beyond what they would get in arm's-length bargaining with a board that had both the inclination to maximize shareholder value and the necessary time and information to perform that task properly."[52]

Even if it could be proven that most U.S. corporate directors are disinclined to maximize shareholder value, or are too ill-informed or busy to do so, that would not explain why CEO pay rose dramatically until 2000, and then declined for three years. *To explain why something changed, such as CEO pay, economists have to connect it with some other variable that changed.*

"The Bebchuk-Fried-Walker hypothesis does not provide a satisfactory reason for the *increase* in CEO pay," wrote Kevin J. Murphy and Jan Zabojni. "Surely, CEOs were trying to extract rents even thirty years ago. But then, one would have to argue that over time the boards of directors became more and more captive. However, if anything, the opposite seems to be true: evidence suggests that the boards of directors are becoming increasingly independent."[53]

The idea that boards are docile captives of each company's managers, said Murphy and Zabojnik "would imply that the executives promoted internally should earn more than CEOs hired from the outside, because, arguably, they have closer ties with their companies' boards of directors." Murphy and Zabojnik found the opposite is true, with CEOs recruited from the outside earning 21.6 percent more than those promoted internally in the 1990s. Moreover, that 21.6 percent premium paid to CEOs recruited from other firms had increased from 17.2 percent in the 1980s and just 6.5 percent in the 1970s. Outsiders, with no prior ties to the board, also accounted for a rising share of new CEOs. "While in the 1970s outside hires accounted for 15 percent of all CEO replacements," they noted, "in the 1980s it was already 17 percent, and in the 1990s more than 26 percent of CEOs were hired from the outside." If boards were becoming more beholding to each company's current executives, why have they grown increasingly inclined to recruit CEOs from outside the firm and to pay extra to do so? The stock market's answer is that paying a premium for an outside CEO can be a bargain. On March 6, 2006, the stock of Krispy Kreme Doughnuts rose 21 percent in a single day on news the company had recruited a new CEO from Kraft Foods.

Bebchuk, Fried, and Walker speculated that "an important factor affecting executives' ability to increase their compensation is the amount of 'outrage' their proposed pay package would create . . . [because] outsiders might become angry and upset." For proof they relied on the scarcity of what *they* defined as "optimal contracting."[54] In particular, scarcely any company paid CEOs with *indexed* stock options that pay off only if the company's stock beats some benchmark, such as the S&P 500 stock index.

Bebchuk, Fried, and Walker concluded that the fact that very few CEO stock options were indexed must prove that CEOs were using market power to extract rent. This is like concluding that the difficulty of finding extra-wide shoes proves there must be something inefficient about the shoe market because everyone knows wide feet are optimal.

Patrick Bolton of Columbia University, and Jose Scheinkman and Wei Xiong of Princeton, analyzed nonindexed options and other supposedly "nonoptimal" features of CEO contracts and explained why such features *are* in the interest of stockholders.[55]

Besides, a 2005 survey by Mercer Human Resources Consulting found that 30 out of 100 major corporations *did* base "a portion" of stock-based executive compensation on performance targets. These were usually company-specific targets for profitability, however, rather than stock performance relative to some index.[56]

Contracts between CEOs and corporations involve two parties at the bargaining table, not just one. To substitute indexed options for nonindexed options greatly increases the risk that such options will end up worthless. That is why Bebchuk and Fried believe that "the performance-conditioned option represents less of a cost to shareholders than the corresponding conventional option because there is a greater chance that it will never be exercised."[57] But why would CEOs *accept* an offer of compensation in the form of options that are very likely to "never be exercised"?

To compensate that extra risk the deal would have to be sweetened. The number of indexed options granted would have to be much larger than the equivalent number of safer nonindexed options, or the salary and bonus would have to be larger.

The notion that indexed options are "optimal" assumes CEO pay can somehow be made much riskier for the CEO without stockholders bearing any extra cost for other parts of the pay package or any extra risk (because CEOs with indexed options would have to take above-average risks to achieve above-average returns). In a review of the Bebchuk-Fried volume, Core, Guay, and

Thomas offer several perfectly sound reasons why indexed options are normally regarded as *mutually* unsatisfactory by corporate boards and executives.[58]

## TWO AGENCY PROBLEMS

Agitation about CEO pay has led those not directly involved to propose various "reforms" of tax policy or accounting regulation, which are designed to influence the *form* of executive compensation. As should have been expected, many such efforts to discourage one form of compensation have had no clear effect on the total amount of CEO pay. Overall compensation is not reduced by changing the mixture of salary, bonus, stock options, restricted stock, deferred compensation, retirement funds, and perks.

Political efforts to alter the way CEOs were paid in the early 1990s, however, had the unintended effect of helping many CEOs collect huge unexpected windfalls when tech stocks soared in the late 1990s.

Back in 1990, an influential study in the *Harvard Business Review* by Michael Jensen, and Kevin J. Murphy concluded that "corporate America pays its most important leaders like bureaucrats." To reward "increased success fostered by greater risk taking, effort and ability," they argued, "would eventually mean paying the average CEO more."[59] They advocated reducing the share of CEO pay from salaries and increasing the share tied to stock prices.

Jensen and Murphy emphasized that corporate managers are *agents* ostensibly acting on behalf of the company's *owners* (stockholders). The fact that mangers (agents) have different interests than owners creates "agency costs." Top executives paid like bureaucrats (mostly in salary and perks) would have personal incentives to waste corporate funds on company jets, yachts, and apartments, and to hire an army of executive assistants to ease their workload. They would also have personal incentives to be overly cautious—to avoid taking chances with potentially lucrative new products or procedures in order to minimize criticism and maximize job security. Such agency costs are the reason for tying a sizable portion of executive compensation to whether or not the company stock provides good returns for stockholders (which is what "pay for performance" means).

When a CEO's pay is mostly dependent on company stock, accumulated gains on that stock can become extremely large after five to ten years if the company does extremely well. Richard D. Fairbank, the founder of Capital One, took a small Virginia bank and in just one decade built it into the 115th most valuable company in the S&P 500. The stock price rose from a few dollars a share to more than $80. Mr. Fairbank received no salary or bonus in 2005, but he decided to exercise about half of his accumulated stock options for $249 million in 2005—one of the largest gains ever.[60] That was a *long-term* payoff for adding something like $100 billion to the company's assets in just five years. Yet surveys of CEO compensation count that sort of rare, multiyear reward as if it was a single year's paycheck. A handful of such atypical gains greatly exaggerate any mean average that includes *exercised* options. In the Piketty-Saez list of top 100 CEOs, Mr. Fairbank's one-year gain would add nearly $2.5 million to the so-called average that year.

When William McGuire became CEO of United Health in 1989, the company had annual revenue of $400 million and the stock sold for about a dollar a share. Annual revenues increased to $45.4 billion in 2005 and the stock topped $98 before being split. Because Mr. McGuire did not exercise options accumulated when the stock was much cheaper, he had *unrealized* capital gains of $1.6 billion by early 2006. That $1.6 billion is instructive once we understand that such *unexercised* stock options are counted as if they were worthless in studies that treat *exercised* options as yearly income (such as Piketty-Saez). What is even more instructive is that such *unrealized* capital gains are also counted as worthless in tax-based income distribution studies that count only realized and taxable capital gains as yearly income (such as the CBO and Strudler-Petska).

The contrast between Mr. Fairbank who sold some shares and McGuire who did not illustrates a fundamental misunderstanding in all studies that count asset sales as yearly income. Selling stock is no different from selling a house—it does not make anyone any richer than before the sale occurred, and proceeds from the sale are not new income.

When Steve Jobs returned as CEO of Apple Computer, his salary was a dollar a year and his pay consisted of 5.4 million shares of restricted stock amounting to less than 1 percent of the company's shares. He ended up being paid extremely well after three years, when the shares became vested (they were then worth $351 million), but only because those who invested in his company were also greatly enriched by the company's astonish- ing revitalization.[61] It is hard to imagine how Mr. Jobs's stock market gains might be said to have been obtained at anyone else's expense. Yet that is what is implied by zero-sum theorists, who insist the top 0.1 percent's increased share of income or wealth was "at the expense of" everyone else.

Stock options only result in these big gains for corporate CEOs (often company founders) if the company and therefore the stock do very well. If actual investors objected to the stock options granted years ago to Messrs. Fairbank, McGuire, and Jobs then investors would have shunned those companies, and the stock options would not have paid off.

In 2000, Brian Hall of the Harvard Business School concluded, "Option grants do not promote a selfish, near-term perspective on the part of busi- nesspeople. On the contrary, options are the best compensation mechanism we have for getting managers to act in ways that ensure the long-term success of their companies and the well-being of their workers and stockholders."[62]

People who make the noisiest public complaints about the executive stock options are rarely actual stockholders, because stockholders in companies such as Apple or Capital One have little to complain about. Critics of stock option gains are more often people who claim to represent the interests of shareholders in general. That includes professional critics such as the Corporate Library, which markets their advice (about how to avoid their criticism) to corporate compensation committees. But it also includes some managers of pension funds or mutual funds who claim to represent everyone with assets invested in their funds.

One big difficulty with "shareholder democracy" is that investment has become increasingly institutionalized. Those who own shares in an S&P 500 mutual fund do not get any chance to vote on who should sit on 500 corporate boards or how each company's executives are to be paid. Those votes are made by fund managers who control the proxy votes of individual investors. The "agency problem" in this case is that managers of pension funds and mutual funds may have personal interests that do not coincide with what stockholders would actually prefer, or they may be subjected to outside pressure from organizations with some axe to grind. As Jensen and Murphy warned back in 1990 that "public disclosure of 'what the boss makes' gives ammunition to outside constituencies with their own special-interest agendas"[63]

The American Federation of State, County, and Municipal Employees got together with the Corporate Library, for example, and got the press to report on their "study" handing out low rating to mutual fund families that did not always vote "yes" on union-backed shareholder proposals and "no" on all executive compensation plans—as if voting "no" settles anything or is always the right answer.[64] There is also some evidence that institutional investors manipulate votes on corporate resolutions by borrowing millions of shares for one day.[65]

There is some evidence that meddlesome bosses of government and labor union pension funds have their own agendas, and are not helpful agents of stockholders. A study from Wayne State's business school looked at firms targeted for monitoring by the monopolistic California Pubic Employees Retirement System (CalPERS) and found that shareholders (including CalPERS pensioners) suffered "significant wealth losses" from such third-party interference with contracts to attract and retain skilled executives.[66] Marilyn Johnson, Susan Porter, and Margaret Shackell found "pension funds like CalPERS appear to be more attuned to what is typically viewed as 'political concerns' about compensation than to what is typically viewed as 'shareholder concerns' about pay-for-performance sensitivities."[67]

In 1993, intense pressure from politicized pension funds, self-styled corporate activists and their contacts in the media resulted in a heavy-handed new tax law explicitly designed to tilt CEO pay away from salary toward stock options. Section 162(m) of the Revenue Reconciliation Act of August 6, 1993, *denied public companies any tax deduction* for the cost of regular compensation in excess of $1 million a year. This soon "led firms to adjust the composition of their pay away from salary and toward performance related pay," Brian Hall and Jeffrey Liebman discovered, but it did *not* decrease "the total level of compensation. . . . Any decrease in salary brought about by section 162(m) was offset by increases in bonuses and stock option grants."[68]

Those over-promoted option grants of the early 1990s, many of which became vested as the stock market peaked, turned out to be *much* more valuable than a higher salary. "Once the $1 million cap was put in place," noted *Fortune*'s Janice Revell, "companies began to dole out options in record numbers, and thanks to the soaring stock market, executives hit the jackpot."[69]

The new 39.6 percent tax rate on marginal salary income offered an extra incentive for executives to prefer stock options in order to defer paying a higher tax. "Because taxes will lead executives to provide less effort for any given level of incentive based pay," noted Hall and Liebman, the increased tax rate "should therefore increase the use of incentive-based pay."[70]

In the early 1990s, economists, pension fund mangers, corporate activists, business journalists, and the Clinton Administration all vigorously advocated changes in tax laws and regulations to encourage companies to tilt executive compensation away from the security of salaries toward risky stock options. But more risk can mean more reward. And in the late 1990s, risk was more rewarding than ever.

A decade later, the same critics of CEO pay feigned surprise and indignation that the biggest increases in executive pay between 1993 and 2000 came from stock options. Yet that was precisely what those seeking to "reform" executive compensation in the early 1990s were trying to accomplish. They simply failed to anticipate what a roaring bull market would do to the value of stock options in the late 1990s, and companies who granted options in the early 1990s were likewise caught by surprise. The result was a *one-time windfall* for CEOs and other stockholders that began to evaporate as the stock market fell for three years after April 2000.

The Joint Committee on Taxation (JCT) issued a 2003 report on the Enron bankruptcy, which concluded, "The $1 million deduction limitation is ineffective at accomplishing its purpose, overrides normal income tax principals, and should be repealed."[71] Instead of undoing their old mistake, however, the critics of CEO pay worked hard to add a new one.

A 2002–2003 backlash against stock options involved politicians, the press, and the same professional activists and pension fund managers that had pushed for the switch to stock options in 1993. This second mission, pursued with same zeal as the first, soon resulted in redefining the "optimal" CEO pay packages in the *opposite* direction from the way Bebchuk and Fried intended. Instead of trying somehow to persuade or compel CEOs to absorb *more* risk, the newer critics of CEO pay have pushed hard to reduce greatly the CEO's risk of losing much money if the company's future stock price falls.

One way they accomplished this strange objective was by besmirching employee stock options in general, and thereby creating a public relations problem for companies that had been generous with stock options. The other way was by lobbying hard and successfully for new rules from the Financial Accounting Standards Board (FASB) to force companies to treat a highly subjective estimate of the value of stock options when they are granted as if that was an immediate expense to stockholders, even though many stock options are never exercised.[72]

The intent and the effect of requiring companies to treat a *potential future expense* as an *actual current expense* was to encourage many of them (notably, Microsoft) to replace option grants with *restricted stock*. Unlike the Bebchuk-Fried indexed options—most of which "will never be exercised"—restricted stock cannot become worthless unless the company goes bankrupt. *Substituting restricted stock for stock options transfers most downside risk from the CEO to stockholders.*

The end result of all the political pressure to "do something" about CEO pay in 1990–1993 was to push public corporations to offer less in salary and more in stock options. Because the stock market boomed after 1995, that "reform" had the ironic effect of making many CEOs much wealthier than anyone had imagined when the companies granted the options.

In 2002–2003, while a sharp drop in CEO went unnoticed in the press, a belated backlash against the windfalls of the late 1990s led to a widespread substitution of restricted stock for stock options. By 2004–2005 it was clear that this "reform" had not reduced stock-based CEO pay, which automatically rebounded when stock prices did. The only thing that substituting restricted stock for stock options accomplished was to reduce the CEOs' risk of being paid nothing but salary if stock prices fell.

Neither the rush into executive stock options in the early 1990s or the rush into restricted stock a decade later might have occurred to the extent that they did if pay arrangements between companies and their executives had been simply allowed to be settled the way pay arrangements are settled for everyone else—by voluntary negotiations among consenting adults.

The best public companies are not about to abandon some form of stock-based compensation for top executives because (1) such incentives get results and stock performance is what it takes to attract investors; and because (2) they have to compete for top managerial talent with other public, private, and foreign firms. Whether pundits and politicians like it or not, a few hundred top executives will continue to report extremely large payouts if and when their company's stock price has increased substantially. Those occasional payouts are *not* annual income, they are financed *entirely* by shareholders rather than by workers, and they never added up to nearly enough money, to begin to explain what happened to the average incomes of even the top one-tenth of one percent.

## NOTES

1. Krugman, "For Richer," p. 64. For many earlier examples of the widespread misuse of income distribution statistics, see Alan Reynolds, "Economic Foundations of the American Dream," in *The New Promise of American Life*, eds., Lamar Alexander and Chester E. Finn, Jr. (Indianapolis: Hudson Institute, 1995), pp. 194–220.

2. David Cay Johnston, "At the Very Top, A Surge in Income in '03," *New York Times*, October 5, 2005. David Cay Johnston, "Richest Are Leaving Even the Rich Far Behind," *New York Times*, June 5, 2005. A 2003 *New York Times* report about the top 1 percent also concealed its source—inaccurately referring to the unnamed Piketty-Saez paper as "a recently updated study on income by the National Bureau of Economic Research" (NBER). Lynnley Browning, "U.S. Income Gap Widening, Study Says," *New York Times*, September 25, 2003. The NBER has *published* thousands of working papers but they all say "the views expressed herein are those of the authors."

3. Johnston, "Richest Are Leaving Even the Rich Far Behind."

4. Dew-Becker and Gordon, "Where Did the Productivity Growth Go?"

5. Emmanuel Saez, "Reported Incomes and Marginal Tax Rates, 1960–2000: Evidence and Policy Implications," *NBER Working Paper* 10274 (January 2004), p. 31.

6. Dew-Becker and Gordon, "Where Did the Productivity Growth Go?" p. 77.

7. "Aging Acts" *Washington Times*, December 28, 2005, p. A18.

8. Lynn Brenner, "What People Earn," *Parade*, March 12, 2006.

9. Bara Vaida, "Pots of Gold," *National Journal*, February 11, 2006.

10. Jacob Hale Russell, "Executive Pay Takes the Stage," *Wall Street Journal*, February 11–12, 2006.

11. "Who Makes How Much," *New York* Magazine, September 25, 2005. http://newyorkmetro.com/guides/salary/14497/.

12. Paul Krugman, "The Sons Also Rise," *New York Times*, November 22, 2002. http://www.pkarchive.org/column/112202.html.

13. Chronicle of Philanthropy, "The 2004 Slate 60: The 60 Largest Charitable Contributions of the Year." http://www.slate.com/id/2112691.

14. Geraldine Fabrikant, "Old Nantucket Warily Meets the New," in *Class Matters* (New York: Times Books, 2005), pp. 167, 169.

15. In the Bebchuk and Grinstein study, the mean average of CEO pay in 2003 is estimated at $9.1 million for the largest 500, $4 million among the next largest 400, and $2

million among the next largest 600. The average would therefore drop to $6.6 million for 1000 firms, $5 million for 1500, etc. Lucian Bebchuk and Yaniv Grinstein, "The Growth of Executive Pay," *Oxford Review of Economic Policy* 21, no. 2 (2005), table 1, p. 285. http://www.law.harvard.edu/faculty/bebchuk/pdfs/Bebchuk-Grinstein.Growth-of-Pay.pdf.

16. "A Payday for Performance: Compensation Is Less Outrageous This Year, Except for CEOs Who Delivered," *Business Week*, April 18, 2005.

17. John A. Byrne, "Getting a Better Handle on Total Compensation," *Business Week*, April 15, 2002.

18. "I define an individual's taxable income as the sum of salary, bonus, options exercised in the year and LTIP [long-term incentive payments]. . . . The compensation data, starting in 1992, also include the Black-Scholes value of options granted . . ." Austan Goolsbee, "It's Not about the Money," in *Does Atlas Shrug?* ed. Joel B. Slemrod (New York: Russell Sage Foundation, 2000), pp. 146–47.

19. Gary Strauss and Barbara Hansen, "CEO Pay Soars in 2005," *USA Today* (April 11, 2006).

20. Board Analysts' Press Release, "The Median Increase in CEO Pay Was over 30 Percent" (Portland, ME, October 27, 2005).

21. Bebchuk and Grinstein, "The Growth of Executive Pay," table 1.

22. Jesse Eisinger, "How the British Rein In Executive Pay," *Wall Street Journal*, February 8, 2006.

23. Standard and Poor's, *SandP 500*. http://www2.standardandpoors.com/spf/pdf/index/500factsheet.pdf; Bebchuk and Grinstein compare CEO pay to *earnings* rather than market cap, but the relevance of that comparison is unclear. Employee compensation in general (a cost of doing business) is typically *much* larger than earnings. Earnings (after paying such costs) are rarely as much as 10 percent of total revenues, and executive compensation is a relatively trivial portion of total labor costs because each CEO typically manages thousands of employees.

24. Ben Stein, "New Front: Protecting America's Investors," *New York Times*, February 12, 2006.

25. Jesse Eisinger, "Memo to Activists: Mind CEO Pay," *Wall Street Journal*, January 11, 2006.

26. "The larger the firm, the greater is the responsibility of the CEO and the greater the probability that a very able person will be needed and, on average, will be chosen." Moreover, "the riskier the situations to which the CEO's reputation, career, and income are exposed, the higher should be the compensation received." Harold Demsetz, *The Economics of the Business Firm* (New York: Cambridge University Press, 1997), p. 112.

27. Eisinger, "How the British Rein in Executive Pay" (2006) and Carol Hymowitz, "To Rein in CEO's Pay Why Not Consider Outsourcing the Post?" *Wall Street Journal*, July 19, 2005.

28. "The Forbes Global 2000," *Forbes*, April 18, 2005, special issue, p. 173.

29. Chet Currier, "Guarding Against Small Caps' Inevitable Decline," *Washington Post*, January 29, 2006.

30. An estimate for CEOs at 100 "major firms" said median *cash* compensation (excluding stock options and restricted stock) was $1.91 million in 2005. Joann S. Lublin, "Boards Tie CEO Pay More Tightly to Performance," *Wall Street Journal*, February 21, 2006. Stock-based pay accounts for the lion's share, on average, but it is received only once in a while if at all. Compensation in any one year is often a very poor guide to each CEOs average pay over many years.

31. "Hot Topic: Are CEOs Worth Their Weight in Gold?" *Wall Street Journal*, January 21–22, 2006. Another sidebar said, "The ratio of the average Fortune 500 CEOs pay to the

U.S. president's salary...is 30-to-1." Since the president is paid $400,000 (plus a house, meals, and other perks), this implies that *Fortune 500* CEOs typically earn $12 million; yet the same article said CEO's in the similar SandP 500 earn $5 million.

32. Median household income for one-earner households was $36,149 in 2004, but that includes millions who worked part-time and/or for only part of the year. Median income among household heads who worked *full-time* year round was $61,601, but that sometimes includes a second salary and/or some investment income. U.S. Census Bureau, "The Effects of Government Taxes and Transfers on Income and Poverty: 2004" (February 8, 2005), table 1. http://www.census.gov/hhes/www/poverty/effect2004/effectofgovtandt2004.pdf.

33. Janice Revell, "Mo' Money, Fewer Problems Is It a Good Idea to Get Rid of the $1 Million CEO Pay Ceiling?" *Fortune*, March 31, 2003.

34. Mishel, Bernstein, and Allegretto, *The State of Working America 2004/2005* (Cornell University Press, 2005), p. 216.

35. From "Superrich," a graph appended to Wlater Kirn, "Way Upstairs, Downstairs," *New York Times Magazine*, April 16, 2006.

36. Chuck Collins and Felice Yeskel, "Billionaires R Us," AlterNet.org (October 24, 2005). http://www.alternet.org/walmart/27168/?comments=viewandcID=50682andpID=50661.

37. "CEO: Worker Pay Ratio Shoots Up to 431:1." http://www.faireconomy.org/press/2005/EE2005_pr.html.

38. Peter Kuhn and Frenando Lozano, "The Expanding Workweek? Understanding Trends in Long Work Hours among U.S. Men, 1979—2004," *NBER Working Paper* 11895 (December 2005), p. 1.

39. The Kuhn-Lozano evidence of a longer work week among college-educated professionals and managers is another reason to doubt the Dew-Becker and Gordon comparison of the distribution of tax-based wage income in 1966 with that of 2001, since it relies on the unspoken assumption that neither the number of workers in top income groups nor their weekly hours have changed in all those years.

40. Krugman, "For Richer," p. 64.

41. Louis Lavelle, "Executive Pay," *Business Week*, April 16, 2002, p. 80.

42. Jerry Useem, "Have They No Shame?" *Fortune*, April 28, 2003.

43. Del Jones and Gary Strauss, "CEOs Are Going, Going, Gone," *USA Today*, June 10, 2002.

44. Joseph A. Challenger, "Where Have All the CEOs Gone?" *Wall Street Journal*, June 25, 2002.

45. The sources of these references can be found in my chapter, "Compensation, Journalism and Taxes," in *After Enron*, ed. William Niskanen (New York: Rowman and Littlefield, 2005), pp. 245–82.

46. National Center for Employee Ownership, "Employee Stock Option Fact Sheet." http://www.nceo.org/library/optionfact.html.

47. Steven Pearlstein, "Going Private on Borrowed Time," *Washington Post*, April 7, 2006.

48. Jay Solomon, "India Poaches U.S. Executives for Tech Jobs," *Wall Street Journal*, February 22, 2005.

49. Nancy L. Rose, "Executive Compensation," *NBER Reporter* (Winter 1994–95), p. 11.

50. Michelle Hanlon, Shivaram Rajgopal, and Terry Shevlin, "Are Executive Stock Options Associated with Future Earnings?" (December 20, 2002). http://papers.ssrn.com/sol3/papers.cfm?abstract_id=318101.

51. John E. Core, Wayne R. Guay, and David F. Larcker, "Executive Equity Compensation and Incentives: A Survey," Federal Reserve Bank of New York, *FRBNY Policy Review* (April 2003), p. 32.

52. Lucian Bebchuk and Jesse Fried, *Pay Without Performance* (Cambridge, MA: Harvard University Press, 2004), p. 62.

53. Kevin J. Murphy and Ján Zábojník, "CEO Pay and Appointments: A Market-based Explanation for Recent Trends," *American Economic Review* (May 2004).

54. Lucian Bebchuk, Jesse Fried, and David Walker, "Managerial Power and Rent Extraction in the Design of Executive Compensation," *University of Chicago Law Review* (2002). http://www.law.harvard.edu/faculty/bebchuk/pdfs/2002.Bebchuk.Fried.Walker.ChicLR .Managerial.Power.pdf.

55. Patrick Bolton, Jose Scheinkman, and Wei Xion, "Pay for Short-Term Performance: Executive Compensation in Speculative Markets," *NBER Working Paper* 12197 (March 2006).

56. Joann Lublin, "Boards Tie CEO Pay More Tightly to Performance," *Wall Street Journal*, February 21, 2006.

57. Bebchuk and Fried (2004), p. 152.

58. John E. Core, Wayne R. Guay, and Randall S. Thomas, "Is U.S. CEO Compensation Inefficient Pay Without Peformance?" *Michigan Law Review* (May 2005).

59. Michael C. Jensen and Kevin J. Murphy, "CEO Incentives—It's Not How Much You Pay, But How," *Harvard Business Review*, vol. 69(3) (May–June 1990), pp. 138–53.

60. Valerie Bauerlin, "Capital One's Results Could Put Formula for Success to the Test," *Wall Street Journal*, April 18, 2006.

61. "Job's Apple Stock Withheld for Tax Reasons," *Washington Post*, March 28, 2006.

62. Brian Hall, "What You Need to Know about Stock Options," *Harvard Business Review*, vol. 78(2) (March–April 2000), p. 122.

63. Jensen and Murphy (1990).

64. Kathy M. Kristof, "Funds' Stances on Exec Pay Criticized," *Los Angeles Times*, March 28, 2006.

65. Mark Hulbert, "One Borrowed Share, But One Very Real Vote," *New York Times*, April 16, 2006.

66. Andrew K. Prevost and John D. Wagster, "Impact of the 1992 Changes in the SEC Proxy Rules and Executive Compensation Reporting Requirements," mimeo, Wayne State University School of Business Administration (September 1999).

67. Marilyn F. Johnson, Susan Porter, and Margaret B. Shackell, "Stakeholder Pressure and the Structure of Executive Compensation" (May 1997). http://papers.ssrn.com/id= 41780.

68. Brian J. Hall and Jeffrey B. Liebman, "The Taxation of Executive Compensation," in *Tax Policy and the Economy*, Vol. 14, ed. James Poterba (Cambridge, MA: NBER/MIT Press, 2002).

69. Revell, "Mo' Money."

70. Hall and Liebman, "The Taxation of Executive Compensation" (2002).

71. Joint Committee on Taxation, "Report of Investigation of Enron Corporation and Related Entities Regarding Federal Tax and Compensation Issues, and Policy Recommendations," vol. 1 (February 2003), p. 723.

72. A critique of the new FASB rules for expensing employee stock options can be found at http://www.expensingisbadaccounting.com.

# Seven

## Wealth Is Not Distributed

All men who can save are industrious, because all men are greedy for wealth.... It is only the guarantee of the ownership and enjoyment of their gains which can put heart into them and make them diligent.
—Francois Quesnay, *Tableau Economique* (1759)

---

A rising percentage of families with a high net worth indicates that wealth is becoming more widely dispersed, not more concentrated. Young college graduates have valuable human capital (education) but big debts. Older people always have accumulated the most financial savings because it takes time to do that, and because they need savings to supplement their depreciating human capital. The ownership of stock and homes has become more widely dispersed, not less so, as has the ownership of college degrees. Financial and housing wealth has not become more concentrated in fewer hands, and ownership of human capital has become far less concentrated.

---

Previous chapters observed that people often confuse a rising percentage of families earning higher incomes with a fixed number of "rich getting richer." That same misunderstanding ("threshold illusion") affects discussions about the concentration of wealth.

A 2005 *Washington Times* report said, "The surge in *income* growth among top earners is corroborated by private studies, including one . . . that found that the number of U.S. households with a net worth of $1 million or more increased by 21 percent last year to a record 7.5 million."[1] But net worth is wealth, not income. A rising number of households with a net worth above $1 million tells us nothing about "income growth." In that report, however, the good news of a large increase in the *percentage* of American families with a net worth above $1 million in 2004 (including home equity) was reported as if it was a problematic "surge in income growth among top earners." People do not have to be "top earners" to have a net worth above $1 million; they just need to be old enough to have seen their savings and home equity grow. Even if it were true that the nation had a record *number* of "top earners," what could be wrong with that? It is not at all clear how anyone would benefit if the nation had fewer top earners or fewer people with a net worth above $1 million.

Another 2005 news report, from the *New York Times*, was intended to demonstrate a widening "gap between the hyper-rich and the rest of America." As evidence of such a gap, the report said, "The group with homes, investments and other assets worth more than $10 million comprised 338,400 households in 2001, the last year for which data are available. The number has grown more than 400 percent since 1980, after adjusting for inflation, while the total number of households has grown only 27 percent.... [S]uch a concentration of wealth can turn a meritocracy into an aristocracy..."[2]

The fact that four times as many households had a net worth above $10 million in 2001 as in 1980 did *not* show the gap between the rich and others had widened or that "concentration of wealth" had increased. On the contrary, it showed that *four times as many* households were wealthy in 2001 as the number who would have qualified as wealthy in 1980 if judged by the same standard. Having four times as many wealthy households in 2001 as in 1980 suggests *wider ownership* of stocks, bonds, and larger homes—less concentration of wealth rather than more.

The rising number of households with a high net worth was not confined to those with more than $10 million. The source of the *New York Times* statistics, Edward Wolff of New York University, also estimated that the number of households with a net worth above $1 million nearly doubled in less than a decade—rising from 3.1 million in 1992 to 5.9 million in 2001—and the number with more than $5 million nearly tripled, from 277,400 in 1992 to 1,067,800 in 2001.[3]

Such increases in the *number* of people with substantial *wealth* appear to encourage what we called "threshold illusion," when discussing the similar confusion about more people leaving "the middle class" and "joining the ranks of the rich." Because the number of wealthy households increased so rapidly, the definition of the amount of money needed to be "very wealthy" has also increased rapidly. Any mean average of wealth among, say, the top 1 percent must appear to increase very quickly whenever the floor defining membership in that top group is raised because there are, for example, nearly three times as many households with more than $5 million than there were just a decade earlier.

Andrew Hacker came close to describing "threshold illusion" when discussing *Forbes* magazine's list of the 400 wealthiest Americans:

To get on the 1982 list, a person needed about $90 million, equal to $150 million in 1996. But by 1996, the amount needed to get into the top 400 had risen to $415 million, in real dollars nearing three times the 1982 figure. This means that many who were on the first list wouldn't have made the most recent one. Stated another way, you must now be a lot richer to be among the very rich.[4]

The *threshold*, or floor, defining the top group (the top 400 in this case) rose from $150 million to $415 million in constant 1996 dollars. That was largely because by 1996 (unlike 1982) the number of people with a net worth above $150 million was much larger than 400. The reason one needed "to be a lot richer" to be counted among the top 400 in 1996 was because there were thousands more very wealthy people in 1996 than there were in 1982, when "very rich" is defined by the unchanged standards of 1982. In this case, as with the earlier 2005 comment from the *New York Times*, increasing *numbers* of people with high wealth demonstrated wider dispersion of wealth rather than greater concentration of wealth in a few hands. By 1996, a much greater number of people had achieved the wealth previously attained by only four hundred.

"Over the period from 1989 to 2001," wrote Federal Reserve Board economist Arthur B. Kennickell, data from the Survey of Consumer Finances (SCF) "show that the distribution of wealth shifted up broadly in real terms— another way of saying that in absolute terms there were fewer poor families and more families who were wealthier."[5]

## WEALTH AND INCOME ARE COUSINS

Although the topics of wealth and income are typically separated, they are intimately interrelated. Income is the flow of value that accrues from wealth— that is, from both *human capital* (training, talent, experience, and skill) and *nonhuman capital* (natural resources, machines, and buildings). Financial wealth is a claim on nonhuman capital that is expected to yield income (dividends, interest, rent, or capital gains). Some income from capital is not received as rent. Owning a house, for example, provides residential services whose value is equivalent to rent (the estimated value of which is "imputed" in the broadest Census Bureau definition of income). Similarly, owning a car provides transportation services equivalent to renting a car. Owning a washer and dryer is equivalent to buying those services from a Laundromat. Doing whatever we please, or doing nothing, also provides value or utility called leisure.

Discussions of income distribution are habitually confined to *money* income (sometimes even to the point of excluding employee benefits and in-kind aid to the poor). Yet the lifetime accrual of money income also depends on wealth. Owning financial assets yields money income over time, in the form of dividends, interest, or capital gains. Owning real assets may yield money income in the form of rent or profit. Owning human capital, such as a formal education and/or experience, yields money income over all of a person's working years. It takes time to acquire human capital—time spent in school or acquiring on-the-job learning. It often requires investing money too—such as college tuition and expenses and foregone earnings (the money that could have been earned in the time spent in school).

There is a "correlation" between income and wealth, which means the two are related to a considerable extent (perfect correlation would be 1.0– 100 percent). People have to have income to acquire real and financial assets, such as homes and stocks. And owning such assets, in turn, generates money income (such as dividends) or in-kind income (the "imputed rent" we pay ourselves by owning our own homes). A Federal Reserve Bank of Minneapolis study of 1998 SCF data, by José-Víctor Ríos-Rull and colleagues, found the correlation between income and wealth weaker than might be imagined, but the correlation between wealth and age is strong:

The correlation between income and wealth is significantly lower (0.60) than that between earnings and income and... the correlation between earnings and wealth (0.47) is even lower. This low correlation between earnings and wealth is justified because there are a large number of retired households in the sample, because they are quite wealthy, and because their labor earnings are mostly zero. ... Average cohort wealth also increases monotonically with the life cycle, but it peaks in the 61–65 cohort, a full 10 years after both earnings and income. Moreover, the over-65 cohort is still significantly wealth-rich: it owns 33 percent more wealth than the sample average, and it is wealth-richer than any of the cohorts age 50 and under.[6]

Older people are often relatively "wealthy" in the sense of having accumulated substantial savings, yet they may not be particularly "rich" in terms of income (because a million dollars invested at 5 percent yields a middling income of $50,000). Conversely, younger people may appear richer than seniors in terms of current income, yet many are heavily indebted at that stage of their life cycle and not yet wealthy at all (except in human capital).

It takes *time* to accumulate much real and financial wealth. Young families start out with big debts and few assets, so their "net worth" (assets minus debts) may even appear to be less than zero for a few years. In addition to a home mortgage and student loan, there may be borrowing for "consumer durables"—real assets such as cars, furniture, and appliances.

What young people have that the old do not, however, is human capital—a long stream of future earnings that may be viewed as the return on investments in formal education and on-the-job training. Each person's stock of human capital in any particular year represents the discounted present value of his or her future earnings. People have the most human capital and the least financial capital when they are young. But those same people usually have the least human capital and the most financial capital when they are old. Human capital depreciates as we age—its value drops to zero at death or retirement—which is why it is prudent to gradually replace human capital with financial capital (by saving for retirement).

Comments that are critical of wealth inequality per se imply that wealth equality is both feasible and desirable. Although the concept of equality of income also makes no distinction between the young and the old, that shortcoming becomes even more impractical when contemplating equality of wealth. In a classic 1975 study, Morton Paglin noted, "[Wealth] equality requires that wealth holdings among families be equal regardless of the age of the head of household. Given a typical age distribution of the population, this means that cumulative annual saving, plus interest compounded, can have no effect on individual family wealth."[7] If some well-intentioned autocrat could equalize wealth among young and old households then nobody would have any incentive to save. Equalizing wealth would have to confiscate wealth accumulated over several decades and give it to the young—a policy that would make capital accumulation useless.

Because wealth is accumulated over decades, it is highly misleading to draw conclusion from a snapshot of who owned what in any particular year. A 2004 *Business Week* article about wealth said, "The top 10% of families, as measured by net wealth own 65% of [the nation's] assets, and the top 50% own a stunning 95% of assets. That means the gains from rising wealth have effectively left out half the population."[8] Actually, it means no such thing. The key fact about wealth is that young people (who have only human capital) do not stay young forever. The "gains from rising wealth" take place over several decades, and so does the average adult lifespan. The top 10–50 percent as measured by net worth will typically spend most of the wealth on retirement, then die and be replaced by an entirely different group of top wealth holders.

The *Business Week* complaint demonstrates the *snapshot fallacy*—the erroneous belief that because half the population had not yet accumulated many assets *in any particular year*, that *same* half of the population (rather than a newer and younger group) would *never* accumulate much wealth over an entire lifetime.

To look at who benefits from rising wealth over a period of years we have to consider the age of the household head. In 2004, a snapshot view of the Survey of Current Finances showed that households headed by someone under age 35 had a median net worth of only $14,200, while those headed by someone aged 45–54 had ten times as much—a median net worth of $144,700. Only 42 percent of the younger group owned their home, while 77 percent of the middle-aged did. Only 40 percent of the younger group had a retirement account, while 58 percent of the middle-aged did. To conclude that future "gains from rising wealth" could benefit only those who had much wealth in 2004 is to forget that the younger group has barely begun to accumulate wealth, while some in the middle-aged group were only a decade or so away from the time when they may be reducing their wealth to pay for retirement.

In a book about changes in wealth in the 1980s, Edward Wolff of New York University wrote that "middle-aged households gained at the expense of both younger and older households." He referred to the young and old as "less privileged age cohorts."[9] But wealth is always lowest among the young, highest shortly before retirement and somewhat lower after a few years of retirement.

A better way to see how *aging* affects conventionally measured wealth (aside from human capital) is to examine one age-based group (cohort) over a series of years. Table 7.1 shows Arthur Kennickell's estimates of wealth distribution for older "baby boomers" defined as the cohort aged 34–43 in 1989 (and therefore 46–55 in 2001). While only 2.9 percent of that group had a net worth above $1 million in 1989, when they were younger, 10.1 percent had passed the million-dollar level a dozen years later (when the group still had

**TABLE 7.1**
**Percent of Baby Boomers with Net Worth above $250,000 (in 2001 Dollars)**

|  | 1989 | 1992 | 1995 | 1998 | 2001 |
|---|---|---|---|---|---|
| $250,000–999,999 | 15.2 | 12.0 | 15.7 | 21.8 | 25.0 |
| Above $1 million | 2.9 | 3.0 | 3.7 | 6.1 | 10.1 |

*Source:* Arthur B. Kennickell, "A Rolling Tide" (2003) http://www.federalreserve.gov/pubs/oss/oss2/method.html.

another 10 and 17 years left before reaching 65). If we could track this same cohort back to 1979, when they were 24 to 33 years old, it is likely that very few had yet accumulated even $250,000, much less a million. In other words, wealth typically rises with age. Even inherited wealth, which is a relatively small part of the total, is commonly received late in life (if the last parent dies at age 85, surviving children are likely to be at least 50 years old).

Rather than viewing financial wealth as an unfair "privilege" of middle age, a more instructive way of looking at wealth accumulation is that it first takes many years to acquire human capital (education and experience), then it takes additional years to acquire real capital (a home and car), and then it requires even more years to build a sizable nest egg of financial capital (a retirement account and other savings). Those who invest the most time, effort, and money in improving their human capital will generally find it easier to acquire real and financial capital later in life, if they choose to build wealth rather than to instead spend more time and/or money enjoying life along the way. All of those stages in life depend on what gifts individuals happen to be born with (such as intelligence and beauty) and what choices they make as adults.

## TOP HEAVY?

Whatever the meaning or significance of annual wealth distribution statistics, popular news reports continue to assert that such wealth distribution has become more unequal. The genesis for that belief appears to date back to 1995, when there was considerable media attention paid to Edward Wolff's ninety-two-page Twentieth Century Fund study, *Top Heavy: A Study of the Increasing Inequality of Wealth in America.*

*Top Heavy* claimed, "The increase in wealth inequality recorded over the 1983–1989 period in the United States was almost unprecedented. The only other period in the twentieth century during which concentration of household wealth rose comparably was from 1922 to 1929. Then inequality was buoyed primarily by the excessive rise in stock values, which eventually crashed in 1929, leading to the Great Depression of the 1930s."[10]

Mr. Wolff's alleged link between wealth inequality and depression seemed to echo Ravi Batra's *The Great Depression of 1990*, which was published with an introduction by Lester Thurow of M.I.T. and became a number one *New York Times* bestseller in November 1987. Mr. Batra claimed that "the seeds of a new depression have already been sown by the Reagan Administration," thanks to "warriors and intellectuals having been reduced to the laboring class by the extreme concentration of wealth" among the "acquisitive class" (businessmen and financiers).[11]

Commenting on Edward Wolff's "very good book," Paul Krugman could not understand why such "a rather dry matter of fact summary of trends in wealth distribution" could "provoke strong emotional reactions."[12] But criticisms of *Top Heavy* were *factual,* not emotional.

From 1982 to 1989, the S&P 500 stock index rose from 119.7 to 322.8, the yield on thirty-year Treasury bonds fell from 15.1 percent to less than 8.5 percent, and the economy grew by 4.3 percent a year. What did such prosperity have to do with the Great Depression? How could such huge improvements have failed to benefit most Americans?

The same 1989 Survey of Consumer Finances that Wolff used as the basis of his book reported that "median real net worth rose by 11 percent" from 1983 to 1989. There was a 40.4 percent median wealth gain among those with incomes between $10,000 and $20,000, compared with a 5.4 percent rise for those earning more than $50,000.[13] Yet Top Heavy nonetheless claimed that "almost all the absolute gains in real wealth accrued to the top 20 percent of wealth holders."

John Weicher found "the distribution [of wealth] was about the same in 1992 as in 1983, or for that matter as in 1962. A modest, insignificant increase in concentration between 1983 and 1989 was completely reversed by 1992."[14] Former Federal Reserve Chairman Alan Greenspan likewise concluded that "inequality of household wealth—that is, net worth—was somewhat higher in 1989 than at the time of our earlier survey in 1963. Subsequently, the 1992 and 1995 surveys—and here our data are statistically more comparable from survey to survey than they were earlier—showed that inequality remained little changed in terms of the broad measures."[15]

A cyclical six-year change in wealth inequality that Alan Greenspan found "little changed" and John Weicher found "modest and insignificant" was nonetheless described by Mr. Wolff as "almost unprecedented." One reason intelligent people could have such different opinions about the same facts was Mr. Wolff's unique "data adjustments." As Arthur Kennickell put it, "Professor Wolff presents a view of the wealth distribution in the U.S. However, his results are quite sensitive to a set of questionable assumptions that are not revealed to the reader." Wolff's *adjusted* estimates claimed "median wealth declined by 17 percent from 1989 to 1995," for example, yet official Fed data revealed no significant decline.[16]

Figure 7.1 shows the actual SCF figures for median and mean wealth. Following Federal Reserve practice, the figures have been converted to 2004 dollars using the consumer price index (which overstates inflation and therefore understates the real wealth gains). Mr. Wolff's alleged 17 percent decline in median wealth from 1989 to 1995 disappears from the original figures. More important, the substantial increase in *median* wealth from

**FIGURE 7.1**
**Average Real Net Worth of Households (Thousands in**
**2004 Dollars)**

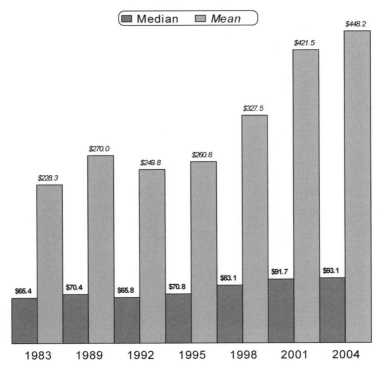

*Note:* Adjusted with CPI-U & rounded to nearest $100.
*Source:* Federal Reserve Bulletin, Feb 1989, Jan 1997 & Feb 2006.

1983 to 1989 and from 1995 to 2001 contradicts his claim (in 2004) that "the only segment of the population that experienced large gains in wealth since 1983 is the richest 20 percent of households."[17]

The supposedly huge increase in inequality from 1983 to 1989 reported in *Top Heavy* was undetectable by Weicher, Greenspan, and Kennickell. One reason was the uniquely narrow concepts of wealth that Wolff relied on. "The most telling finding," wrote Wolff, "is that the share of marketable net worth held by the top 1 percent... rose to 39 percent in 1989, compared with 34 percent in 1983." He also wrote, "The most telling statistic is that virtually all the growth in (marketable) wealth between 1983 and 1989 accrued to the top 20 percent of households."[18]

Marketable wealth means "only assets that can be readily converted to cash." That excludes consumer durables, such as cars and furniture, and also the value of retirement benefits from private pension plans and Social Security. Yet people view ownership of luxury cars and big-screen HDTVs as wealth—not because of their resale value but because they yield real income in the form of transportation and entertainment. Future retirement benefits are wealth in a more conventional sense—assets that yield future income. What Wolff means by marketable wealth is similar to what is usually called "liquid assets"—assets that can quickly be converted into cash with little risk of loss. But this is a matter of degree; stocks and bonds are not as liquid as a money market fund.

Wolff also alludes to the concentration of "financial wealth"—a measure that leaves out home-owner equity because, he claims, "one's home is difficult to convert into cash in the short-term." Mr. Wolff does not apply that rule consistently, however. He counts ownership (equity) in a business as "financial wealth" even though businesses are quite difficult to convert to cash in the short-term because of leases and other long-term contracts. Table 7.2 uses Mr. Wolff's figures from a 1998 publication to show how excluding home equity but keeping business equity biases the conclusions. Home equity accounted for 65.9 percent of the assets owned by the bottom 80 percent of households in 1995, while equity in unincorporated business was 36.8 percent of all assets among the top 1 percent (as gauged by wealth rather than by income). Arbitrarily *excluding* home equity while *including* business equity clearly exaggerates the share of *actual* wealth held by the top 1 percent.

An appendix to *Top Heavy* provided a less restrictive measure of "augmented wealth," including pension wealth and homes. Figure 7.2 presents

**TABLE 7.2**
**The Composition of Household Wealth in 1995**
**(Percent of Gross Assets)**

| The Composition of Household Wealth in 1995 (Percent of Gross Assets) | Bottom 80% | Top 1% |
| --- | --- | --- |
| Principal residence | 65.9 | 6.4 |
| Other real estate | 5.0 | 11.4 |
| Unincorporated business equity | 3.1 | 36.8 |
| Pension assets | 8.5 | 4.7 |
| Corporate stock, financial securities, mutual funds, and personal trusts | 4.1 | 30.3 |
| Miscellaneous assets | 2.2 | 2.7 |

*Source:* Edward Wolff, *Journal of Economic Perspectives* (Summer 1998).

**FIGURE 7.2**
**Share of "Augmented Wealth" Held by the Wealthiest
1 Percent of Households**

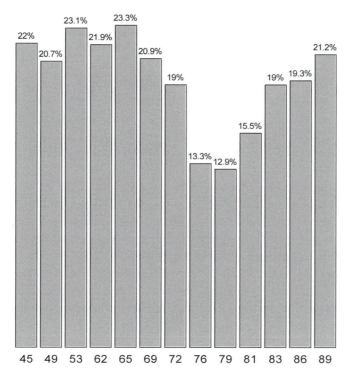

*Source:* Edward N. Wolff "Top Heavy," table A-1.

Wolff's estimates of the share of augmented wealth owned by the top 1 percent. By this measure, the share of wealth held by the top 1 percent rose from 19 percent in 1983 to 21.2 percent in 1989. Far from being "unprecedented," however, those figures were the norm from 1945 to 1972—before two virulent episodes of stagflation collapsed the value of stocks and bonds. In fact, the Dow Jones stock index was substantially lower in 1982 (884.4) than it had been in 1965 (910.9).

If the objective of wealth equality is to reduce the share of wealth held by top wealth-holders, regardless of what happens to the wealth of other people as well, there is no question that soaring interest rates and a prolonged crash in the stock market will indeed reduce wealth most dramatically for those who have the most wealth. Since tax-deferred and tax-exempt retirement and college savings plans have become far more widespread than in the past, however, there are millions more middle-income stakeholders in the stock and bond markets than there were in 1974–1982. Yearning for another period in which the top 1 percent suffers a stock market calamity of the magnitude of 1968–1982 seems as destructively spiteful as expressing nostalgia about the "great compression" of incomes that occurred during the Depression and World War II.

Both mean and median wealth soared from 1995 to 2000, largely because of the stock market boom. When the 2004 survey came out, several business reporters seemed alarmed that wealth was not much higher than it had been in 2001. This should have been no surprise because most stock prices were still lower in 2004 than in 2001. The S&P 500 averaged 1194.2 in 2001, for example, and 1130.7 in 2004. The NASDAQ index was 2035 in 2001 and 1986.5 in 2004.

The untenable notion that wealth had become unusually "top heavy" in the 1980s continued to be echoed a decade after that book was published in 1995. As the earlier references to such news reports showed, however, the erroneous evidence for this view usually consisted of showing that much larger numbers of Americans had more wealth—not that only a few had more wealth.

The *Top Heavy* allegation of "almost unprecedented" wealth concentration from 1983 to 1989 was exaggerated at best. Since then, there has been no evidence of significantly greater gains in wealth among top wealth holders than among households in general. There are many more people with a million dollars or more than there were in 1983 or 1989, but that is not evidence of wealth concentration or inequality.

Comparing the Surveys of Consumer Finances between 1992 and 1998, the previously mentioned Minneapolis Fed study found "earnings inequality and income inequality decreased slightly, and wealth inequality increased, also slightly."

Comparing the same surveys between 2001 and 2004, the *Wall Street Journal* erroneously reported "a widening gap between households at the top and the bottom of the economic ladder," because, "the net worth of the typical family in the bottom 25% fell 1.5%."[19] But a correction the following day noted that net worth among the bottom 25 percent had instead *increased* by 41.7 percent.

Citing data from estate tax returns, Piketty and Saez concluded that "the increase in wealth concentration has been modest since the 1970s."[20] Updating that finding in 2006, Emmanuel Saez told the *Wall Street Journal* that "the share going to the broader class of rich Americans has been stable for the past couple decades."[21] Edward Wolff also found "wealth inequality . . . remained virtually unchanged from 1989 to 2001."[22] Yet journalists often continued to write as though the United States had long experienced a widening gap between the wealth owned by a few and the wealth owned by many, sometimes mistakenly citing Emmanuel Saez and Edward Wolff as their source.

If the concept of wealth is properly expanded to include human capital, not just homes and stocks, it is clear that total wealth has become far less concentrated and more widely dispersed than it used to be. Percentages of narrowly defined wealth held by some top percentile do not begin to capture how much more widespread the ownership of real capital, financial capital and human capital has become. Fewer than 8 percent of those above the age of 25 had a college degree in 1960, but that fraction doubled to more than 16 percent by 1980 and nearly doubled again to almost 28 percent by 2004. Although rewarding investments are never risk-free, investments in education normally pay dividends just as surely as blue-chip stocks do. A much larger fraction of Americans own stock than was true in the past, and a much larger fraction own air-conditioned houses and cars, and a much larger fraction also owns valuable human capital. Wealth has not become concentrated in fewer hands, as some have claimed, but has instead become increasingly dispersed among a widening share of the population.

## NOTES

1. Patrice Hill, "Income Gap Grows in U.S.," *Washington Times*, July 31, 2005.

2. Johnston, "Richest Are Leaving Even the Rich Far Behind," reprinted in *Class Matters* (Times Books, 2005), chapter 12.

3. Edward N. Wolff, "Changes in Household Wealth in the 1980s and 1990s in the U.S." (working paper 407, The Levy Economics Institute, May 2004), table 2, p. 30.

4. Andrew Hacker, *Money: Who Has How Much and Why* (New York: Touchstone, 1998), p. 92.

5. Kennickell, "A Rolling Tide."

6. José-Víctor Ríos-Rull et al., "Updated Facts on the U.S. Distributions of Earnings, Income, and Wealth," *Federal Reserve Bank of Minneapolis Quarterly Review* (Summer 2002).

7. Morton Paglin, "The Measurement and Trend of Inequality: A Basic Revision," *American Economic Review* (September 1975).

8. Michael J. Mandel, "Where Wealth Lives: The Productivity Boom Has Made Asset Owners Rich—And Left Many Wage-Earners Behind," *Business Week*, April 19, 2004.

9. Wolff, *Top Heavy* (1998), pp. 15–16.

10. Edward N. Wolff, *Top Heavy: A Study of the Increasing Inequality of Wealth in America* (New York: Twentieth Century Fund Press, 1995), p. 13.

11. Ravi Batra, *The Great Depression of 1990*, rev. ed. (New York: Simon and Schuster, 1987), pp. 51, 171. My review of this book is at http://www.worldandi.com/specialreport/1988/january/Sa14126.htm.

12. Krugman, "An Unequal Exchange," *Accidental Theorist*.

13. Arthur B. Kennickell and Janice Shack-Marquez, "Changes in Family Finances from 1983 to 1989: Evidence from the Survey of Consumer Finances," *Federal Reserve Bulletin* (January 1992). http://www.federalreserve.gov/pubs/oss/oss2/89/bull0192.pdf.

14. John C. Weicher, "The Distribution of Wealth, 1983–1992: Secular Growth Cyclical Stability," *Federal Reserve Bank of St. Louis Review* (January–February 1997). http://reseach.stlouisfed.org/wp/1996/96-012.pdf.

15. Alan Greenspan's opening remarks in *Income Inequality: Issues and Policy Options* (symposium sponsored by The Federal Reserve Bank of Kansas City, Jackson Hole, WY, August 27–29, 1998), pp. 2–3.

16. Arthur B. Kennickell, "Comments on 'Recent Trends in the Size Distribution of Household Wealth,' by Edward N. Wolff," Federal Reserve Board (1998). http://www.federalreserve.gov/PUBS/oss/oss2/papers/jep.wolff.3.pdf.

17. Wolff, "Changes in Household Wealth," p. 1.

18. Wolff, *Top Heavy* (1998), pp. 10, 13, 51.

19. Christopher Conkey, "Typical Family's Net Worth Edged Up Only 1.5% in '01–'04," *Wall Street Journal*, February 26, 2006. (The correction appeared February 27, 2006.)

20. Thomas Piketty and Emmanuel Saez, "Income Inequality in the United States, 1913–2002" (November 2004), p. 14. http://emlab.berkeley.edu/users/saez/piketty-saez OUP04US.pdf.

21. David Wessel, "Rich Get Richer, But Not as Fast as You Think," *Wall Street Journal*, March 2, 2006.

22. Wolff, "Changes in Household Wealth," p. 6.

# Eight

## Consumption Inequality, Lifetime Income, and Mobility

If we label the bottom 30 percent of the population "the poor" and the top 30 percent "the rich," we find that 13.8 percent of the annually poor are lifetime rich, and 2.6 percent of the annually rich are lifetime poor.

—Don Fullerton & Diane Lim Rogers, *Who Bears the Lifetime Tax Burden?* (1993)

In the end, what really matters is not whether there has been some small change in the degree of mobility in America but whether the level of mobility remains high. After all, it cannot rise infinitely—if it did, at some point income distribution would become purely random, with no linkage whatsoever to family, education, or anything else. Complaining that mobility is not rising is akin to lamenting that baseball batting averages are no higher today than they were a generation ago. There is no reason to think they should be.

—Bruce Bartlett, *Commentary* (2005)

Differences in living standards are measured more accurately by what consumers spend than by any of the many measures of income. Because people can consume out of past income (savings) or future income (debt), consumption is a better gauge of lifetime income. Gini coefficients for consumption show increased inequality from 1981 to 1986, but that was largely cyclical. From 1986 to 2001, consumption inequality declined, and wage inequality was unchanged. Press reports in 2005 about a decline in mobility between income groups were based on faulty evidence. Mobility appears artificially easy in Sweden because there is very little difference between income in adjacent quintiles after high taxes and generous transfer payments are taken into account. Studies comparing incomes of siblings indicate that inequalities between U.S. families do not persist for even one generation—because at least one of each family's two children will fall behind the other.

Annual income is a snapshot, but life is a motion picture. As Anthony Atkinson of Oxford University points out, "Equality or inequality should be measured in terms of the distribution of *lifetime* and not just *current* wealth."[1]

Statistics about the distribution of income or wealth in any particular year are of interest only to the extent that they tell us something about differences in *living standards*. Yet living standards are most directly measured by *consumption* rather than by income—that is, by the quantity and quality of each household's food, clothing, housing, transportation, and entertainment.

Living standards do not depend on just one year's income but also on past and future income. *Past* income can be accumulated, which adds to a person's stock of savings (financial wealth). Mortgages and auto loans permit consumption to occur out of expected *future* income.

Most discussions about income distribution implicitly assume that *annual* income (and sometimes just *labor* income) is either the only measure of living standards or the best available measure. As Cleveland Fed economists Peter Rupert and Chris Telmer explained, however, "[I]ncome and wealth are so interesting because they affect consumption inequality and, as a result, inequality in economic welfare."[2] If so, why not focus directly on the end game—namely, *consumption* inequality?

There are, in fact, several reasons to believe that *consumer spending* is a far more accurate measure of economic well-being over time.

First of all, a household's annual income in any particular year may be much *lower* than usual because of transitory difficulties such as job loss or illness. On the other hand, another household's annual income may be much *higher* than usual that year because of a one-time windfall from an unusually clever or lucky investment. People smooth their consumption over the years by selling assets or borrowing in hard times and saving in good times.

Second, there is a typical *life-cycle* pattern to income from work and savings. Young people start out with wages or salaries that are much lower than what they will earn when they reach middle age. Young people also have had no time to accumulate significant savings, and often have to borrow against their human capital (future earnings) to finance costly start-up expenditures on a car, home, furniture, and appliances. By the time they reach middle age, these same households or families will typically be earning about three times as much as they did when they were younger, they will have accumulated home equity and consumer durables, and they will be augmenting their labor income with investment income. By old age, labor income usually stops with retirement, or is reduced by semi-retirement, but there may be sizable savings to draw upon to finance consumption—thereby smoothing consumption over the life cycle.

Third, most measures of annual income (particularly those relying on individual tax returns) reveal comparatively little about nonhuman wealth, such as a family's home equity, retirement savings, ownership of rental property, and other investments. They may also fail to measure even current income. Studies have found that many people seriously underreport certain types of income, on both surveys and tax returns, such as income from tips and other cash income, from means-tested government transfer payments and from illegal activities.

Summarizing these and other advantages of using *consumption* rather than *income* to measure differences in living standards, Bruce D. Meyer and James X. Sullivan concluded that "consumption captures permanent income, reflects the insurance value of government programs and credit markets, better accommodates illegal activity and price changes, and is more likely to reflect private and government transfers."[3]

The *Economic Report of the President* for 2003 noted, "Research has shown that, when a longer view is taken, differences in well-being, whether measured by income or by consumption, tend not to be as great, because of the fluidity of household incomes over time."[4] Former Federal Reserve Chairman Alan Greenspan also observed, "There is a surprising difference between the trends in the dispersion of holdings of claims to goods and services (income and wealth) and trends in the dispersion of actual consumption, which is, of course, the ultimate determinant of material or economic well-being."[5]

For all of these reasons, questions about differences among household living standards (and about the growth of living standards) are better measured by annual consumption than by annual income. It would be better still if we could measure income or consumption over each adult's lifetime. There have been a few heroic efforts to do that with "panel studies" that survey what happens to some representative group of people (called a cohort) over time. One particularly provocative example of this approach is the quote at the top of this chapter from a book by Don Fullerton and Diane Lim Rogers, which found that 13.8 percent of those in the *bottom* 30 percent in any particular year actually end up in the *top* 30 percent over their lifetimes. When we look at statistics describing people as rich or poor in any one year, we are often describing the same people at different ages.

Studies of lifetime income are daunting and good ones are scarce. By simply using consumption in place of income, however, it is possible to minimize many of the problems associated with the far more common practice of measuring inequality and poverty by *annual* income alone.

Those who look only at annual incomes before taxes and transfers contend that income inequality became much "worse" *after* 1986 (thus invoking the implicit value judgment that greater equality of annual income is always an improvement, even if a decline in high incomes results from recessions that also reduce the lowest incomes). Writing in 2002, for example, Paul Krugman said, "For at least the past 15 years [1986 to 2001] it has been hard to deny the evidence for growing inequality in the United States."[6]

To prove inequality has been growing for fifteen to thirty years it is customary to use the Gini coefficient, despite its shortcomings, because it offers a broad measure of equality that encompasses broad trends for the entire population (rather than just the top 10 percent). Recall from the description of Gini coefficients in the first chapter that a larger number means more inequality and a smaller number means less. There are several ways to define economic well-being, however, and therefore several ways to define the Gini coefficient.

Table 8.1 shows four of the seven sets of Gini coefficients prepared by David Johnson and Barbara Boyle Torrey of the Bureau of Labor Statistics and Timothy Smeeding of Syracuse University. "Most studies of well-being and its inequality are still based on annual income data," they observe; "This is partly because of history and also partly because of habit."[7] History and habit are not very good reasons to stick with income alone, so they also measured *consumption* inequality from the Consumer Expenditure Survey from the Bureau of Labor Statistics.

Since 1980, the Consumer Expenditure Survey has surveyed consumer spending for about 7,500 representative consumer units by having one group keep a detailed diary of what they buy over two weeks, then conducting

**TABLE 8.1**
**Alternative Measures of Inequality (Gini Coefficients)**

|                                | 1981 | 1986 | 1990 | 1994 | 1999 | 2001 |
|--------------------------------|------|------|------|------|------|------|
| Household income               | .406 | .425 | .428 | .456 | .458 | .466 |
| Income after taxes & transfers | .358 | .409 | .386 | .400 | .408 | .412 |
| Consumption expenditures       | .273 | .316 | .314 | .313 | .305 | .307 |
| Consumption                    | .256 | .283 | .293 | .294 | .281 | .280 |

*Source:* Johnson, Smeeding, and Torry, *Monthly Labor Review* (April 2005).

a quarterly survey of another 7,500 to fill in the gaps, such as big-ticket items and infrequent outlays (such as vacations or annual insurance premiums).

Unlike the tax-based estimates of income inequality criticized in previous chapters, the Gini coefficients from this survey are not corrupted by the massive measurement problems in tax-based data surrounding the 1986 Tax Reform and the related evidence of (in James Poterba's summary) a "substantial reporting response to changes in tax rates."[8] What people actually purchase is a broader and more reliable indicator of their well-being than what they report as annual individual income to the IRS.

The first row shows the usual measure of Gini coefficients for *pretax* and *pretransfer* household income. These figures naturally show more inequality than those in the second row, which subtract taxes from higher incomes and add cash transfer payments at lower incomes. That is because taxes and transfers *do* reduce inequality, unless their offsetting effect on work incentives makes pretax and pretransfer inequality even larger.

Since taxes and transfers clearly affect households' ability to purchase goods and services, the figures in the second row measure actual differences in living standards more accurately than the figures in the first row. People with little or no earnings from work can buy goods and services with food stamps and Medicaid, and with money received from Social Security, TANF, or the EITC. People with higher earnings from work or investments can buy goods and services only after they pay their taxes.

Inequality of annual income, regardless how it is measured, is still a round-about and short-term way of measuring differences in living standards. The third and fourth rows provide Gini coefficients for two measures of consumption expressed in "equivalent" terms—adjusted for family size with a formula commonly used for this purpose. Ending any hope that "two can live as cheaply as one," for example, the formula finds that two have to spend about 41 percent more than one in order to have an equivalent level of consumption per person.

A 2005 study by Dirk Krueger of the University of Pennsylvania and Fabrizio Perri of New York University concluded that the apparent increase in income inequality from 1980 to 2003 "has not been accompanied by a corresponding rise in consumption inequality."[9] Table 8.1, by contrast, shows an increase in consumption inequality from 1981 to 1986–1990, followed by a decline in consumption inequality since then (presumably through 2003, judging by Krueger and Perri). Three British economists questioned the whole idea that U.S. consumption inequality has not increased. But they were able to come to that unique conclusion only by excluding "from our definition of consumption expenditures on durables, health, education, as well as mortgage and rent payments."[10]

The third row of Table 8.1, by contrast, measures inequality in what people normally think of as (equivalent) consumption—namely, how much money consumers spent on *all* goods and services during a year, including durable goods such as cars and appliances. The Gini coefficients in the fourth row deal with a criticism sometimes made about figures such as those in the third row. The objection is that buying a home and car is not actually consumption in a single year but an *investment* that yields a flow of housing and transportation services over many years—in-kind income equivalent in value to renting that home or car. For such reasons, the authors explain, the fourth row measures the inequality of "consumption expenditures less the costs of home ownership and the purchase price of vehicles plus the rental equivalence of owned homes and the service flows from vehicles."

The first thing to notice about these Gini coefficients for consumption is that they are markedly lower (more equal) than for any measure of income, partly because one year's income does not measure longer-term ability to consume. That is particularly true for those who own their homes, for example, which is one reason why inequality is so low in the last row.

The second thing to notice is that both Gini coefficients for consumption show more inequality in 1986 than in the boom of 1999 or the recession of 2000. In contrast to Mr. Krugman's comment about income inequality, there was clearly a *reduction* in consumption inequality from 1986 to 2001 (even though the last measure shows a slight rise between 1986 and 1990). Even when it comes to income and wealth, a survey of the evidence for the Federal Reserve Bank of Minneapolis, by Jose-Victor Rios-Rull and others, found that "economic inequality in the United States did not change much during the 1990s."[11]

Since wages and salaries are by far the largest source of income, it is also significant that one major study on inequality of *wages* by David Card and John DiNardo found that *wage inequality* did not increase before 1980 and that 85 percent of the increase during the 1980s happened "before 1985." Card and DiNardo conclude that "none of the three series [measuring wage differences] . . . shows a noticeable change in inequality between 1988 and 2000."[12]

Evidence that *consumption* inequality and *wage* inequality have not increased since around 1985–1988 contrasts sharply with some commonly expressed strong beliefs about what happened to *income* inequality.

A 2002 paper on income mobility by Katharine Bradbury and Jane Katz of the Federal Reserve Bank of Boston, for example, began by doubting whether "we still deserve our reputation" as a land of opportunity "in light of the fact that over the last thirty years Americans' household incomes have become increasingly unequal." "Increasingly unequal" suggests this was not a problem of, say, 1975–1985, but something that was a minor problem back then and a much greater problem by 2001. As if to foreclose any doubts or questions, they declared, "The pattern stands virtually undisputed among researchers."[13]

Their evidence of this supposedly undisputed pattern of increasing inequality was a graph showing real income by quintiles from 1967 to 2000. The line showing average real income in the top quintile does appear to rise much more than the line for the second quintile. But this is a trick—an optical illusion. Suppose, hypothetically, that income in the top quintile doubled from $50,000 to $100,000 while income in the second quintile also doubled from $25,000 to $50,000. A graph of the sort that Bradbury and Katz used would show that as a *widening gap*—the distance between the top and second lines would widen from $25,000 to $50,000. Yet both the top and second quintiles would have experienced exactly the same percentage increase in real incomes, and if that also happened to all other quintiles then their income shares would have remained unchanged. This provides a useful lesson in why things are not always as they seem.

The top fifth's share of pretax and pretransfer income increased from 43 percent in 1969 to nearly 47 percent in 1989–1992, but that was mainly because by 1992 there was a much larger percentage of two-earner, college-educated families in the top income households. Since the 1993 change in Census survey methods spiked the number to 49 percent, it varied negligibly from 49 percent to 50 percent through 2004. The top 5 percent's share has likewise fluctuated narrowly between 21 percent and 22 percent since 1993. Estimating income shares *before* taxes and transfers was never a credible measure of living standards. Yet even that dubious measure does *not* show that "household incomes have become increasingly unequal"—at least not since 1993. And that, in turn, brings us back to *consumption* inequality and *wage* inequality, and the fascinating issue of what happened when.

Dew-Becker and Gordon believe the debate about *consumption* inequality "has not yet been resolved," although they had not yet considered the impressive contribution of Johnson, Torrey, and Smeeding. After adopting an agnostic position on consumption inequality, unfortunately, they adopt the sweeping Bradbury-Katz declaration about something that supposedly happened to some measure of income over a period of thirty years. "Whatever their thoughts on consumption inequality," they write, "nobody debates that income inequality has increased in the United States over the past three decades."[14] The trouble with nobody debating that sort of comment, however, is that it still leaves two enormously important questions unanswered.

The first key question is, *when* during the past three decades did the alleged increase in inequality occur? The second is, what sorts of income were involved in this increase in inequality? Was it increased inequality of income from *work*, or from investments in 401(k) plans, or was it increased inequality from exercised stock options, taxable capital gains and Subchapter-S corporations?

Since they cited Card and DiNardo favorably, Dew-Becker and Gordon appear to agree that wage inequality has *not* increased since 1985, or 1988 at the latest. Using their tax data for "wages" (and exercised stock options), Dew-Becker and Gordon also found *no increase in wage inequality within the bottom half* from 1966 to 2001. Like another recent study they cited, they found that "all the increase in inequality was occurring above the [median wage] level." Specifically, there was a "dramatic increase in inequality within the top 10 percent."

If wage inequality has not increased since 1985–1988 as Card and DiNardo found, and has not increased since 1966 for the bottom half as Dew-Becker and Gordon found, then the only way *total* income inequality could have increased would be as a result of *business and investment income.* That would be consistent with Dew-Becker and Gordon's finding that inequality in *tax return income* is visible only within the top 10 percent, because private businesses and taxable investments account for a very small portion of income in the bottom half. As we found in previous chapters, however, big changes in tax-based income data from private businesses (Subchapter-S corporations) and from investments (taxable stock options and capital gains) makes credible comparisons of these types of income extremely suspect when talking about years before and after 1986.

It seems clear that exercised stock options (not just those of executives) accounted for much of the ephemeral surge in top incomes in 1996–2000. But four years of one-time windfalls at the expense of other shareholders can scarcely be considered a *trend* toward inequality. We know that billions of dollars of business income has been shifted from the corporate tax to the individual income tax since 1986. But we do *not* know if that bookkeeping adjustment for tax purposes meant anyone had more income than before.

When it comes to the *other* 90 percent—the portion that used to be a matter of greater concern—it remains an (politically incorrect) open question whether or not inequality *of living standards* has increased or *decreased* since the mid-1980s. A 2006 survey by Meyer and Sullivan concluded, "some researchers argue that overall inequality has fallen" although "most argue that it has risen."[15] The reason there is "a fair amount of disagreement," as they put it, about whether inequality has risen or fallen is because some economists are measuring inequality by using a sample of income tax returns for the top 10 percent of taxpayers; while others are using money income alone with no adjustment for taxes or transfer payments; and still others are looking at goods and services that people actually own and consume. The first two measures cannot describe relative living standards among large numbers of people during even a single year, much less over many years.

If the supposedly undisputed increase in inequality (of something or other) happened sometime between 1980 and 1988—as both wage and consumption data suggest—that was (1) too brief and too cyclical to be described as a trend and (2) too long ago to be of much current significance.

From 1981 to 1986, however, these measures of consumption inequality and wage inequality *do* show increasing inequality. But Gottschalk and Moffitt "found that one-third to one-half of the increase in income inequality during the 1980s was accounted for by transitory income changes and not from changes in permanent income."[16]

Before jumping to the conclusion that 1981 was therefore a "better" year than 1986, simply because of lower inequality, it is important to understand just how dreadful the 1981 economy really was and how that resulted in low inequality.

From the *Economic Report of the President*, one of the handy sources highlighted in the first chapter, it is easy to verify historical facts such as these: Even if energy is excluded, consumer price inflation was 11.6 percent in 1980, 10 percent in 1981 and 3.9 percent in 1985–1986. That squeeze on inflation was accomplished by the Federal Reserve, which pushed the interest rate on bank reserves (federal funds) to 16.4 percent in 1981 before finally letting it fall to 6.8 percent by 1986. With short-term interest rates falling by nearly 10 percentage points, the yield on ten-year Treasury bonds fell from 13.9 percent in 1981 to 7.7 percent by 1986.

What did inflation and interest rates have to do with low inequality in 1981 and higher inequality in 1986? With long-term interest rates near 14 percent on Treasury bonds, and much higher than that on mortgages and corporate bonds, the stock market and business profits collapsed. Three years of inflationary recession from 1980 to 1982 reduced inequality, but not by helping the poor. Unemployment hit 9.7 percent in 1982, and the poverty rate rose to 22.3 percent by 1983, before slowly declining to 19.9 percent in 1997. Stagflation in the late 1970s and early 1980s reduced inequality *at the top*—replacing business profits with losses, and creating massive *capital losses* for anyone who owned stocks, bonds, or real estate.

Economists who keep declaring it indisputable and undebatable that some measures of inequality have increased since some date about thirty years ago are leaving the most important questions unanswered. Even if such a thirty-year comparison was unambiguously true we should nonetheless remain very curious about just *when* the increased inequality happened and why. Otherwise, one might end up believing 1981 was a wonderful year simply because inequality was low.

Tax-based studies of income distribution *within* the top 10 percent cannot be properly compared before and after 1986, and they certainly cannot help us understand whether or not there has been a significant and sustained increase in broadly defined "inequality" among the other 90 percent since 1986.

Regardless of what the various pretax annual income statistics may show, the facts allow no disagreement that average *consumption* per household has risen very substantially in real terms since 1973 or 1981. That broad and obvious improvement in living standards could not have been possible without a substantial increase in average incomes unless real net worth had somehow declined for three decades (which is both impossible and the opposite of what wealth surveys show).

## MOBILITY MANIA

Major newspapers and business magazines often stumble upon surprisingly similar stories about some sensational new research about anemic growth of income or wages, soaring inequality of income or wealth, or diminishing social mobility. Readers wade through these changing fads and fashions of seemingly terrible news, each of which is soon forgotten and replaced with some newer series about some other deplorable failure of the U.S. economy.

Recent journalistic fascination with "income mobility" can be traced to a December 1, 2003, article by *Business Week* writer Aaron Bernstein. It was called, "Waking Up from the American Dream: Meritocracy and Equal Opportunity Are Fading Fast." Bernstein's article, in turn, became the source of Paul Krugman's "The Death of Horatio Alger" in The *Nation.* Such brilliant titles made this a hot story, so other journalists began to jump on the bandwagon. By May 2005, the *Wall Street Journal* and *New York Times* launched a strikingly similar *series* of articles—just two days apart— suggesting that upward mobility had stalled. If you were born poor, they all argued, you would probably end up stuck in that situation forever (or at least until you turned 30).[17]

Newspapers and magazines are called "secondary sources" for a reason. The problem with all these second-hand, shorthand political interpretations of economic research is that nearly everything can be lost in translation.

According to Mr. Bernstein's seminal *Business Week* article, for example,

new research suggests that, surprisingly, the best economy in 30 years did little to get America's vaunted upward mobility back on track. The new studies, which follow individuals and families over many years, paint a paradoxical picture: Even as the U.S. economy was bursting with wealth in the 1990s, minting dot-com millionaires by the thousands, conventional companies were cutting the middle out of career ladders, leaving fewer people able to better their economic position over the decade.

During the 1990s, relative mobility—that is, the share of Americans changing income quintiles in any direction, up or down—slipped by two percentage points, to 62%, according to an analysis of decade-long income trends through 2001 by Jonathan D. Fisher and David S. Johnson, two economists at the Bureau of Labor Statistics. While two points may not sound like much, it's bad news given how much progress might have been made amid explosive growth.

An innocent *Business Week* reader would never guess that what Jonathan Fisher and David S. Johnson actually concluded was strikingly different:

Overall, we see that income and consumption mobility more than offset the increases in income and consumption inequality, as measured by the Gini coefficient. Between 1984 and 1999 and using this one social welfare function, the data shows that welfare increased despite the relatively large increase in income inequality. The results suggest that the relatively high degree of income inequality may not be as worrisome if it continues to be accompanied by what now appears to be relatively high levels of income mobility.[18]

"A man hears what he wants to hear and disregards the rest," as the philosophers Simon and Garfunkel explained. But a man cannot always believe what he reads—even if it is exactly what he wants to hear.

David Wessel's *Wall Street Journal* piece in May 2005 was the first to depict the United States as a caste society. He worried that "Americans are no more or less likely to rise above, or fall below, their parents' economic class than they were 35 years ago." What "no more or less likely" meant, however, was that Mr. Wessel was trying to make front-page news out of something that had not changed for *at least* thirty-five years.

The *Wall Street Journal* found it strangely interesting that some economists "have come to see America as a less mobile society than [others] once believed." *New York Times* readers must have had a sense of déjà vu when reading that "new research on mobility ... shows there is far less of it than economists once thought." In both cases what economists "once thought" referred to one speech by one economist (Gary Becker) in 1987. The "new research" was published in 1992 by Gary Solon of the University of Michigan.[19] Mr. Solon estimated that 60 percent of earnings differences between two families are eliminated in one generation; Gary Becker had thought it was closer to 75 percent. By 1992 it did indeed appear there was less mobility than one economist "once believed" in 1987. But this was very old news by 2005, and nothing much had changed since 1992.

In the context of income distribution, mobility is of interest only because *annual* income figures ignore opportunities to climb upward into higher income groups through hard work and study. Since the 1960s opportunities have opened up to many more people (such as women and blacks) in ways not captured by estimates of intergenerational mobility. If a larger percentage of parents live better, and their children do too, the linkage between parents and children becomes a secondary issue.

In 1997, Urban Institute scholars Daniel McMurrer, Mark Condon, and Isabel Sawhill wrote an article called "Intergenerational Mobility in the United States." After surveying considerable evidence before and after Mr. Solon's study appeared, their conclusion was that "[o]verall, the evidence suggests that the playing field is becoming more level in the United States. Socioeconomic origins today are less important than they used to be. Further, such origins have little or even no impact for individuals with a college degree, and the ranks of such individuals continue to increase."[20]

The most novel element of the 2005 media blitz about mobility was that the *definition* of mobility had changed. Previous popular articles on this topic, including the 2003 *Business Week* story, were about *family* mobility—the difficulty or ease of "individuals and families" climbing up the ladder of economic opportunity after leaving school.

In marked contrast to previous discussions of personal or family mobility, the initial *Wall Street Journal* piece and *New York Times* sequel were mostly about "class" or what economists call *intergenerational* mobility. This involves estimating the odds of rising above your "parents' economic class."[21] To make the case that the United States is now a rigid caste society, the *Journal* relied on a table on "Family Fortunes," attributed to a chapter by Bhashkar Mazumder of the Federal Reserve Bank of Chicago in the Russell Sage foundation book *Unequal Chances*.[22] Yet another chapter in that same book by Christopher Jencks and others surveyed the evidence and critiqued another study by Mazumder and Levine, concluding, as the Urban Institute scholars had in 1997, that "almost all of these studies suggest that the inheritance of economic advantages has declined."[23] The editors, including Samuel Bowles and Herbert Gintis, founders of Union for Radical Political Economy, noted that the study by Jencks and others found "the income gap between those raised by advantaged and disadvantaged parents narrowed during the 1960s but has shown no trend since."[24]

Mr. Mazumder's table in the *Wall Street Journal* nonetheless compared some measure of "wages" for young *men* between the ages of 30 and 32 in the late 1990s with supposedly comparable wages of their fathers. What that table purported to show is that if fathers were in the bottom *fourth* of the earnings distribution then "only" 32 percent of their sons (not daughters) managed to climb to the top *half* by the age of 30–32. For those born in the top fourth, 34 percent ended up in the bottom half in an equally short time.

To move upward from the bottom 25 percent to the next highest 25 percent by age 30 (rather than jumping over into the top 50 percent) would not count as upward mobility in this scheme, even though such a move could mean a very large pay increase at such an early age.[25] In any case, it is doubtful that incomes at age 30–32 tell us much about the *lifetime* earnings of sons. It certainly says nothing about the upward mobility of *daughters*; yet young women have scored far more impressive gains than men in both education and income over the past few decades.

Mr. Wessel, to his credit, did not pretend to have found any evidence that it has become any harder to get ahead than it has always been. Two days later, however, the *New York Times*' launched the inaugural essay for its new series *Class Matters* by Janny Scott and David Leonhardt. They first wrote that "mobility seems to have stagnated," but that simply confirmed Wessel's scoop that it had not changed. So they took a bridge too far and claimed that "Americans are arguably more likely than they were thirty years ago to end up in the class to which they were born." The authors allowed that "some economists consider the findings of the new studies murky." But that polite understatement still left the impression that there were new studies indicating that Americans in 2005 were "arguably" more likely than before to "end up in the class to which they were born." That was a strong statement based on scraps of weak evidence. As we will later see, those scraps had been rigorously and thoroughly discredited by the economist who started the whole discussion—Gary Solon.

## WHAT MOBILITY STUDIES MEAN

To see what is right or wrong and true or false about these so-called "new studies" (which end with 1994 or 1998) we first need to see how such studies are usually put together.

Mobility studies use survey data to track the incomes of the same individuals or families over time, as far as possible (many people get divorced, or they die and become replaced with someone else). The Panel Study on Income Dynamics (PSID) from the University of Michigan is by far the most common source, but there are others such as the National Longitudinal Survey of Youth (NLSY).

Comparisons of the incomes of siblings are sometimes used in studies of *intergenerational* mobility, on the theory that if brothers and sisters ended up with similar incomes that might indicate some shared advantage or disadvantage from their parents (genetic brains or beauty) or their community (such as peers or schools).

In studies of *family* mobility, such as Bradbury and Katz, the incomes of each family are ranked by quintiles in some starting year, such as 1969, and then reranked for later years (often just a few years, which makes results murky). The percentage of individuals who change income quintiles between these years is then used as an indicator of mobility.

In studies of *intergenerational* mobility, the incomes of parents at some narrow range of ages (fathers averaged age 41 in Solon's 1992 paper) are compared with incomes of children (usually males) at the same or different range of ages. If the relative ranking of fathers and sons were always identical (such as both being in the bottom quintile), such a 100 percent correlation would be expressed as an "intergenerational elasticity" of one. If there was no connection at all between parents and children, then the elasticity would be zero. But that is not really possible because there are only five groups for children to wind up in, so random luck alone ensures that intergenerational elasticity must be well above zero.

## HAS MOBILITY DECLINED?

The *New York Times* cited Mazumder, as the did the *Journal*, but two different papers coauthored with David I. Levine of U.C. Berkeley. One of those studies dealt with differences or similarities in incomes between brothers, which is a topic saved for the end of this chapter. The other used three different surveys to gauge changes in mobility, claiming one of them might provide "some suggestive evidence that the rate of inheritance of economic status rose in recent decades [1980 to 1994]." For the other two, however, "the change over time is statistically insignificant and of inconsistent signs" [meaning mobility appeared to increase, not fall].[26]

In a paper available in draft form by October 2004—before the 2005 articles appeared—Gary Solon and Chul-In Lee note that "Levine and Mazumder's PSID results, like some of those of Mayer and Lopoo and Fertig, show a large but statistically insignificant decline (from 0.45 to 0.29) in the estimated intergenerational elasticity. In contrast, their NLS estimates show a statistically significant increase from 0.22 to 0.41. This result, however, may be distorted by the differential reporting of parental income between the two periods."

Scott and Leonhardt believe Bradbury and Katz "found that fewer families moved from one quintile, or fifth, of the income ladder to another during the 1980s than during the 1970s and the still fewer moved in the 1990s than in the 1980s." The pace at which families moved between income quintiles over seven to ten years may tell us something about how volatile the economy was, but it provides no information about anyone's ease or difficulty of earning a higher income. Because of the *relative* nature of mobility among quintiles, no family can move up unless another moves down in relative ranking, even though both may be moving ahead.[27] To say that movement between quintiles was less common between one pair of years than it was between some earlier pair of years does *not* mean there was less *upward* movement. It just means there were *fewer ups and downs* of the sort that necessarily cancel each other out.

It would not be surprising if there was more churning of incomes in the 1980s than in the 1990s, given the unusual way Bradbury and Katz defined these "decades." The 1980s were defined by a pair of years, 1980 and 1987—a seven-year decade that was bound to show a lot of "mobility" because it consisted of three years of recession and four years of strong recovery. The 1990s were defined by comparing 1988 with 1998—a period spanning three presidencies, the first Iraq war and a mild recession. Only the 1970s ended with a cyclical peak, 1979.

Dew-Becker and Gordon draw the correct conclusion that "Bradbury and Katz shows clearly that there was substantial income mobility across income quintiles over decade-long periods in the 1970s, 1980s and 1990s."[28]

In a more detailed and interesting 2005 paper, Bradbury and Katz showed that the percentage of couples under age 55 in which both husband and wife were working rose from just 54 percent in 1969 to 78.9 percent by 1988 (when the top tax on spouses' earnings was 28 percent). The percentage of two-earner couples then *fell* to 74.5 percent in 1998 (when the top tax on second incomes was 39.6 percent).[29] To have 4.4 percent of couples under age 55 switch from being two-earner families to one-earner families would have had an adverse effect on mobility between 1988 and 1998 (the dates of the final decade in their 2002 study). An appendix to this study (their table A-1) nonetheless showed that the percentage of married couples under age 55 that fell into the poorest quintile declined from 18.5 percent in 1969 to 16.6 percent in 1979, 14.5 percent in 1988, and 13.6 percent in 1998. If that does not count as *upward* mobility, what would?

With so many more college-educated, two-income couples in the 1990s than in the 1970s, much of the large real income gain reported in top decile between those decades was the result of *increased hours of work* per family (and per joint tax return). The greatly increased hours in the top 10–20 percent highlights a critical flaw in Dew-Becker and Gordon's effort to convert total W-2 income into *hourly* income, sorted by income groups, by incorrectly assuming no change in the *distribution* of hours.

Efforts to estimate intergenerational mobility began with the 1992 paper by Gary Solon, whose statistical work has long been considered a model of clarity and precision that others should emulate. The *New York Times* and *Wall Street Journal* identified Solon as the leading authority on intergenerational mobility. Yet neither bothered to mention his latest research and what it shows about the so-called "new research" they chose to publicize. It seems appropriate to let Gary Solon have the last word.

In a paper that was readily available online by October 2004, Gary Solon and Chul-In Lee lamented the fact that "the research conducted so far on intergenerational mobility trends has produced wildly divergent estimates," They found this was largely "an artifact of imprecise estimation." Many previous studies used only a small portion of the information available in the PSID. Some used only two separate years to define a "trend," for example, or some arbitrary selection of a few years, such as the 2002 Bradbury-Katz definition of decades in the 1980s and 1990s.

"By drawing more fully on the information in the Panel Study of Income Dynamics," Lee and Solon explained, "we generate more reliable estimates of the recent time-series variation in intergenerational mobility. For the most part, these estimates do not reveal major changes in intergenerational mobility."

The odds that children will end up in a higher or lower income group than their parents are no different than they were 10, 20, or 35 years ago. The major media's sudden fascination with "class" in 2005 showed no class at all. Something that never changes is not news, and certainly not a topic that justified all the agitated media misinformation it received in 2003–2005.

## WHAT ABOUT SWEDEN?

U.S. income mobility within families and between families is remarkably fluid and no different from any earlier era for which we have comparable data. Those determined to worry about mobility have come up with two popular ways of changing the subject.

The first diversionary tactic is to deplore the fact that mobility has not sped up, year after year. But it never did and ultimately never could, for reasons explained by Bruce Bartlett in the opening quote. If the sacrifices that most parents make to help their children succeed in life had no effect on results, then who would bother to read to their kids, help them with homework, and put money away for their college?

The second diversion is to say it is easier to move between one quintile and the next in other countries, with Sweden being the favorite example. Sweden is said to be at least as mobile as the United States, maybe more so. But this may be just another statistical illusion.

The reason it is so easy to move from one quintile to the next in Sweden is that the quintiles are not very far apart after you subtract Sweden's famously high taxes and add the famously large transfer payments of the Swedish welfare state. Over half the economy consists of government

**TABLE 8.2**
**Increase in Mean Disposable Income Needed to Move to a Higher Group in 1992–1994**

|  | 1st to 2nd Quartile | 2nd to 3rd Quartile | 3rd to 4th Quartile | Bottom to Top 10% |
|---|---|---|---|---|
| United States | $11,471 | 14,225 | 31,242 | 80,185 |
| Sweden | $6,372 | 12,643 | 19,382 | 52,178 |

*Source:* Adapted from De Nardi, Ren, and Wei, *Economic Perspectives* (Q2, 2000).

spending and transfers, and it is anybody's guess what government services are really worth (particularly in U.S. dollars).

Table 8.2 is adapted from "Income Distribution and Inequality in Five Countries" by Mariacristina De Nardi and others at the Federal Reserve Bank of Chicago.[30] The data are from the Luxembourg income study for 1995, which means 1994 for Sweden and 1992 for the U.S. Changes in Swedish incomes are in U.S. dollars (a minor problem because exchange rates do not capture differences in purchasing power) but the years are close enough that inflation adjustment is not required.

In terms of *disposable* income—after taxes and transfers—the top 10 percent earned 9.8 times as much as the bottom 10 percent in the United States, but only 3.6 times as much in Sweden. The study emphasizes that this difference is *not* because of Swedish taxes. Swedish taxes are very high but (unlike in the U.S.) they are "not very progressive." The average tax on the *poorest* 10 percent was 16 percent in Sweden, for example, compared with 2.5 percent in the United States

The biggest difference in the distribution of disposable income is because Sweden devotes much more of its tax revenue to *cash* transfer payments (partly to offset the high taxes on the poor) while the United States relies on *in-kind* transfers like Medicaid and food stamps that are not counted.

Since it is easier for people to raise their income by 360 percent in Sweden than it is to raise it by 980 percent in the United States, mobility between the bottom and top is surely easier in Sweden than in the United States. Moving from the bottom 10 percent to the second lowest quartile requires more than doubling income in the United States, but only a 43 percent gain in Sweden.

If the allure of moving easily between quintiles without really getting anywhere makes you eager to move to Sweden, do not forget to check those taxes. There is a flat tax of 40 percent on payrolls, a flat tax of 30 percent on investment income, a flat tax of 1.5 percent on wealth, and a flat municipal tax on incomes of 29–37 percent. And then there is a nominally progressive national income tax—25 percent on high incomes and 20 percent on everyone else.[31] This is quite egalitarian—everyone is equally overtaxed. Yet it seems like a high price to pay just to make mobility statistics look artificially good.

## SIBLING RIVALRY

"The incomes of brothers born around 1960 have followed a more similar pattern than the incomes of brothers in the late 1940s," according to *New York Times* writers Janey and Scott, alluding to Mazumder and Levine.[32] Janey and Scott concluded, "Whatever children inherit from their parents—habits, skills, genes, contacts, money—seems to matter more today."

First of all, notice that this comparison is only between "brothers," reflecting once again the surprisingly common practice of ignoring the inconvenient fact that employment opportunities, incomes, and educational attainment of *women* have improved dramatically for decades. That does not imply that differences in income between sisters has widened, because *most* sisters have been doing much better lately (while past differences in earnings between sisters were more likely because only one went to college).

Second, the first group of brothers reached 18 in 1962–1970 when it was still relatively unusual to send more than one son (often the eldest) to college. College enrollment was much higher when the group turned 18 in 1975–1983. It is no surprise that incomes between two college-educated brothers are apt to end up more similar than in the past when one went to college but the other often did not.

Third and most important, "whatever children inherit from their parents" is the key issue, not some minor and insignificant detail. To the extent that the link between parents and children is *anything other than parental income*, then differences or similarities between brothers' earnings provide *no* evidence that children of poor parents are any more or any less likely to end up poor.

Janey and Scott cited this allegedly "more similar pattern" between brothers as evidence for their statement that "Americans are arguably more likely than they were thirty years ago to end up in the class to which they were born." Yet Mazumder concluded that sibling correlation of earnings was mainly due to "family background and community influences that appear to be independent of family income." Similarity of the brothers' education and reading and math scores was by far the most important factor (although similar score results could be due to inherited intelligence). Also, "time spent in jail has a large effect."[33]

Mazumder opined that his finding of a 50–50 chance that two brothers will earn similar incomes "suggests that inequalities between families persist strongly from generation to generation and that the U.S. is a less mobile society than is commonly believed." That preordained conclusion was totally disconnected from his evidence.

Leading studies of comparative sibling incomes *do not* find the similarities more informative than the differences, and *do not* find the similarities and differences can simply be explained by how much money their parents made. *Good parenting* is very important (and apparently differs between siblings), but high-income couples may be so wrapped up in their careers that they neglect their children while lower-income families with a stay-at-home mom may be more attentive.

New York University sociologist Dalton Conley wrote a book on this topic, *The Pecking Order,* which was on the list of recommended readings for the *New York Times* series "Class Matters."[34]

"In explaining economic inequality in America," says Mr. Conley, "sibling differences represent about three-quarters of all differences between individuals. . . . What this means is that if we lined everyone in America up in rank order of how much money they have—from the poorest homeless person to Bill Gates himself—and tried to predict where any particular individual might fall on that long line, then knowing about what family they came from would narrow down our uncertainty by about 25 percent (in the case of income). . . . What do sibling disparities as large as these indicate? They imply an American landscape where class identity is ever changing and not necessarily shared between brothers and sisters."[35]

Dalton Conley's conclusions are the exact opposite of those drawn by the *New York Times*. He also found that "sibling correlation has not changed much." Conley includes sisters in his estimates, uses a larger survey than the one Mazumder used, and also draws upon Gary Solon and other respected sources. Whatever the reasons, Conley's estimates show larger differences between *siblings* than Mazumder's estimates for *brothers*. Yet switching to Mazumder's estimates would not fundamentally alter Conley's conclusion.

Even if sibling differences represented half of all differences between individual incomes, rather than three-quarters, that would still "imply an American landscape where class identity is ever changing." Sibling differences definitely do *not* "suggest that inequalities between families persist strongly from generation to generation," as Mr. Mazumder believed. As often as not inequalities between U.S. families do not persist for even *one* generation—because at least one of each family's two children, and possibly as many as three out of four, will fall behind.

## NOTES

1. Atkinson, "On the Measurement of Inequality," p. 162.

2. Peter Rupert and Chris Telmer, "Life Cycle Income and Consumption Variability," *Federal Reserve Bank of Cleveland Economic Commentary* (March 1, 2001). http://www .clevelandfed.org/research/Com2001/0301rupert.htm.

3. Bruce D. Meyer and James X. Sullivan, "Consumption, Income and Material Well-Being after Welfare Reform," *NBER Working Paper* 11976 (January 2006), p. 5.

4. *Economic Report of the President* (2003), p. 177.

5. Quoted in Johnson, Smeeding and Torrey, "Economic Inequality." http:// www.bls.gov/opub/mlr/2005/04/art2abs.htm.

6. Krugman, "For Richer."

7. Johnson, Smeeding and Torrey, "Economic Inequality," table 3, p. 14.

8. James M. Poterba, "Public Economics," *NBER Reporter* (Winter 2005/6), p. 3.

9. Dirk Krueger and Fabrizio Perri, *Does Income Inequality Lead to Consumption Inequality? Evidence and Theory* (Federal Reserve Bank of Minneapolis Research Department Staff Report 363, June 2005). http://minneapolisfed.org/research/common/pub_detail.cfm? pb_autonum_id=1034.

10. Orazio Attanasio, Erich Battistin, and Hidehiko Ichimura, "What Really Happened to Consumption Inequality in the U.S.?" *NBER Working Paper* 10338 (March 2004), p. 13.

11. Ríos-Rull et al., "Updated Facts on the U.S. Distributions of Earnings, Income, and Wealth."

12. David Card and John E. DiNardo, "Skill Biased Technological Change and Rising Wage Inequality: Some Problems and Puzzles," *NBER Working Paper* 9769 (February 2002), p. 17.

13. Katherine Bradbury and Jane Katz, "Are Lifetime Incomes Growing More Unequal? Looking at New Evidence on Family Income Mobility," *Federal Reserve Bank of Boston Regional Review* (fourth quarter, 2002).

14. Dew-Becker and Gordon, "Where Did the Productivity Growth Go?" p. 72. Their comments on consumption inequality appear only in a longer version than their NBER working paper.

15. Meyer and Sullivan, "Consumption, Income and Material Well-Being."

16. Johnson, Smeeding, and Torrey, "Economic Inequality," p. 13.

17. I wrote a quick critique of both articles: Alan Reynolds, "For the Record," *Wall Street Journal*, May 18, 2005. See also the critical letter about my article by Mazdumer and Levine on May 24, 2005 and my reply on May 25, 2005.

18. Jonathan D. Fisher and David S. Johnson, Consumption Mobility in the United States: Evidence from Two Panel Data Sets (U.S. Bureau of Labor Statistics, June 19, 2003), p. 27.

19. Gary Solon, "Intergenerational Income Mobility in the United States," *American Economic Review* 82(3) (1992).

20. Daniel P. McMurrer, Mark Condon, and Isabel V. Sawhill, *Intergenerational Mobility in the United States* (Urban Institute, May 1, 1997). http://www.urban.org/url .cfm?ID=406796.

21. In the novel and simultaneous efforts of the *New York Times* and *Wall Street Journal* to redefine the United States as a rigid caste society, both relied uncritically on Bhashkar Mazumder who had reason to believe that U.S. caste discrimination is genuine. His father, engineering professor Pinaki Mazumder, had sued the University of Michigan in 2003

alleging that he had been discriminated against (not paid enough) because he had been a member of the Kayastha caste. Tarun Udwala, "Caste Discrimination Case in Univ of Michigan Dismissed," *Zestcaste*, April 27, 2005. http://www.mail-archive.com/zestcaste@ yahoogroups.com/msg00542.html.

22. Bhashkar Mazumder, "The Apple Falls Even Closer to the Tree than We Thought," in *Unequal Chances: Family Background and Economic Success*, eds., Samuel Bowles, Herbert Gintis, and Melissa Osborne Groves (Princeton, NJ: Princeton University Press, 2005), chapter 2.

23. Bowles, Gintis, and Groves, *Unequal Chances*, p. 103.

24. Ibid., p. 20. Even though this good news appeared in the same book as Mazumder's chapter, it did not receive 0.01 percent as much press attention. That was not a matter of liberal press bias, but of negative press bias. Jencks, Bowles, and Gintis are veteran leaders of the "radical left" and proud of it. Similarly, optimistic 1997 comments from the "liberal Democrat" Urban Institute were likewise shunned by the mainstream media.

25. The salary in my first job after college increased from $5,400 to $9,900 just before I turned 30. But that would show up as no improvement at all in the Mazumder table because I would have needed about $13,000 in the early seventies to make it into the top half with a family of four.

26. David I. Levine and Bhashkar Mazumder, "Choosing the Right Parents: Changes in the Intergenerational Transmission of Inequality between 1980 and the Early 1990s," WP 2002-08 (Federal Reserve Bank of Chicago working paper, 2002), p. 24.

27. Downward changes in relative shares, which can be caused simply by income remaining about the same but the threshold defining the top of a family's income group moving up—thus dropping them into the next lower quintile. That would be another example of "threshold illusion." *Absolute* downward mobility means a lower real income. That is uncommon except during severe recessions, and a bit off topic. Downward mobility normally reflects hopefully temporary spells of bad luck (such as serious illness or career setbacks) or self-destructive behavior (such as gambling, alcoholism, or drug addiction).

28. Dew-Becker and Gordon, "Where Did the Productivity Growth Go?" p. 45.

29. Katharine Bradbury and Jane Katz, "Wives' Work and Family Income Mobility," *Federal Reserve Bank of Boston Public Policy Discussion Papers* No. 04-3 (May 12, 2005).

30. Mariacristina De Nardi, Liquian Ren, and Chao Wei, "Income Inequality and Redistribution in Five Countries," Federal Reserve Bank of Chicago *Economic Perspectives* (Q2, 2000).

31. Pricewaterhouse Coopers, *Individual Taxes 2004–2005* (New York: John Wiley & Sons, 2004).

32. Earnings data for the older group of brothers (born 1944–52) ended with a couple of tumultuous years in 1981, while earnings for the younger brothers (1957–65) ended in the peak year of 2000. Bhashkar Mazumder and David I. Levine, "The Growing Importance of Family and Community: An Analysis of Change in the Sibling Correlation in Men's Earnings" (working paper, revised draft October 2004).

33. Bhashkar Mazumder, "What Similarities between Siblings Tell Us about Inequality in the U.S.?" Chicago Fed Letter No. 209 (December 2004).

34. *New York Times* website for the "Class Matters" series is http://www.nytimes.com/ pages/national/class/index.html.

35. Dalton Conley, *The Pecking Order: Which Siblings Succeed and Why* (New York: Pantheon, 2004), pp. 6–7.

# Nine

## Causes and Cures

Politicians, pundits, historians, sociologists and Wall Street analysts have jumped in. The debate pops up all the time, in articles and books and on talk shows. Policy prescriptions fill the air: regulate trade, restrict immigration, levy higher taxes on the rich to subsidize the poor and improve educational standards in an attempt—perhaps vain—to make everyone highly skilled and well paid.

—Louis Uchitelle, "Like Oil and Water"
*New York Times* (February 16, 1977)

Consumers decide who is paid more and who is paid less, and their choices may not always seem fair. Evidence of increased wage inequality is confined to the early 1980s, except at the very top of the job ladder. The loss of manufacturing jobs was greater in Japan, Germany, and China than in the United States, and U.S. manufactured output doubled since 1979. The fastest-growing service jobs pay better than manufacturing jobs, and labor's share of national income was no higher when more workers belonged to unions. When the minimum wage was increased in 1997, the number of workers paid *less than* the minimum shot up. The textbook trade-off between "equity and efficiency" is not actually about efficiency but about incentives and economic growth. And the trade-off can be huge. Countries that decided to go for growth after 1980, such as India, South Korea, and Russia cut their highest tax rates in half since 1979, to 13–25 percent in several cases. Income in fast-growing economies like India and China is now distributed far less equally than it is in places like Ethiopia, Burundi, and Tanzania, where there is very little income to distribute.

Life is not fair. But that is largely because people are not fair. Consumers ultimately decide who gets paid more, less, or not at all. Consumers decide what we are paid by putting a low or high value on the products and services we offer for sale. Employers are just middlemen.

Thousands of people have been willing to pay $215 a seat to listen to Elton John sing and play his red piano in Las Vegas, while few are willing to pay even $10 a seat to listen to a Nobel Laureate lecture about economics, so Elton John earns a higher income than famed economists. Because nobody is willing to pay much for a quick hamburger and fries, those who prepare and serve fast food earn much less than master chefs and head waiters at elegant restaurants.

The way we spend our money often leaves more of it in the hands of beautiful women, tall men, and thin people in general. We shamelessly place an unfair emphasis on intelligence when choosing between hedge-fund managers, surgeons, and college professors even though intelligence partly depends on luck in winning a genetic lottery. We spend billions on entertainment and sports, but fail to distribute that money fairly to the hardest-working or most needy singers, actors, and athletes.

For those most deeply troubled by all this unfairness, statistics about whether various measures of inequality have gone up or down between two dates are beside the point. Nobody who uses income distribution figures as an argument for adopting their pet government policies would advocate different policies even if they could be persuaded their statistics are wrong. Besides, new estimates tend to pop up as quickly as old estimates are shot down, because economists supply what is demanded.

To hold a monomaniacal attachment to *any* single measure of economic performance (such as *shares* of income, regardless of income going up or down) is to forget the essence of economics. Economics deals with scarcity, with tough choices among limited opportunities.[1]

Previous chapters found that inequality of income, consumption, and financial wealth increased between 1981 and 1986, give or take a year or two. Yet inflation and unemployment and poverty were also greatly *reduced* between those dates. There can be *big* trade-offs to be made, and *not* simply between economic efficiency and social equity alone. There was nothing "equitable" about high inflation, unemployment, and poverty in 1981.

Those most deeply concerned about inequality were just as concerned about it in 1981 as they were in 1986 or any other year. It is not really *rising* inequality that bothers them, but the *level* of inequality—the sheer coexistence of people with very high and very low incomes. And that focus on inequality—on gaps between high and low incomes—makes it a matter of indifference whether inequality increases because more people are becoming rich or because more are becoming poor. In fact, recent academic discussions of income and wage inequality are almost entirely about what has happened among the top 1–10 percent.

To condemn economic inequality *per se* implies that equality would be ideal (regardless of work effort, age, schooling, etc.), or at least possible. Yet some people have always had higher incomes than others in every civilized society throughout history. And some people have always accumulated greater wealth than others.

Utopian promises to end inequality just replaced the unfair choices of consumers with the selfish choices made by an elite cadre of autocrats and bureaucrats.[2] In the former Soviet Union, for example, special access to housing, health care, education, and special shops was often granted to the Communist Party hierarchy and the bribe-prone bureaucratic elite. Incomes may still be closest to the Utopian ideal of equality in Kim Jong Il's North Korea or Fidel Castro's Cuba, since the vast majority of people are more-or-less equally impoverished. But intransigent Party bosses in such places are (as in George Orwell's *Animal Farm*) "more equal than others." To assume *political* allocation of goods or incomes is "fairer" than *market* allocation is to forget world history.

Most non-Utopian proposals to reduce income inequality fall into one of two categories, direct and indirect. The "direct approach" is to spend more money on means-tested transfer payments—those targeted toward people who report low incomes. Such payments usually come with strings attached, such as going only to those with children, those who work a little, or old people who did not work enough to collect Social Security.

The direct approach is sometimes said to require higher taxes on the rich (unlike Sweden). But reducing the net incomes of the rich does not give one dollar to the poor—that depends entirely on the allocation of public spending. The complex issues of taxing and spending for redistributive purposes will be addressed later in this chapter.

Most recent proposals on what to do about U.S. inequality have stressed the "indirect approach." That refers to a catch-all of proposals ostensibly aimed at affecting the labor market in ways intended to increase the lowest wage rates. Such proposals include protecting manufacturing industries from foreign competition, restricting immigration, promoting unionization, and raising the minimum wage. The indirect approach also encompasses education, since advocates of additional subsidies to certain types of schooling often claim their proposals would reduce measured inequality.

Each of these direct and indirect fixes for inequality has filled many books. This chapter is only intended to highlight a few problems with various proposed solutions and to question how those proposals relate to actual problems. In other words, this chapter is about "causes and cures."

## THE INDIRECT APPROACH

When seeking explanations for inequality, previous chapters have emphasized such unexciting facts as the increased number of prime-age workers in top income groups and their improved average levels of education. The more lively academic discussions of inequality, by contrast, often seem to follow each scholar's particular area of interest.

Labor economists look for causes of inequality in terms of wages and salaries and therefore suggest labor market solutions such as increased unionization and a higher minimum wage. Trade specialists are more likely to focus on international issues, such as promoting trade adjustment assistance for those who lost jobs because of foreign competition (rather than those who lost their jobs because of domestic competition). Education specialists naturally focus on greater funding for schools or students, not to mention the urgent need for larger research grants to themselves. Immigration experts emphasize tighter restrictions on unskilled immigration and/or reduced restrictions on skilled immigration.

Labor economists' papers on inequality often begin with some stylized facts about *income* inequality then quickly switch to providing various explanations for *wage* inequality. Income inequality is often treated as though it was virtually synonymous with wage inequality. That is because wages and salaries accounted for 55.8 percent of personal income in 2005 and benefits for another 13.7 percent. Income from transfer payments accounted for 14.9 percent of personal income—slightly more than income from interest and dividends (14.2 percent).[3]

Although wages and benefits account for nearly 70 percent of personal income, however, estimates of wage inequality often exclude benefits. And estimates of income inequality often exclude transfer payments. The many different sources of wage, income, and consumption statistics also generate distinctly different "trends" toward more or less inequality since 1986, as the last chapter demonstrated.

Summarizing a half-dozen books and studies on inequality in 1995, Barry Bluestone of Northeastern University wrote that "in our rogue's gallery we have ten suspects: skill-biased technological change, deindustrialization, industry deregulation, the decline of unions, lean production, winner-take-all labor markets, free trade, transnational capital mobility, immigration, and a persistent trade deficit."[4] What all those explanations have in common is that the assumed increase in inequality of *incomes* must be due to the assumed increase in inequality of *wages*.

To visualize the problem with treating wage inequality as equivalent to income or consumption inequality, imagine what would happen if most low-income workers lost their jobs. Since their wages would no longer be counted in wage surveys, the inequality of wages would appear to have "improved." But those without jobs might disagree.

To support the idea that inequality of *wages* has increased, it has become commonplace to recycle some crude estimate of the ratio of CEO pay (mostly stock options) to worker salaries. Yet it is irrelevant to wage inequality if business founders or managers have been making millions from the stock market. Nobody's wage or salary would be a dollar higher if Steve Jobs earned millions less than he has from Apple's stock.

Each of the many competing explanations for *low* wages is invariably attached to competing *policy advice*. One group says the cause of the problem is A so the cure is B; another says the cause is C so the cure is D. A cynic (or realist) might suspect that the policy being advocated came first, before work began on defining the problem in a way that fits that policy.

A little skepticism seems prudent when interest groups are so obviously involved. Manufacturing industries play the inequality card when lobbying for tariffs, subsidies, and tax breaks. Union organizers cite inequality as a rationale for public policies to facilitate their job of organizing workers who appear unwilling to be organized. Critics of immigration sometimes use inequality inconsistently as a reason to limit work visas for highly skilled immigrants and also to toughen border control for low-skilled illegal immigrants.

The academic emphasis on *wage* inequality is nonetheless puzzling. Policies aimed at raising wage rates would be an extremely unlikely means of increasing the bottom quintile's share of total income, because higher wages cannot help people who are not working. Chapter Two showed that few households among the poorest fifth have any member working, and fewer still have anyone working full time. The poverty rate among full-time workers is negligible. A few more low-income people might *seek* employment if hourly wages were higher, but it is doubtful if many would find a higher-paying job since they have not found a lower-paying job. Besides, many of the poor are *unable* to work because of advanced age, infirmity, substance abuse, or the burden of child care.

The other peculiarity about the academic emphasis on labor markets is that the evidence that wage inequality has *increased* was never persuasive for women and is now quite debatable for everyone—aside from stock options at the top and a brief increase in inequality following the economic debacle of 1980–1982.

The evidence most often cited to support the idea of rising wage inequality was a survey written in 1992 about earlier studies, which relied on even earlier data.[5] We now know that some of those old studies were incorrectly viewing 1980–1985 as the beginning of an endless trend. They often used annual income data to estimate hourly wages, which confused a rising share of part-time workers with a lower hourly wage. In his introduction to a 2001 collection of studies on wage inequality, Finis Welch of Texas A&M noted that "when the population is restricted to full-time, full-year workers, the increased dispersion [inequality] that has occupied so much attention disappears."[6]

In the Chapter 8 we referred to a 2005 study by David Card and John DiNardo that found wage inequality only increased from 1980–1988, with 85 percent of that increase ending by 1985. That one-time spurt in inequality was a cyclical rebound from an unusually depressed base of 1980–1982, which, among other things, had wiped-out most managerial bonuses or stock options linked to the stock market.

Robert Lerman of the Urban Institute was one of first to question the claim that wage inequality had increased *after* the mid-1980s. He examined the Census Bureau's Survey of Income and Program Participation (SIPP) as well as the Current Population Survey (CPS). "Contrary to the conventional wisdom," wrote Lerman, "wage rate inequality for all workers actually fell between 1987 and 1994. SIPP data reveal that the Gini coefficient, measuring overall wage rate inequality, fell by 5.5 percent. The 90/10 ratio, measuring the disparity between the very highly paid and the very poorly paid, fell by 7.1 percent. A similar pattern emerges for men ages 25 to 54.... The CPS data show a somewhat different picture, but still no evidence that overall wage rate or earnings inequality increased." Citing supporting work by Robert Haveman, Katharine Bradbury, and the OECD, Lerman noted that "when other studies measure earnings as payments per hour or include all workers, they also find no increases in inequality since 1984.[7]

Increasing inequality of wages is an *old* story, but one that refuses to die.

## IDEALIZING ASSEMBLY LINES AND SWEAT SHOPS

The absence of convincing evidence of increased wage inequality after 1985–1988 has not diminished the intense passion with which many people continue to advocate solutions for increased wage inequality. We are left with an abundance of theoretical solutions in search of a factual problem.

Whenever facts conflict with an appealing theory, many prefer to cling to that theory and discard the facts. But the tenacious faith in rising *wage inequality* and *wage stagnation* is not driven by economic theory, but by historical mythology. That myth concerns the decline of assembly-line jobs in manufacturing and sewing, which are said to have provided an easy springboard into the middle class in the 1950s and 1960s.

The shift into service sector jobs from about 1983 to 2006 was supposedly equated with low-wage employment, and therefore caricatured as "McJobs." In 2004, *Business Week* announced, "[T]here's a new name for the downward pressure on wages: the so-called Wal-Martization of the economy."[8] Clever names are no substitute for facts. Such caricatures assert something demonstrably untrue—namely, that the reduction in national *share* of jobs in the manufacturing sector were offset by an increase in the *share* of jobs in retailing.

The *Washington Post*, on April 15, 2006, nonetheless repeated this familiar mantra that high-wage, union manufacturing jobs have been replaced by low-wage, nonunion retail jobs:

The quarter-century decline in manufacturing jobs, which often paid middle-class wages and benefits, is one factor that has contributed to the fall during that period in average hourly earnings, adjusted for inflation, economists say.... The shrinking of the manufacturing sector has also corresponded to a drop in union membership to 13 percent of the workforce currently from 24 percent in 1979, weakening labor's power to bargain for better wages.[9]

The loss of industrial employment was called "The Deindustrialization of America" in a 1982 book by Barry Bluestone and Bennett Harrison, but the thesis soon faded as the economy grew by 4 percent a year for the next seven years. The idea was revived in 1996 in "The Downsizing of America," another gloomy *New York Times* series that *Washington Post* columnist Robert Samuelson described as a "selective collection of information to buttress what editors and reporters had already concluded."[10] Yet 1996 was the dawn of the Internet Age and a four-year stock market boom. The ill-timed chatter about "downsizing" in 1996 was out of touch with reality, even by the low standards of election-year journalism.

Employment in U.S. manufacturing industries peaked at 19.4 million in 1979, falling to 14.3 million by 2005.[11] The decline is somewhat exaggerated because manufacturing companies used to hire more people to perform services such as payroll, law, and accounting that are now usually done more effectively and cheaply by specialist firms (the biggest of which, in New York and D.C., also export such "outsourcing" to many foreign corporations).

Anxiety about deindustrialization or downsizing is usually linked to international trade through catch-words like "globalization" or "offshoring." The United States is widely imagined to have "exported jobs" to countries

**TABLE 9.1**
**Number of Manufacturing Jobs (Thousands)**

|      | United States | Japan | Germany |
|------|---------------|-------|---------|
| 1992 | 20,120 | 15,650 | 10,731 |
| 2005 | 16,253 | 11,393 | 8,144* |

*Note:* *The measure is for the year 2004.
*Source:* http://www.bls.gov/fls/flscomparelf.htm.

that export more than they import, such as Japan and Germany, even though *manufacturing* employment declined even more dramatically in those countries (and their overall job growth has been abysmal). That is what investments in "labor-saving" equipment do—they save labor. Manufacturing employment in China fell from more than 98 million in 1995 to 80.8 million by 2000 before recovering to 89.6 million in 2003.[12]

Table 9.1 shows manufacturing employment figures adjusted by the BLS to make them comparable among countries. From 1992 to 2005 manufacturing employment fell by 19 percent in the United States, but by 24 percent in Germany and 27 percent in Japan.

Those who blame "globalization" or "free trade" for whatever they believe happened to wages or jobs usually emphasize competition with other countries for manufacturing jobs, citing the U.S. trade deficit as evidence. Since Japan and Germany have run chronic trade surpluses for many years, particularly in manufactured goods, Table 9.1 contradicts *all* trade-related explanations for the (unproven) belief the United States has long been suffering wage stagnation or increasing wage inequality.

The erroneous "wage stagnation thesis" was nonetheless repeated once again in the previously quoted *Washington Post* comment about the "quarter-century decline in . . . average hourly earnings." As usual, that article blamed wage stagnation on the "shrinking of the manufacturing sector." But that could make sense only if wages in manufacturing are typically higher than wages in sectors famous for having added millions of jobs—such as health, education, construction, information technology, and "FIRE" (finance, insurance, and real estate).

When people decry the disappearance of "high-wage jobs" they must mean jobs that paid better than average. But jobs that pay better than average have *always* been relatively scarce or else they would have been described as *average* jobs. In any case, the commonly repeated generalization that *manufacturing* pays higher wages than the most rapidly expanding service occupations is blatantly untrue. Table 9.2 shows average hourly earnings at the end of 2005 for production or nonsupervisory workers in ten

**TABLE 9.2**
**Average Hourly Earnings in December 2005 by Production or Nonsupervisory Workers**

| | |
|---|---|
| Utilities | $27.03 |
| Information | 22.79 |
| Construction | 19.72 |
| Wholesale trade | 18.43 |
| Professional & business services | 18.37 |
| Financial activities | 18.27 |
| Education & health services | 17.01 |
| Transportation & warehousing | 16.97 |
| Manufacturing | 16.82 |
| Private service-producing | 15.98 |

*Source:* http://www.bls.gov/news.release/pdf/realer.pdf.

large industries. Several industries with the highest wage rates in this table were rapidly growing *service* industries—such as Internet-based information services, banking and securities, insurance, law, accounting, real estate sales, cellular phones, and other telecommunications, education, and medical services. In this league, manufacturing wage rates were near the bottom, only marginally higher than miscellaneous other *private* services (which excludes, by definition, many highly paid service jobs in *government*).

What is missing from Table 9.2 are *retailing* and hospitality industries, which do indeed offer lower wage rates than typical manufacturing jobs. But such jobs have *not* accounted for a rising share of employment, so they could *not* have replaced the declining share of jobs in manufacturing. Retailing, for example, accounted for the same 11.3 percent of total payroll employment in both 1979 and 2005.[13] By contrast, those service industries with a rapidly *rising share* of employment have included health, education, FIRE, professional and business services, and numerous new services related to computers and the Internet (such as Google).

Manufacturing jobs have been lost through automation in *every* major industrial economy, but in the United States those jobs have been replaced by a much larger number of higher-skilled, higher-paying jobs in service industries of the sorts listed *above* manufacturing in Table 9.2. As we discovered with "the vanishing middle class," a rising percentage of American families left the "middle class" manufacturing jobs by moving *up*.

Anecdotal reports of industrial layoffs nonetheless get all the press attention, while growth of new industries (including high-tech manufacturing) gets almost none. The United States is a very dynamic and mobile economy, so *job creation* and *job destruction* are always going on simultaneously at a hectic pace.[14] The fact that U.S. employment keeps growing nearly all the time proves that the net effect is for job creation to exceed job destruction (except during recessions). In 1979, when manufacturing employment peaked, total employment was 98.8 million. In 2005, total employment was 141.7 million.[15] Comments about the United States "losing jobs" go beyond mythology into sheer fantasy.

The fact that U.S. manufacturing employment declined certainly does not mean *manufacturing* declined. Output per worker improved—that is what increased productivity means. Table B-13 in the *Economic Report of the President* provides an index of the *real* gross domestic product (GDP) of U.S. manufacturing industries, where the year 2000 (a cyclical peak) is set as equal to 100. That same index was 50.8 in 1979 (another cyclical peak) and rose to 103.7 by 2005. In other words, the real value of U.S. manufactured products *more than doubled* from 1979 to 2005 (as did real GDP in general). Similarly, Table B-51 shows the manufacturing component on the industrial production index, where the year 2002 is set at 100. By this measure manufacturing output also doubled, rising from 53.7 in 1979 to 109.5 in 2005. The common belief that U.S. manufacturing has been declining since 1979 is another historical hoax.

Manufacturing has raised productivity by mechanizing and automating much of the mindless routine, leaving fewer but better jobs. Robert Reich, the former Secretary of Labor, explained this very well:

Go into a modern factory today and what do you see? A lot of numerically controlled machine tools and robots, and a few technicians sitting behind computer consoles. The old-style assembly line factory worker is going the way of the bank teller, telephone operator, and service-station attendant. . . .

Take a close look at any manufactured item—a pen, a cup, a car, a dress—and see who's actually earning what portion of its purchase price. Much of it goes to Americans, even if the factory that made it is located in Asia. More and more of any item's value is going to researchers and designers, engineers, entrepreneurs, marketers, advertisers, distributors, bankers, lawyers, wholesalers, retailers. None of them is considered a manufacturing worker, but they are the future of manufacturing.[16]

## UNIONS AND LABOR'S SHARE

The April 2006 *Washington Post* article, and a few labor economists, assert that wage stagnation was caused by the "drop in union membership." The argument is that workers had more "bargaining power" in the past and therefore captured *a larger share of national income.* It is not enough to say that unions pushed their wages above those of other workers, because such *relative* wage gains were obviously not shared by "labor" as a whole.

Unless labor's share of national income has declined since union membership declined, we must reject the hypothesis that declining union membership has caused wage growth in general to slow down or "stagnate."

A 2004 graph from the Federal Reserve Bank of St. Louis shows that "labor's share of income has averaged 70.5 percent [of national income] over the past fifty years and has remained within a narrow range of that average."[17] Dew-Becker and Gordon likewise conclude, "Contrary to the widespread impression that labor's share has been squeezed, there was no change in labor's share from 1996:Q3 to 2005:Q1.... Labor's income share... fluctuated around a mean of 71.2 percent between early 1984 and early 2005. The average during the past decade (1996:Q2–2005:Q1) was almost exactly the same, 70.8 percent."[18]

There is no evidence that the reduction in manufacturing jobs or the reduction in union membership since the 1970s has reduced labor's share of national income.

## LESS THAN MINIMUM WAGE

There is always an ongoing academic contest between one season's favorite explanation for wage inequality and the next. A favorite theme has long been "skill-based technological change" (SBTC), which its fans described as the "consensus" view.

The SBTC hypothesis tried to solve a puzzle. The puzzle was that so many millions more people have been graduating college (particularly in the 1970s) that this should have created a glut in the market for college graduates, and a relative shortage of those with a high school diploma or less. By itself, that should have narrowed the pay gap between increasing scarce of high school dropouts and increasingly abundant college graduates (which, if it happened, would have discouraged college enrollment). Yet the wage premium between college and high-school graduates widened, as did the gap between those with and without a high school degree.

One reason the assumed scarcity of unskilled labor did not push up the lowest wage rates is that immigration greatly increased the supply of high school "dropouts" (who are miscounted as having dropped out of *U.S.* schools).[19] That seemed obvious by 2006, yet it was missed by many of those writing about SBTC. At the higher end of the salary ladder, however, it does appear that demand for well-educated employees grew even faster than growth of supply.

Where "skill-based technological change" went too far was to tie it all to computer skills and the Internet (rather than to, say, MBA, JD, and MD degrees). The clearest evidence of increased wage inequality was from 1980 to 1985; scarcely anyone still thinks it continued beyond 1992. Yet very few people had a personal computer in 1984 and the Internet was not popularized until 1996.

The SBTC hypothesis was mainly developed by Frank Levy and David Autor of MIT, and Lawrence Katz and Richard Murnane of Harvard. That Ivy League consensus nonetheless began to be eroded by "revisionists," such as Thomas Lemieux of the University of British Columbia. He found that "experience and education . . . only explain about a third of the variance in wages." As for the other two-thirds, "a large part of the increase in residual wage inequality is a spurious consequence of the fact that the workforce has grown older and more educated since the early 1980s."[20]

A rebuttal by Autor, Katz, and Melissa Kearney began by citing evidence of increased inequality from three studies published from 1991 to 1996 based on data from several years earlier. They seemed to realize those references were outdated and to concede that rising inequality was "a one-time ('episodic') event of the early 1980s, which plateaued by the mid-1980s and did not recur."[21] That should be the end of the story, but the urge to fix something persists.

The SBTC economists and their critics (which include Dew-Becker and Gordon) seem to agree on one thing—that a higher minimum wage might fix something. But what? Autor, Katz, and Kearney (like Dew-Becker and Gordon) find no increase in inequality after the mid-1980s aside from "upper tail inequalities." That is, some among the rich were getting richer than others among the rich.

Even if tax-based income data about the top 1 percent were not so terribly flawed, why does anyone care if 13,000 super-rich are leaping ahead of the other 1.3 million who are also decidedly well-off? The increasingly narrow academic fascination with the upper tail totally ignores the "bottom tail"— the poor. While the focus on "inequality" does indeed imply *total indifference* about whether inequality is caused by the rich getting richer or the poor getting poorer, such indifference may have gone too far. Perhaps that explains the odd gesture of pretending the minimum wage is an effective policy.

Lemieux thinks failure to increase the minimum wage explained whatever increase in wage inequality there was in the early 1980s. Autor, Katz, and Kearney prefer to include "SBTC, the minimum wage, declining unionization, immigration, international shifts in labor composition." That seems like a few too many explanations for "a one-time ('episodic') event of the early 1980s."

The minimum wage is a particularly strange choice, since all these economists (including Dew-Becker and Gordon) found no increase in income inequality among the bottom half—only "upper tail inequalities."

Lemieux found "the gap between high school graduates and dropouts remained more or less constant (or even declined in some cases)." He also
found a "dramatic increase in the return to post-secondary education," and
believes that helps explain why "changes in wage inequality are increasingly
concentrated in the very top end of the wage distribution."[22] But how is a
higher minimum wage supposed to narrow the increasingly concentrated
inequalities between those with a bachelor's in philosophy and those with
an MBA?

The minimum wage may appear statistically related to changes in wage
inequality because a higher minimum wage could put many of the lowest-
wage workers out of work—or at least shove them into obscure subminimum
wage jobs unlikely to be counted. That would narrow wage inequality because a lot of low-wage work would disappear from the data. And that, in
turn, shows why studies of wage inequality are no substitute for surveys of
consumption inequality or income inequality. Firing many low-wage workers could greatly improve the apparent equality of measured wages. But it
would *not* improve equality of income or consumption.

If the only thing that mattered was to reduce wage disparity—the spread
between high and low wages—that could doubtless be accomplished by
raising the minimum wage to $100 an hour, and severely punishing anyone
who offered a job at any lower wage. Anyone incapable of producing more
than $100 an hour would not have a job, of course. That is the bad news.
But the good news is that *those who do not have a job with a reasonably large,
established business are not included in BLS surveys of hourly or weekly earnings.*
As a result, the gap between high and low wages would narrow dramatically—
because only those with extremely high wages would still be included.

One little-noticed effect of an increased minimum wage is that it always
increases the percentage of workers who end up earning *less than* the minimum wage. Subminimum wage jobs are usually too obscure to be counted
in wage surveys, even if the jobs are legal. Any employer with an annual
income below $500,000 is free to ignore the federal minimum wage. The
federal minimum wage does *not* apply to workers on small farms or at
seasonal amusement or recreational facilities. It does not apply to newspaper
deliverers, companions for the elderly, outside salesmen, U.S. seamen on
foreign-flag ships, switchboard operators or part-time babysitters. There is
sure to be some outright evasion of minimum wage laws, since it is impossible
to police all the casual day labor, migrant farm work, and home cleaning in
this country.

The *Statistical Abstract of the United States* shows that among 73 million workers still paid by the hour in 2003, only 545,000 or 0.7 percent
earned the federal minimum wage. Three times as many—1.6 million or

2.2 percent—earned *less than* the minimum wage. What happens when the minimum wage is increased is that some are priced out of a job, such as replacing supermarket clerks with self-checkout machines. But many are simply shoved into jobs that pay even *less than* the minimum, legally and otherwise.

The federal minimum wage was increased to $4.75 in October 1996 and to $5.15 a year later. What happened? The *Statistical Abstract* from that period shows that percentage of workers earning *less than* the minimum wage jumped from 2.5 percent (1.7 million) in 1995 to 4.2 percent (3 million) by 1997. The percentage of teens working for *less than* the minimum rose from 7.2 percent to 19.8 percent. The increased minimum wage is the only plausible explanation, since unemployment was low and falling in 1996–1997. The higher minimum wage increased competition for subminimum wage jobs, pushing the lowest wages even lower. Good intentions do not always produce good results.

## GLOBAL DEMOGRAPHICS

Economic growth depends on the quantity and quality of both labor and capital. Workers cannot produce as much without good equipment.[23] And equipment is useless without workers with the skill and motivation to use it.

In some parts of the world, such as China, India, and Mexico, labor will be relatively abundant and capital relatively scarce for many decades. In other parts of the world where the population is rapidly aging, such as Japan, Europe, and the United States, capital will be abundant in comparison with an increasingly scarce supply of qualified workers. How willing and able those workers will actually be, however, is more a matter of incentives than demographics.

Demographics alone present no fundamental economic problems for free and open economies. Nations relatively short of *labor* can either import workers through open immigration policies or they can import labor-intensive goods and services through open trade, including electronic imports of services. Nations relatively short of *capital* can either import financial capital by providing secure property rights and competitive taxation, or they can import capital-intensive goods and knowledge-intensive skills through open trade.

If a labor-short country, such as the United States, became highly restrictive toward both immigration and imports of labor-intensive goods, then domestically produced labor-intensive goods would become increasingly expensive, reducing real U.S. wages and incomes. If a capital-short country such as Mexico became restrictive toward both foreign investment and imports of foreign equipment and know-how, then real output and income per worker would remain depressed. Trading labor and capital is not a problem but a mutually essential win-win solution.

Taxes and transfers could greatly complicate this picture.[24] Aging populations in countries like the United States could help provide a more skilled and stable workforce even though young workers will be unavoidably scarce (because not enough were born eighteen years earlier). Yet more senior workers cannot substitute for fewer younger workers if steep taxes on their work and generous subsidies for retirement make work unattractive.[25]

In the decades ahead, Japan, Europe, and the United States are going to have to take work incentives very seriously.[26] If immigration policy in the United States turns toward greatly restricting the *number* of immigrants, regardless of their employability or job skills, then it will be even harder for companies to find enough willing and able workers in the United States.

## TAXING AND SPENDING

The "direct approach" to redistributing income involves more government spending intended to help the poor. It may also involve *trying* to collect more taxes from the rich, but the taxing and spending decisions are separate. Federal, state, and local governments could easily spend more on the poor by spending less on something else. They could also "soak the rich" and spend all the extra loot on pork-barrel spending, wars, and bureaucratic salaries.

In any case, both the tax and spending side of fiscal redistribution are more difficult than they sound. Taxes and transfers affect behavior in ways that can result in unintended consequences. Trying to tax the stuffing out of rich people cannot work if it makes it too difficult to find many rich people to tax—the dilemma of taxable income elasticity discussed in Chapter 5. Trying to be generous to poor people also has some limits. Many might find themselves stuck in a "poverty trap" because even a little extra income from working or saving results in a large reduction of valuable government benefits (the loss of Medicaid, food stamps, housing allowances, etc.)

A subtle variation on the direct approach is not really about redistribution from rich to poor, although that rhetoric is used, but about politicizing as many choices as possible. The argument is that a larger fraction of the economy's benefits (food, housing, health care, gasoline, etc.) should be distributed by government rather than by markets. In theory, we could turn over all of our income to democratically elected officials and let them decide who gets what. But Communism demonstrated that distribution on the basis of *political criteria* and political power is not often "fairer" than distribution on the basis of voluntary market arrangements. Political allocation of goods and services not only leans toward inefficient, one-size-fits-all solutions, but also toward favoritism for those with the most political clout (which does *not* include the poor).

The more familiar direct approach proposes taking much more in taxes from those with higher incomes (such as college-educated, two-earner couples) and using the money to subsidize those with low incomes (such as single parents, graduate students, and seniors who failed to save for retirement).

Some point to Sweden as a practical example of redistribution through the *tax system* (as opposed to the transfer payment system). But Chapter 8 showed that Sweden is most egalitarian when it comes to using income and payroll taxes to punish everyone equally, including the poor. If poor Swedes have anything left to spend after paying those taxes, they also face another 25 percent value-added tax (VAT) on whatever they buy.

Besides, as Abba Lerner explained in 1961, "the tax itself doesn't redistribute income. It only takes income away from rich people."[27] Redistribution occurs only through government *spending*, particularly transfer payments.

The only *federal* spending specifically targeted for low-income people are *means-tested* programs—Temporary Assistance to Needy Families (TANF), which is mainly for single parents, Supplemental Security Income (SSI), which is mainly for elderly poor who do not qualify for Social Security, and the Earned Income Tax Credit (EITC) which is refundable and therefore supplies a check to low-income people who work. There are no federal cash subsidies for nonelderly people without children who are not working, unless they qualify for unemployment or disability insurance.

Aside from Medicaid, the means-tested programs account for a fairly small portion of the U.S. Budget. "In 2004," the CBO reports, "federal outlays for TANF totaled $18 billion, compared with $24 billion for Food Stamp benefits, $30 billion for SSI benefits for nonelderly recipients, $33 billion for the EITC, and $114 billion for the federal share of Medicaid spending on benefits for nonelderly people."[28] Medicaid is by far the biggest of these programs, but the means testing has been expanded in many states to cover people well above the poverty line.

The total spent on all the major means-tested programs was $219 billion in 2004, with less than 37 percent ($81 billion) in cash, the rest in kind. There are a few other in-kind programs that could be included, such as housing allowances and school lunches, and states and counties spend significant sums on such programs too. But the $219 billion figure captures the bulk of redistribution by the federal government—about 10 percent of the $2.2 trillion budget that year. Even the broadest definition of poverty programs does not exceed 16 percent of federal spending.

Many other federal programs affect the distribution of income, of course. The government cannot spend a dollar without someone receiving that dollar. But there would not be all those high-priced lobbyists and lawyers in Washington, D.C., if much of the loot was going to the poor.

In a well-named 1972 book, *Redistribution to the Rich and the Poor*, Kenneth Boulding and Martin Pfaff explained, "The political economy of redistribution... comes fully into its own in those areas that use political power not only as an ameliorative device equalizing income between the rich and the poor but, on the contrary, as an exploitive device leading to the transfer of income from the poor to the middle class, or from the middle to the wealthy."[29]

## MORAL HAZARD AND GENERAL EQUILIBRIUM

Redistribution can have unexpected consequences on both the spending side and the tax side. Programs intended to be of help to those with low incomes can create what economists call a "moral hazard." Subsidized flood insurance encourages people to build in risky areas. Extending unemployment benefits for a longer period has been shown to increase the duration of unemployment and the unemployment rate.

Tax-free savings plans were introduced to encourage people to save money for their children's college education. But students applying for college will not qualify for financial aid if their family has saved much money, so they will be charged much higher tuition than other students whose parents were not so frugal. So, financial aid programs end up discouraging parental saving thereby offsetting to some extent the incentive effect of 529 plans.[30]

On the tax side, programs *intended* to tax the rich may end up having the opposite effect. This was first explained in a 1978 paper in the *Journal of Political Economy*, "Notes on the Estate Tax," by Nobel Laureate Joseph Stiglitz.

The burden of a tax on capital may initially *appear* to fall on the rich, he noted, because they own most claims to property such as stocks and bonds, as well as real estate. But that conclusion would be premature, an illustration of *partial* equilibrium—not seeing beyond the initial impact. General equilibrium has to consider how people will react to such a tax. A tax on capital, Stiglitz emphasized, will discourage capital accumulation and therefore make capital scarcer. But anything that becomes scarcer also becomes more valuable: Those who owned real property could charge higher rents; those with savings could demand higher interest rates.

Those who own capital, Stiglitz concluded, do not really bear the long-term burden of the capital tax. In a world of increasing capital mobility, after all, the *after-tax* return on capital has to rise to an internationally competitive level in any event, or capital will stay scarce (or flee the country) until it does.

Because capital becomes scarcer, and the cost of capital gets higher as a result of a higher tax on capital, businessmen will make fewer investments in productivity-improving equipment. With less capital per worker, there must be less real *output* per worker and therefore less real *income* per worker. The tax on capital, in short, holds back the growth of productivity and real wages.

In general equilibrium, the capital gains tax ends up being shifted to labor—in the form of slower growth of wages and/or faster growth of consumer prices. As a result, Stiglitz concluded that "reductions in savings and capital accumulation will, in the long run, lead to a lower capital-labor ratio; and the lower capital-labor ratio will . . . lead to an increase in the share of capital. Since income from capital is more unequally distributed than is labor income, the increase in the proportion of income accruing to capital may increase the total inequality of income."[31]

We always need to think very carefully about how *incentives* would change if the government either attempted to collect much more tax revenue from those with high incomes or tried to provide much larger transfer payments to those with low incomes.[32]

## A TRADE-OFF BETWEEN FAIRNESS AND PROSPERITY?

In welfare economics, any change that makes even one person better off without making anyone else worse off is considered "Pareto optimal" (named for the Italian economist Vilfredo Pareto). Martin Feldstein, president of the National Bureau of Economic Research, invoked the concept of Pareto optimality to explain a core issue in the income distribution debate:

When professional economists think about economic problems we generally start with the Pareto principle that a change is good if it makes someone better off without making anyone else worse off. . . . A change that increases the incomes of high-income individuals without decreasing the incomes of others meets that test: it makes some people better off without making anyone else worse off. . . . There is nothing wrong with an increase in well-being of the well-off or with an increase in inequality that results in higher incomes.[33]

It has become commonplace to suggest there is a simple trade-off between greater equality and economic efficiency, so that choosing one over the other is just a matter of taste. That trade-off actually refers to the types of distortions and disincentives that reduce economic growth, not efficiency per se.

The relevant trade-off is between governmental efforts to equalize incomes and private incentives to work hard, to learn new skills, start new businesses, and to accumulate capital by saving and investing. Government efforts to redistribute income through taxes and transfers tend to discourage productive activity among both those paying the taxes *and* those receiving transfer payments. If work is taxed and nonwork is subsidized, we should expect less work and more nonwork.

A prominent columnist believes it is not "unreasonable for a society to decide that it is willing to sacrifice a half percentage point of GDP growth to achieve greater social harmony."[34] Deliberately sacrificing even a half percentage of GDP growth every year would take a greater and greater toll on the actual real incomes of *future* generations. Because of compound interest, a half percentage point a year would add up to a substantially smaller economy in twenty years but a *much* smaller economy in fifty years.[35] Besides, those who set out to trim economic growth by just a tiny bit often end up being far more successful than they expected.

Since about 1980, many countries abandoned the notion that high marginal tax rates produce equity or harmony. Quite a few cut their highest income tax rates in *half*, sometimes more. They found the trade-off turned out to be a great deal more dramatic than a mere half percentage point of added economic growth each year.

There is more to economic growth than tax policy of course—including sound money, secure property rights, and free trade (import competition keeps efficiency high and costs low). Yet lowering the highest tax rates is one thing all "economic miracles" had in common.[36]

## THE LIMITS OF REDISTRIBUTIVE TAXATION

If high marginal tax rates on high incomes were an *effective* way to collect tax revenue (whether for redistribution or just to pay government salaries), it would be puzzling to explain why at least fifty countries dramatically *reduced* their highest individual income tax rates in the 1980s and/or the 1990s. Table 9.3 shows a very small sample of the most dramatic changes in top individual income tax rates (and it does not show the *corporate* tax rate, which was slashed to 12.5 percent in Ireland).

*Economic Growth* by Robert J. Barro and Xavier Sala-i-Martin lists among the world's twenty fastest growing economies Taiwan, Singapore, South Korea, Hong Kong, Botswana, Thailand, Ireland, Malaysia, Portugal, Mauritius, and Indonesia.[37] *All* of them slashed top tax rates dramatically, often by half. By now we would surely have to add India and Russia to the

**TABLE 9.3**
**Maximum Marginal Tax Rates on Individual Income**

|                | 1979 | 1990 | 2004 |
|----------------|------|------|------|
| Botswana       | 75   | 50   | 25   |
| Hong Kong      | 25   | 25   | 16   |
| India          | 60   | 50   | 30   |
| Ireland        | 65   | 56   | 42   |
| South Korea    | 89   | 50   | 36   |
| Mauritius      | 50   | 35   | 25   |
| Russia         | NA   | 60   | 13   |
| Singapore      | 55   | 33   | 22   |
| United Kingdom | 83   | 40   | 40   |
| United States  | 70   | 28   | 35   |

*Source:* Price Waterhouse Coopers, *Individual Income Taxes.*

list of economies that began expanding *much more rapidly* after their highest marginal tax rates were sharply reduced.

That linkage between policy and results might be dismissed as mere coincidence, but the people and governments of these countries do not think so. Their political leaders discovered that a growing economy means a growing tax base. Because the value of incomes, sales, and property rose more rapidly after top tax rates came down, so did tax receipts collected from incomes, sales, and property. Rather than continue trying to extract a large *average* share of a slow-growing economy (and a tax-avoiding underground economy), these governments found it *more effective* to instead have their tax collectors claim a reasonable *marginal* share of a rapidly expanding economy. A larger economy has more income, and more to redistribute.

Never before in world history has there been so rapid a reduction in poverty as that experienced by India and China in the very recent past.[38] If we had good statistics on income distribution before and after India and China decided economic growth was more important than *enforced equality*, however, they would surely show a dramatic increase in inequality. The Russian economy (and stock market) has also grown very rapidly since the top tax rate was reduced to 13 percent. In Russia too, income inequality is doubtless much higher than it was in the Soviet Union (aside from the Party elite).

What such stark before-and-after contrasts show us is that in countries where nearly everyone is poor, and the government makes it impossible or illegal to get rich by starting a new business, most measures of inequality are bound to look "good." That was true of India and China during their impoverished socialist past, and it is still true of many of the world's poorest nations.

The World Bank's *World Development Indicators* for 2006 shows that the poorest fifth received an unusually large 6.4 percent share of all income in Guinea, 6.5 percent in Mozambique, 7.3 percent in Tanzania, and 9.1 percent in Ethiopia. The latest available Gini index was an egalitarian 30 in Ethiopia, 34.4 in Egypt, compared with 44.7 in China. The top 10 percent earn 28.5 percent of total income in India, 34.9 percent in China, but only 25.5 percent in Ethiopia.[39] Despite their statistically lower level of inequality, the Ethiopians would gladly change places with the Chinese because the Chinese are making rapid progress.

## CONCLUSION

Throughout this book we have encountered several dismal descriptions of the U.S. economy. They are often assembled in a package that includes the following strange beliefs about what has happened in the U.S. economy since the stagflation of the 1970s:

- Some 80–90 percent of U.S. households are said to have experienced no increase, if not a decline, in real income for twenty-five to thirty years such income stagnation is said to have been caused by twenty-five to thirty years of stagnation in average real wages.

- Stagnation of average wages is said to have been caused by the replacement of high-paid, union factory jobs with low-paid, nonunion retail jobs, and a related drop in labor's share of national income.

- Only the top 1–10 percent is said to have received any significant benefit from the growth of productivity or from the rise in prices of stocks and homes.

- And those in the top 1–10 percent are said to have somehow obtained those gains at the expense of the shrinking middle class.

Not one of those statements is even remotely close to being true, as this book has tried to explain. It is difficult to imagine how so many of the nation's leading economic journalists and economists claim to believe not just one or two of these incredible ideas but the entire package.

There have certainly been a few nasty oil shocks and/or recessions since 1983, but they have been *much* milder than those of 1974–1975 and 1980–1982. The long-term economic trend since 1983 has been far stronger than any other major industrial country, and the gains in labor income, investment income, and wealth have been widespread.

No matter what one thinks ought to be done about taxes, spending, unions, immigration, trade, minimum wage laws, and so on, the first thing that needs to be done is to get the facts right. If that happens there will still be plenty of room for lively debates about all sorts of public policies. And they will be *honest* debates.

## NOTES

1. Kaplow and Shavell offer rigorous economic and legal arguments for *not* basing public policy on "fairness," particularly when doing so conflicts with efficiency as defined by the new welfare economics. Louis Kaplow and Steven Shavell, *Fairness versus Welfare* (Cambridge, MA: Harvard University Press, 2002). See also Edward E. Zajac, *Political Economy of Fairness* (Cambridge, MA: MIT Press, 1995), particularly chapters 7–12.

2. David R. Henderson, Robert M. McNab and Tamás Rózsás, "The Hidden Inequality in Socialism," *Independent Review*, vol. 9(3) (Winter 2005). http://www.independent.org/publications/tir/article.asp?issueID=40andarticleID=503.

3. *Economic Indicators* (March 2006), p. 5. http://www.gpoaccess.gov/indicators/index.html.

4. Barry Bluestone, "The Inequality Express," *American Prospect*, vol. 6(12) (December 1, 1995).

5. Frank Levy and Richard Murnane, "U.S. Earnings Levels and Earnings Inequality: A Review of Recent Trends and Proposed Explanations," *Journal of Economic Literature*, vol. 30(1) (September 1992).

6. Finis Welch, ed., *The Causes and Consequences of Increasing Inequality* (Chicago: University of Chicago Press, 2001), p. 2.

7. Robert I. Lerman, "Is Earnings Inequality Really Increasing?" (Washington, DC: The Urban Institute, March 1997).

8. Michelle Conlin and Aaron Bernstein, "Working . . . And Poor," *Business Week*, May 31, 2004. This error-filled cover story said, "Wal-Mart pays its full-time hourly workers . . . about a third of the level of the union chains." A later correction said it "should have described the average hourly pay at Wal-Mart Stores Inc. ($9.64) as one-third less than the union chains (not one-third of their level)."

9. Nell Henderson, "Effect of Immigration on Jobs, Wages Is Difficult for Economists to Nail Down," *Washington Post*, April 25, 2006.

10. Robert J. Samuelson, "News Cut to Fashion," *Washington Post*, March 13, 1996.

11. *Economic Report of the President* (February, 2006), table B-46.

12. Asian Development Bank, *Key Indicators of Developing and Asian Pacific Countries* (2005), p. 214. http://www.adb.org/Documents/Books/Key_Indicators/2005/pdf/PRC.pdf.

13. *Economic Report of the President* (February 2006), table B-46.

14. Steven J. Davis, John C. Haltiwanger, and Scott Schuh, *Job Creation and Destruction* (Cambridge, MA: MIT Press, 1996).

15. *Economic Report of the President* (February 2006), table B-37.

16. Robert Reich, "Bringing Back Manufacturing," *American Prospect*, vol. 14(9) (September 17, 2003). http://www.prospect.org/webfeatures/2003/09/reich-r-09-17.html.

17. Michael R. Pakko, "Labor's Share," Federal Reserve Bank of St. Louis National Economic Trends (August 2004). http://research.stlouisfed.org/publications/net/20040801/cover.pdf.

18. Dew-Becker and Gordon, "Where Did the Productivity Growth Go?" p. 22.

19. See Alan Reynolds, "Dropout Nation?" *Townhall.com* (April 14, 2006). http://www.cato.org/pub_display.php?pub_id=6352; Alan Reynolds, "Immigration as Random Rationing," in *Blueprints for and Ideal Legal Immigration Policy*, eds., Richard D. Lamm and Alan Simpson(Washington, DC: Center for Immigration Studies, 2001). http://cis.org/articles/2001/blueprints/reynolds.html.

20. Thomas Lemieux, "Increasing Residual Wage Inequality" (May 2005). http://www.econ.ubc.ca/lemieux/papers/within.pdf.

21. David H. Autor, Lawrence F. Katz, and Melissa S. Kearny, "Trends in U.S Wage Inequality: Re-Assessing the Revisionists" (September 2005). http://econwww.mit.edu/faculty/download_pdf.php?id=967.

22. Thomas Lemieux, "Post-secondary Education and Increasing Wage Inequality," *American Economic Review* (May 2006).

23. Robert E. Lucas, Jr., "Supply-Side Economics: An Analytical Review," *Oxford Economic Papers* (April 1990), pp. 293–316. http://ideas.repec.org/a/oup/oxecpp/v42y1990i2p293-316.html.

24. Jagadeesh Gokhale, Laurence Kotlikoff, and Alexi Sluchynsky, "Does It Pay to Work?" *NBER Working Paper* w9096 (August 2002). http://www.nber.org/papers/w9096.

25. See Alan Reynolds, "The Future of Jobs in the United States and Europe," in *OECD Societies in Transition: The Future of Work and Leisure* (Paris: OECD, 1994). http://www.oecd.org/dataoecd/26/32/17780767.pdf.

26. See Edward C. Prescott, "Why Do Americans Work So Much More Than Europeans?" Federal Reserve Bank of Minneapolis *Quarterly Review* (July 2004). http://minneapolisfed.org/research/qr/qr2811.pdf; Philip A. Trostel, "The Effect of Taxation on Human Capital," *Journal of Political Economy*, vol. 101(2) (1993), pp. 327–50. http://econpapers.hhs.se/article/ucpjpolec/v_3A101_3Ay_3A1993_3Ai_3A2_3Ap_3A327-50.htm.

27. Lerner, *Everybody's Business*, p. 99.

28. Congressional Budget Office, "Changes in Participation in Means-Tested Programs" (April 20, 2005).

29. Kenneth E. Boulding and Martin Pfaff, *Redistribution to the Rich and the Poor* (Belmont, CA: Wadsworth Publishing, 1972), p. 5. Benjamin Okner, on page 65, reported that even the distribution of social welfare spending was "fairly close to 50-50 between the poor and nonpoor." A lot of other federal spending (such as subsidies to farmers and ethanol producers) is clearly tilted toward the rich.

30. See Alan Reynolds, "The Real Cost of Higher Education, Who Should Pay It and How?" in *Straight Talk about College Costs and Prices* (The National Commission on the Cost of Higher Education, Phoenix, AZ: Oryx Press, 1999).

31. Joseph E. Stiglitz, "Notes on Estate Taxes," *Journal of Political Economy* 86, no. 2 (1978).

32. See Bernard Salanie, *The Economics of Taxation* (Cambridge, MA: MIT Press, 2003) and Joseph E. Stiglitz, *Economics of the Public Sector*, 2nd ed. (New York: W.W. Norton, 1988). Stiglitz is the easier of these two; the second edition has the advantage of having been written before he became politically involved (as CEA chairman in the Clinton Administration).

33. Martin Feldstein, "Is Income Inequality Really a Problem?" in *Income Inequality: Issues and Policy Options* (The Federal Reserve Bank of Kansas City, 1998), pp. 357–60.

34. Steven Pearlstein, "Solving Inequality Problem Won't Take Class Warfare," *Washington Post*, March 15, 2006.

35. Measured in constant 2000 dollars, real GDP per capita rose from $22,666 in 1980 to $36,596 in 2004, or about 2.6 percent a year. If per capita economic growth had been just 0.5 percent slower each year, real GDP per capita would have been $34,089 in 2004—7 percent smaller than it actually was. With less real output per person, there would have to be less real income per person. In only 24 years, a half percentage difference in economic growth would have amounted to about $2500 less for every man, woman, and child.

Louis D. Johnston and Samuel H. Williamson, "The Annual Real and Nominal GDP for the United States, 1790–Present," Economic History Services (October 2005). http://www.eh.net/hmit/gdp/.

36. Alan Reynolds, "National Prosperity Is No Mystery," *Orbis* (Spring 1996). http://www.findarticles.com/p/articles/mi_m0365/is_n2_v40/ai_18338846.

37. Robert J. Barro and Xavier Sala-i-Martin, *Economic Growth* (Cambridge, MA: MIT Press, 2004), p. 514.

38. Surjit Bhalla, *Imagine There's No Country* (Washington, DC: Institute for International Economics, 2002). http://bookstore.iie.com/merchant.mvc?Screen=PROD&Product_Code=348; Xavier Sala-i-Martin, "The World Distribution of Income: Falling Poverty and . . . Convergence, Period," *Quarterly Journal of Economics* (forthcoming, 2006). http://www.columbia.edu/~xs23/papers/pdfs/World_Income_Distribution_QJE.pdf.

39. World Bank, *World Development Indicators*, 2006, Table 2.8. http://devdata.worldbank.org/wdi2006/contents/Section2.htm.

# Glossary

**Adjusted Gross Income (AGI).** The broadest concept of income reported on individual income tax returns. The largest "adjustments" that make AGI smaller than actual income are for contributions to tax-deferred retirement accounts. Since such accounts barely existed before 1980, and allowed contributions are much larger than they used to be, this is one of many reasons why AGI cannot be legitimately compared between 1970–1980 and any recent years. Adjustments for student loan interest also make recent AGI different from past AGI.

**Agency Problem.** Also known as the principal-agent problem, this refers to the fact that corporate executives are agents of the owners (stockholders). The interests of agents and owners may not be the same unless incentives are put in place to align them (such as paying executives with stock or options to buy stock). Similar agency problems may include pension fund managers acting as agents of pension fund investors.

**Asset.** In the context of household rather than business wealth (which includes goodwill, copyrights, and other intangible capital), assets normally refer to homes, consumer durables, stocks, bonds, and money in the bank.

**Average.** The word "average" usually refers to a "mean" or arithmetic average. Total income earned by the top 20 percent of households divided by the number of households in the top 20 percent, for example, equals that group's average (mean) income per household. See *median* and *mode*.

**Bureau of Economic Analysis (BEA).** Part of the Commerce Department, the BEA produces estimates of GDP, personal income, corporate profits, and so on. See *GDP* and *PCE*.

**Bureau of Labor Statistics (BLS).** Part of the Labor Department, the BLS produces consumer and producer price indexes, estimates of productivity (output per hour worked) and real compensation per hour, international comparisons of labor costs, and others. See *CPI*.

**Capital.** Any asset that produces real or in-kind income in the future. Capital can mean financial capital such as stocks and bonds; real capital such as a factory, office, or apartment building; and human capital such as education and experience. Owning your own home is capital that produces *in-kind* income in the form of implicit rent (the value of which is imputed in some studies). See *Asset* and *Net Worth*.

**Census Bureau.** The premier source of detailed estimates of the U.S. population, income, poverty, health, and housing as well as economic indicators by sector such as manufacturing, retailing, and construction. See *CPS* and *Statistical Abstract*.

**Chain-weighted.** The prices within every price index are given higher or lower weights depending on each item's relative importance in a "typical" budget. If the weights are rarely changed, as is the case with the CPI, the index is called a fixed-weight index. A chain-weighted index reflects changes in the way consumers spend their money by using an average mix (a smoothed moving average) of the quantities bought in the current and prior years.[1] There is a relatively new chain-weighted CPI, but a longer time series is available for the PCE deflator. See *CPI* and *PCE*.

**Constant dollars.** Every price index defines some year or set of years (such as 1982–1984) as the base year where the index is set at 100. If the weighted average of prices rises by 2.5 percent in the following year, then the index equals 102.5. If prices then rise by another 2 percent in the second year, the index would be 104.5. Unless inflation was zero or less (deflation), years before the base year are *smaller* than 100 (much smaller if we look back enough years). If the base year is 2000, and all *nominal* figures have been adjusted for inflation, then they can be said to be expressed in *constant* 2000 dollars.

**Consumer durables.** Goods expected to last for about three years or more, such as cars, appliances, and furniture. See *Assets*.

**Consumer Expenditure Survey (CEX).** A quarterly panel survey by the BLS.

**Consumer Price Index (CPI).** The most commonly used measure of inflation is the CPI-U. Another measure, the CPI-W for Urban Wage Earners and Clerical Workers is narrower in scope, but still in use to adjust annual Social Security benefits and to estimate real average weekly wages (a major topic of Chapter 4 of this book). The 1996 Boskin Commission estimated the CPI exaggerated inflation by more than 1 percent per year, but subsequent changes appear to have reduced the upward bias to less than 0.7 percent per year.[2] The improved series (CPI-U-RS) is available for years going back to 1978.[3]

**Current Population Survey (CPS).** A monthly survey of about 50,000 households conducted by the Bureau of the Census for the Bureau of Labor Statistics for more than fifty years. It represents the civilian noninstitutional population age 16 and up showing estimates of employment, unemployment, earnings, and hours of work. The data are available by age, sex, race, marital status, educational attainment, occupation, and industry. Supplemental questions cover school enrollment, income, previous work experience, health insurance, and other employee benefits.

**Earned Income Tax Credit (EITC).** A refundable federal tax credit for qualified low-income workers, including those who worked part-time for a short period. In 2005, a single parent with two children under age 19 (or 24 if students) be eligible for $4,400 if income was below $35,263. A married couple without children would need an income lower than $13,750 and receive only $399. Investment income could not exceed $2700, which imposes an implicit marginal tax on frugality (if you save, you lose the EITC).[4]

**Egalitarian.** Someone who advocates that everyone should receive more-or-less equal shares of income and/or wealth regardless of effort (see incentives) or personal merit (see meritocracy).

**Elasticity.** An estimate of responsiveness of one variable to another. If the two variables are X and Y, then elasticity equals the percentage change in X divided by the percentage change in Y. The elasticity is sometimes negative (more of X is associated with less of Y) but minus signs are nonetheless often omitted.

**Empirical.** Factual observations. Common references to "empirical evidence" are redundant, since there is no other kind of evidence. The phrase "theoretical evidence" is sometimes used, but it is quite ambiguous. We may need theory to explain evidence, and to make predictions about what the evidence will show, but theory without evidence is just hypothetical—a *hypothesis*.

**Employee and/or Executive Stock Options.** These are "call" options, meaning they confer the right to *buy* a certain number of corporate shares in the future—usually at the market price at the time the options are granted ("put" options confer the right to sell). If the stock prices rise after the options are vested (usually 3–4 years) and before they expire (usually 10 years), the difference between the grant price and the selling (or "strike") price results in a capital gain. With *incentive stock options* (ISOs) the exercised shares have to be held long enough to qualify for the gain to be taxed at the tax rate for long-term capital gains, which was lower than the ordinary income-tax rate except from 1988 to 1990. Other options are "nonqualified" for capital gains taxation because the shares are sold soon after they are exercised. Gains from nonqualified options are taxed the same as salaries, and therefore became more popular after ordinary income tax rates came down (and/or capital gains tax rates went up).

**Employee Compensation.** Total employee compensation includes wages and salaries plus benefits, including mandatory government benefits (notably, the employer's half of the Social Security tax). The BLS provides an index of real hourly compensation for the private business, nonfarm business and nonfinancial corporate business sectors in conjunction with estimates of output per hour (productivity). The BLS offers an employment cost index, which is a gauge of what firms pay for wages, salaries, and benefits. The difference between what employers pay (including work-related taxes) and what employees receive (after income and payroll taxes) is called a "tax wedge."

**Equilibrium.** When changes are complete and the situation is restored to balance it is considered in equilibrium. For example, an increased price will normally reduce demand and increase supply, but equilibrium is restored after that happens. If price controls kept the price too low the result would be "disequilibrium" (a shortage). If price controls kept the price too high the result would be a surplus or glut. See *General Equilibrium*.

**Expanded Income.** In addition to the Census Bureau's fifteen experimental measures of income, several federal agencies measure income (and income distribution) quite differently.[5] The Congressional Budget Office's version of expanded income is adjusted gross income from tax returns plus taxable capital gains (including the 50–60 percent that was excluded from 1978 to 1986) and "certain tax preference items." The Joint Committee on Taxation (JCT) begins with AGI and adds tax-exempt interest, employer contributions for life and health insurance, the employer's share of Social Security and Medicare payroll tax, and "preference items" (the largest of which are state taxes and personal exemptions). These additions greatly increase measured income among the top two quintiles, yet the JCT *excludes means-tested transfer payments* from the bottom two quintiles. The Treasury's Office of Tax Analysis (OTA) also includes interest on tax-exempt bonds when estimating how many taxpayers with nominal "expanded incomes" above $200,000 did not pay income tax, which makes it incorrect for journalists (e.g., at the *New York Times*) to compare such figures before and after 1987—the first year interest on tax-exempt bonds was reported.

**401(k) Accounts.** One of the largest of many tax-deferred savings plans for retirement.

**529 Accounts.** Tax-deferred savings plans for education. The investment income is currently tax-exempt rather than tax-deferred if used for approved educational expenses.

**Family.** Two or more people who are related and living together. Unlike the Census Bureau, income distribution studies by the Congressional Budget Office define a one-person household as a "one-person family," except among the highest-income groups (such as the top 1 percent) where CBO estimates make no effort to adjust for family size.

**General Equilibrium.** Changes in taxes and transfer payments affect incentives and therefore have secondary effects on the whole economy. Yet a partial equilibrium analysis (of the sort commonly used to estimate who will bear the burden of higher tax rates) assumes that only direct and immediate effects matter, and that no other prices or wages are affected. "General equilibrium effects have important distributional consequences," Joseph Stiglitz explained, "sometimes in a direction quite opposite of the intent of the legislation. A tax on capital may reduce the supply of capital, thereby increasing the return to capital; in some instances, the degree of inequality may actually be increased by such a tax."[6]

**Gini Coefficient.** A broad measure of the degree of inequality of various measures of income, wages, or consumption. Zero would be total equality (each percentile gets the same 1 percent share) and the number one would mean total inequality (one person has all the income). Because there are many ways to measure incomes, wages, and consumption, there are many Gini coefficients, and therefore no one measure can be considered definitive evidence that inequality has increased or decreased (an often neglected question is —inequality of *what?*).

**Great Compression.** A phrase from a 1992 paper by Claudia Goldin and Robert A. Margo referring to 1940–1950, when differences in labor income became much narrower than they were in the late 1920s or late 1980s.[7] This period starts during the Great Depression and Thomas Piketty and Emmanuel Saez found, "In contrast to capital income, the Great Depression did not produce a reduction in top wage shares. On the contrary, the high middle class fractiles benefited in relative terms from the Great Depression."[8] The compression after 1942 included severe wage controls and rationing during World War II, which (equal suffering aside) was no more an idyllic "golden age" than the Depression. Goldin and Margo mainly attribute wage compression in the 1940s to the scarcity of unskilled labor. Millions of young men were shipped overseas to fight and hundreds of thousands never returned, even as postwar rebuilding and pent-up requirement raised the demand for scarce manpower.

**Gross Domestic Product (GDP).** An estimate of the market value of all goods and services produced within a country (including many services of governments and nonprofit institutions that are not sold and therefore have an unknown market value). It is "gross" product because it includes an estimate of the depreciation (wear and tear), while net national product or income does not. It is "domestic" because, unlike Gross National Product (GNP), it does not consider imports or exports. GDP is habitually described by its uses (how money is spent) rather than its sources (how money is earned). Purchases of consumer goods and services account for a very large share of the way GDP is *used*, but production of goods and services (mainly by businesses) creates the incomes and wealth that enable consumers to spend.

**Household.** One or more people sharing the same housing (see family). Income distribution estimates are by household, family, or taxpaying unit because to construct such estimates for individuals would make it appear that *all* children and nonworking spouses were poor regardless of the income of the head of the household.

**Human Capital.** To acquire valuable job skills requires investing time and/or money in acquiring education (formal schooling) and on-the-job training (experience). As in the case of investments in real capital (land) or financial capital (stocks and bonds), investments in human capital are expected to pay a return in the form of a higher future income over a person's remaining years of working life.

**Imputed Income.** Since income is not always received as money, the IRS requires that the value of some employer-provided benefits (such as life insurance policies above $50,000; child care above $5,000) be considered income when calculating taxes. Economists likewise impute (ascribe) income in some studies, such as the "imputed rent" that home owners pay to themselves.

**Incidence.** Those who write checks to pay taxes are not necessarily the ones who actually bear the burden. And some who do not appear to be paying taxes (such as owners of tax-exempt bonds) actually bear the burden.

**Income.** There are at least eighteen official definitions of income used in income distribution studies, and several other private definitions. There are also several sources of income statistics, including Census Bureau and Federal Reserve surveys and a sample of income tax returns. Income may or may not subtract some taxes, and may or may not include transfer payments, taxable capital gains, tax-exempt interest income, imputed rent on homes, employer-financed benefits, and the like. When investigating what happened to the growth or distribution of income, we first have to ask what is meant by "income." See *Expanded Income* and *Imputed Income.*

**In-kind income.** This refers to income not received as cash, such as (1) Medic-aid, food stamps, and housing allowance, but also (2) employer-paid benefits and perquisites for higher-income employees. "*Expanded income*" usually counts the second type of in-kind income but not the former, thus exaggerating inequality.

**Intergenerational mobility.** The degree of similarity or difference in income, wealth, education, and/or status between parents and their children.

**Keogh plan.** A tax-deferred retirement savings plan for the self-employed.

**Labor force and the labor-force participation rate.** In the BLS survey of house-holds, everyone over the age of 16 who says they are working or looking for work are members of the labor force. That number divided by the population over age 16 is the labor force-participation rate.

**Longitudinal or Panel study.** Observing the same people and/or families over time. See *PSID* and *NLS.*

**Marginal Tax Rate.** The tax on the next dollar earned. In 2004, married couples paid 10 percent on the first $14,300 of *taxable* income (after exemptions, deduc-tions, and adjustments). After that the tax was 15 percent on additional (mar-ginal) dollars earned up to $58,100, then 25 percent above that up to $117,250 when the next dollar would be taxed at 28 percent, and so on up to the top rates of 33 percent and 35 percent. Those in the highest 35 percent tax bracket also pay 10 percent on the first $14,300, then 15 percent on the next $43,800, so the *average* tax rate (taxes paid divided by income) is always lower than the marginal tax rate. Largely because the EITC and child tax credit are phased-out as low-income families earn more, *marginal* income and payroll taxes on an *extra* dollar earned could reach a discouraging 51 percent on four-person families earning only half the median income if the United States reverted to pre-2001 tax law.[9]

**Market Capitalization.** The market value of all outstanding shares of a corporation. If there are 10 million shares and the stock is selling for $10 a share, the firm's market value is $100 million.

**Means-tested.** Government programs that require that income and/or savings be below certain level as a condition of eligibility for benefits. Examples include the food stamp program run by the Department of Agriculture, housing allowances run by the Department of Housing and Urban Development, Medicaid and TANF run by the Department of Health and Human Services, SSI run by the Social Security Administration, and the EITC run by the Treasury Department. Each program has different criteria for eligibility, and criteria for some programs (notably Medicaid) differ by state. Poverty alone is almost never a sufficient condition for federal as-sistance. For example, "the Medicaid program does not provide health-care services, even for very poor persons, unless they are in one of the designated eligibility groups." (http://www.cms.hhs.gov/MedicaidGenInfo/)

**Median.** A median (also known as the 50th percentile) is the mid-point dividing a group, so that half the group is above the median and half, below. Because only the top 1–20 percent has no income ceiling, a mean average for any top-income group is substantially larger than the median. Median incomes or wage rates can be *diluted* by adding more low-income people to the mix through welfare reform or immigration. Suppose there were nine people on an island and one earned $10 an hour, another $20, another $30, and so on up to $90. Together they earn a total of $450 an hour or a *mean* average of $50 apiece. The median happens to be $50 because half earn more than that and half earn less. If two new people move in and they each earn $20 an hour, then the mean hourly wage would fall to $45 but the median would fall to $40—without anyone's wage being reduced.

**Mode or Modal.** A modal average leaves off the extremes, because a small number of outliers might give a distorted picture of the average. Leaving off the top and bottom ten or 10 percent, for example, might be done to approximate a "middle" income level. Tax-based studies of income distribution usually leave out taxpayers with negative incomes (net losses), and a case could be made for also excluding the top 1 percent for similar reasons.

**National Longitudinal Surveys (NLS).** These BLS surveys follow a sample of people over time as they grow older. There are two of youth, one starting in 1979 (followed by another study of their children), the other in 1997. There are also earlier studies of young and older women, and of men.

**Net Worth or Wealth.** Assets minus liabilities (debts). Human capital is rarely counted as an asset (which would be difficult). But it is logically incorrect to consider student loans as a liability, for example, without putting the offsetting value of higher education on the other side of the ledger.

**Noncognitive skills.** Cognitive skills related to reasoning ability are approximated by IQ tests. However, Nobel Laureate James Heckman finds noncognitive skills developed early in life, such as patience and perseverance, may be just as important to on-the-job performance and, therefore, lifetime income.[10]

**Panel Study of Income Dynamics (PSID).** Begun in 1968 at the University of Michigan, this is a longitudinal study consisting of repeated interviews over the years of a sample of individuals in 4,800 U.S. families (the number has since grown to nearly 8,000, largely because births exceeded deaths). The PSID is the leading source used in income mobility studies. See *Intergenerational mobility* and *longitudinal studies*.

**Pareto Optimality.** A situation in which nobody can be made better off without making someone else worse off. If a change in the allocation of income (goods) would be preferred by some but not by others, it is not Pareto optimal.[11] Gains from greater efficiency or economic progress, by contrast, *can* make some better off without making others worse off.

**Percentiles, Deciles, Quintiles, and Quartiles.** There are 100 percentiles in any sample, but there can also be fractions of a percentile, such the top 0.01 percent. The tenth percentile is the same as the first decile; the fiftieth percentile is the same as the median. There are four quartiles in any sample, five quintiles (fifths) and ten deciles (tenths). The name depends on whether the pie is sliced into four, five, ten, or hundred pieces.

**Personal Consumption Expenditures Deflator (PCE).** The price index used to convert *nominal* spending on personal consumption into *real*, inflation-adjusted dollars. The more comprehensive GDP deflator, which includes business expenses, the PCE deflator is chain-weighted, while the usual CPI is not. See chain-weighted.

**Price Index.** All price indexes have trouble dealing with *new* products, *improved* products (a new pill is not just more expensive, it may be much more effective), and changes in unseen discounts (such as free shipping). But fixed-weight indexes like the CPI also have particular trouble dealing with *substitution* (of apples for oranges if the price of oranges rises). That is why chain-weighted indexes measure inflation more accurately. See *Chain-Weighted, CPI, PCE Deflator*, and *Constant dollars*.

**Quintiles (fifths).** See *Percentiles*

**Real and Nominal.** To estimate "real" income, wealth, or GDP, one begins with a time series of *nominal* values (in dollars) and adjusts those figures for inflation by using the most appropriate and accurate price index available.

**Redistribution.** Spending tax receipts collected from people with average and above-average incomes on programs intended to raise the money income or in-kind income of people with low or below-average incomes. See *Means-Tested*.

**Roth IRA and Roth 401(k).** Under a traditional IRA or 401(k), contributions are not taxed. If a taxpayer earned $40,000 and contributed $4,000 to such a plan, that taxpayer's "adjusted" gross income (AGI) would be $36,000. After age 59½, money can be withdrawn from such plans without penalty but such withdrawals are taxed as ordinary income. By contrast, contributions to Roth plans are made with income that has already been taxed so there is no additional tax when the money is withdrawn. And all accumulated investment income ("inside build-up") is tax-free. Both the traditional and the Roth approaches result in savings being taxed only once—either when the money is first saved or when it is later withdrawn (presumably to finance consumer spending).[12]

**Securities and Exchange Commission (SEC).** The federal agency that regulates the financial reporting and activities of publicly traded corporations. Such corporations sell shares on a stock exchange such as the New York Stock Exchange and NASDAQ, and are called "Subchapter C" corporations because they pay taxes under the corporate income tax before distributing any earnings to owners (called shareholders or stockholders) as dividends or capital gains.

**Standard & Poors 500 (S&P 500).** An index created by Standard and Poors to measure the average prices of 500 large corporations. This index is weighted by market capitalization, which explains why high-tech stocks gained an increasing weight (had more effect on the average) during the tech boom of 1996–2000.

**Statistics of Income (SOI).** The data-gathering arm of the Internal Revenue Service (IRS).

**Supplemental Security Income (SSI).** A program run by the Social Security Administration, SSI is designed to help aged, blind, and disabled people who have little income and are ineligible for Social Security retirement or disability benefits. Means testing includes some assets, but not a home and car. The program covers mental disability of children and adult children, which created some controversy regarding SSI payments to parents of hyperactive children (considered a learning disability).

**Survey of Consumer Finances (SCF).** A Federal Reserve Board survey of U.S. households that collects information on their wealth (assets and debts) and incomes. This survey has been conducted every three years since 1983. See *Net Worth*.

**Tax Bracket.** Under a graduated or progressive income tax, successive additions to income are taxed at higher (marginal) tax rates as income rises. As income increases into higher tax brackets, the same extra $100 of income will be taxed at higher rates (currently ranging from 10–35 percent).

**Temporary Assistance for Needy Families (TANF).** TANF provides monthly cash assistance (welfare) for poor families with children under age 18. This program replaced Aid to Families with Dependent Children (AFDC) as a result of welfare reform in 1996. Recipients are normally required to work as soon as they are able, and no later than two years after coming on assistance. There is a lifetime limit of five years of benefits.

**Thesis and Hypothesis.** A thesis is a statement of belief about some fact not yet proven (an *academic* thesis, by contrast, begins with a thesis but then attempts to prove it). Within the scientific method, a *hypothesis* refers to a statement of fact that yields predictions capable of being tested by anyone and potentially falsified by factual observation. If the hypothesis is that an increase in variable X (budget deficits) will be followed by an increase in Y (inflation), then inability to demonstrate such a relationship empirically would constitute falsification. Hypotheses cannot be definitively proved true because alternative hypotheses may be equally consistent with the evidence.[13]

**Threshold.** Estimates of the distribution of income commonly involve grouping and ranking households by quintiles (fifths). During periods in which most incomes have been increasing in real terms, the income "threshold" defining the minimum income needed to be in higher income groups also increases. At such times, households whose income remained unchanged may nonetheless be reassigned to a lower income group simply because the thresholds have increased. (The income thresholds defining the amount of taxable income needed to fall into higher or lower tax brackets is an unrelated topic).

**Threshold Illusion.** The author's expression for misinterpreting a long-term change in any top income group's share as having been caused entirely by increased income *within* that group rather than having been partly caused by increased income among those with *lower* incomes. If it used to require only $50,000 to get into the top fifth but now it takes $100,000, that is not simply because those in the top fifth made more money but because there are many more households earning more than $50,000 than there were in the past—shoving the bar higher from below.

**Time Series.** A sequence of data over time—such as monthly, quarterly, or annual.

**Top-Coded.** To preserve confidentiality, public use files from the Census Bureau do not reveal much detail on high incomes—lumping together all income above $100,000, for example. Because the percentage affected by such top coding changes, this might conceivably distort income inequality estimates. Yet the only suggested instance of such a distortion coincided with a 1993 change in Census survey methodology that clearly led to a *one-time* jump in measured inequality.[14]

**Transfer Payments.** Government programs that transfer money or in-kind income from some people to others. Recipients of transfer payments do not necessarily have lower incomes or wealth than those who paid the taxes, except in the case of *means-tested* programs. The largest transfer payments are called "entitlements," because meeting some criterion (such as having worked for the military or having reached certain age) automatically entitles a person to a monthly check or a heavily subsidized service.

**Unemployment Rate.** The percentage of the labor force who say that they are looking for work. In 2005, about 48 percent were unemployed *at some time* during the year because they lost a job, 40 percent were unemployed because they had not worked before or not for quite a while, and 12 percent were unemployed because they quit. And half the unemployed were in that situation for 8.9 weeks or less.

**Variables.** Something that varies, as opposed to a "constant," which does not. In an if-then statement (which typically *implies* but does not necessarily *prove* cause and effect), a change in an *independent* variable is said to be associated with a change in a certain *dependent* variable. A change in the unemployment rate may be associated with a change in the poverty rate; a change in stock prices may be associated with a change in executive compensation. It would not be logical to hypothesize that a change in some *variable* (such as inflation or profits) is associated with a *constant* (such as "greed").

**Wage Inequality.** Wage inequality is only part of income inequality, since it excludes income from investments (which is often very important at high incomes) and from transfer payments (which is often very important at low incomes). Differences in wages per week or year can be due to differences in hours worked, rather than differences in hourly compensation, but some studies not confined to full-time workers obscured this key distinction.

## NOTES

1. For more information, see Charles I. Jones in the *Federal Reserve Bank of San Francisco Economic Letter* (August 2, 2002). http://www.frbsf.org/publications/economics/letter/2002/el2002-22.html.

2. Robert J. Gordon, "The Boskin Commission Report and Its Aftermath," *NBER Working Paper* 7759 (June 2000). http://www.nber.org/papers/W7759.

3. The CPI-U-RS. http://www.bls.gov/cpi/cpiurstx.htm.

4. From the IRS rules. http://www.childpc.org/eitc/docs/p596.pdf.

5. David F. Bradford, *Distributional Analysis of Tax Policy* (Washington, DC: The AEI Press, 1995), particularly chapters 2, 3, 10.

6. Stiglitz, *Economics of the Public Sector*, pp. 393, 430–32.

7. Claudia Goldin and Robert A. Margo, "The Great Compression: The Wage Structure in the United States at Mid-century," *Quarterly Journal of Economics*, vol. 107(1) (1992). See the reference to The Great Compression in Krugman, "The Death of Horatio Alger."

8. Piketty and Saez, "Income Inequality in the United States, 1913–2002," p. 18.

9. Elaine M. Maag, "Marginal Tax Rates, 1955–2005," Tax Notes (February 13, 2006). http://www.urban.org/UploadedPDF/1000875_Tax_Fact_02-13-06.pdf.

10. Some of James Heckman's work on noncognitive skills can be found at: http://www.nber.org/cgi-bin/author_papers.pl?author=james_heckman.

11. On Vilfredo Pareto (1848–1923), see http://cepa.newschool.edu/het/profiles/pareto.htm.

12. Stephen J. Entin, "Growth-Friendly Tax Systems," in *Unleashing America's Potential* (The National Commission on Economic Growth and Tax Reform, New York: St. Martin's Griffin, 1996), pp. 77–91.

13. A classic reference, *The Logic of Scientific Discovery* by Karl Popper, is ably discussed in David Miller, *Critical Rationalism: A Restatement and Defence* (Chicago: Open Court, 1994).

14. Robert Lerman, "Earnings Inequality: An Addendum to 'Is Earnings Inequality Really Increasing?'" Urban Institute (July 1, 1997). http://www.urban.org/publications/307031.html.

# Online Resources

Many of these website links are useful for economic research in general, including a few international links. Other sites are specifically related to the topic of this book—the growth and distribution of income and wealth in the United States. Nearly all these sites are free (with the exception of AEA, WEAI, and NBER). Within each category the links are in order of relative importance, from top to bottom, but the inclusion of a link is not intended to imply the information is accurate.

## INDISPENSABLE STATISTICAL SOURCES

Bureau of Economic Analysis, http://www.bea.gov/bea/interactive.htm.

Bureau of Labor Statistics, http://www.bls.gov. The consumer price index, real compensation per hour, median wages, etc.

Census Bureau, http://www.census.gov or http://www.census.gov/main/www/srchtool.html (search tool). Income distribution by household or family; median household income, etc.

Economic Indicators, http://www.gpoaccess.gov/indicators/index.html. Monthly data updates key figures in the *Economic Report*.

Economic Policy Institute data (EPI), http://www.epinet.org/content.cfm/datazone_dznational.

*Economic Report of the President,* http://www.gpoaccess.gov/eop/. Tables going back to 1929 or 1959 for GDP, employment, real per capita income and consumption, stock market, and others. This site includes the past ten annual reports, each of which contains the Council of Economic Advisors' analyses of topics of interest at the time. For the oldest reports, going back to 1947, see FRASER.

Education Statistics, http://nces.ed.gov/programs/digest/.

FRASER, http://fraser.stlouisfed.org/about/. Federal Reserve archival system for economic research. Mainly useful for historical research, particularly about the Federal Reserve and monetary policy.

FRED, http://research.stlouisfed.org/fred2/. More than 3,000 U.S. economic time series, past and current, covering industrial production, GDP, interest rates, oil prices, inflation, and much more. The data can be downloaded in Microsoft Excel and text formats or viewed as a chart.

*Historical U.S. GDP heroic estimates back to 1790*, http://www.eh.net/hmit/gdp/.

*Statistical Abstract of the United States,* http://www.census.gov/statab/www/.


## ECONOMISTS' ARTICLES AND WORKING PAPERS

Alan Reynolds (Cato Institute), http://www.cato.org/people/reynolds.html. Archive of my weekly columns and other articles.

Alberto Alesina (Harvard), http://post.economics.harvard.edu/faculty/alesina/alesina.html.

American Economics Association (AEA), http://www.aeaweb.org/e-pubs/. An AEA membership provides an inexpensive way to access JSTOR.org to search economic literature, plus the *American Economic Review, Journal of Economic Literature*, and *Journal of Economic Perspectives*.

Economics Research Network, http://www.ssrn.com/ern/index.html.

*Encyclopedia of Economics* http://www.econlib.org/library/CEE.html. This is a good place to start—a remarkable collection of short explanations of almost every imaginable economic topic by a wide variety of experts. See the editor's home page, http://www.davidrhenderson.com/index.html.

James Heckman (University of Chicago & University College, London), http://www.econ.ucl.ac.uk/displayProfile.php?staff_key=258.

Karl Marx, http://libcom.org/library/critique-of-the-gotha-program-karl-marx. Unlike those that Karl Popper dubbed "vulgar Marxists" (and whom Marx called "vulgar socialists"), Karl Marx was a revolutionist *not* a redistributionist. In this widely misunderstood essay, Marx considered the whole notion of "fair distribution" to be "obsolete verbal rubbish." In response to the notion that society's production should be equally distributed to all, Marx asked, sarcastically, "To those who do not work as well?"

National Bureau of Economic Research (NBER), http://www.nber.org. A searchable source of timely papers and books on economics.

Research Papers in Economics/Econ Papers, http://econpapers.repec.org/ or http://repec.org/. Search hundreds of working papers by topic or author.

Resources for Economists (AEA), http://rfe.org/.

Robert Lerman (Urban Institute), http://www.urban.org/bio/RobertILerman.html.

Steven D. Levitt (University of Chicago; author and subject of *Freakonomics*), http://pricetheory.uchicago.edu/levitt/LevittCV.html.

Thomas Sowell (UCLA), http://www.townhall.com/columnists/thomassowell/archive.shtml.

Walter Williams (George Mason), http://www.gmu.edu/departments/economics/wew/index.html.

Western Economics Association International (WEAI). A $25 membership for students includes *Economic Inquiry* and *Contemporary Economic Policy*. http://weainternational.org.

## INCOME DISTRIBUTION

Class Matters, http://www.nytimes.com/pages/national/class/index.html.

Compensation (labor), http://www.bls.gov/opub/cwc/cm20030124ar01p1.htm. On the difficulty of measuring real wages and benefits over long periods of time.

Consumer Expenditure Survey, http://www.bls.gov/cex/csxfaqs.htm.

Current population survey (income), http://www.census.gov/hhes/www/income/dinctabs.html.

Distributive Justice, http://plato.stanford.edu/entries/justice-distributive/. The Stanford Encyclopedia of Philosophy's remarkable summary of the ethical issues.

Employment by industry, http://www.bls.gov/web/cesbmtab.htm#Tab2.

Family Income, http://www.census.gov/hhes/income/4person.html. Median income for four-person families.

Green Book, http://www.gpoaccess.gov/wmprints/green/2004.html. House Ways & Means Committee's program descriptions and historical data on Social Security, employment, earnings, welfare, child support, health insurance, the elderly, families with children, poverty, and taxation. Not always politically neutral.

Hillary W. Hoynes (UC Davis) http://www.econ.ucdavis.edu/faculty/hoynes/.

Household Income, http://pubdb3.census.gov/macro/032005/hhinc/new01_001.htm. Money income by age, education, number of workers, etc.

Income (fifteen definitions), http://www.census.gov/hhes/www/income/histinc/rdi6.html. Even these fifteen definitions of income are insufficient. What is needed for historical comparisons is the Census Bureau's fourteenth or fifteenth definition *without capital gains*. Reporting of capital gains on tax returns is extremely sensitive to changes in tax rates, which greatly distorts data that include such gains (particularly in 1986–1988).

Income Distribution Tables, http://www.census.gov/hhes/www/income/histinc/h03ar.html. The distribution of pretax, pretransfer income by quintiles (and top 5 percent) from 1967 to 2004, and in 2004 dollars.

Income Mobility, http://www.ncpa.org/pub/st/20050801-laffer.pdf. Survey article by Bruce Bartlett with many references.

Institute for Research on Poverty, http://www.irp.wisc.edu/home.htm.

Labor Market Data explained, http://www.richmondfed.org/publications/ economic_research/macro_economics/labor.cfm.

Panel Study on Income Dynamics (PSID), http://psidonline.isr.umich.edu/.

Poverty Guidelines, http://aspe.hhs.gov/poverty/05poverty.shtml.

Survey of Consumer Finances (SCF), http://www.federalreserve.gov/Pubs/oss/oss2/scfindex.html.

Wages (Mean and Median), http://www.ssa.gov/OACT/COLA/central.html. From the Social Security Administration; *see also* http://www.bls.gov.

Working Poor, http://pubdb3.census.gov/macro/032005/pov/new22_100_01. htm.

## INTERNATIONAL

BLS Chartbook of International Labor Comparisons, http://www.dol.gov/asp/media/reports/chartbook/index.htm.

Global Competitiveness (by Paul Krugman), http://pages.stern.nyu.edu/~nroubini/COMPKRUG.HTM.

Luxembourg Income Study, http://www.lisproject.org/keyfigures.htm. International comparisons of income distribution, poverty by age, wealth, etc. But read the "Methods and Warnings."

OECD Factbook, http://oberon.sourceoecd.org/vl=2830229/cl=12/nw=1/rpsv/factbook/. Easy source for international comparisons among major countries.

Xavier Sala-i-Martin, http://www.columbia.edu/~xs23/home.html. Entertaining home page of a Columbia University economist who studies income growth and distribution from a global perspective.

## TAX FACTS AND TAX POLICY

Average taxes, http://www.census.gov/hhes/www/income/histinc/rdi2.html. Average taxes paid as a percentage of average income by type of tax 1980–2003.

Capital Gains taxes (Alan Reynolds), http://www.asx.com.au/about/pdf/cgt.pdf.

Fiscal Facts and Figures, http://www.cato.org/research/ fiscal_policy/facts/tax_charts.html.

Individual Income Tax sample data, http://www.nber.org/~taxsim/gdb/. You can actually look at old income tax forms here, to see they did not use to have an adjustment for IRA saving, for example, or a line to report tax-exempt interest income (which is now added to some measures of "expanded income").

Institute for Research in the Economics of Taxation, http://www.iret.org/.

Optimal (and Pareto-Efficient) Taxation (Joseph Stigliz), http://papers.nber.org/papers/w2189.

Statistics of Income Bulletin (SOI), http://www.irs.gov/taxstats/article/0,,id=117514,00.htm.

*Supply-Side Economics* (readings), http://www.yorktownuniversity.com/grad_libraries_supply_side.cfm.

Tax Foundation, http://www.taxfoundation.org/.

*TaxProf Blog* think tank reports, http://taxprof.typepad.com/taxprof_blog/think_tank_reports/index.html. University of Cincinnati law professor Paul Caron provides handy summaries and links to think tank research from all perspectives.

## MATH TOOLS

Compound annual growth calculator, http://www.investopedia.com/calculator/CAGR.aspx.

Consumer Price Index calculator, http://www.aier.org/colcalc.html or http:// woodrow .mpls.frb.fed.us/research/data/us/calc/. These calculators use the consumer price index to compare how much money would be needed today to purchase as much as some dollar amount did in the past. Yet they also reveal the cumulative effect of the CPI's chronic overstatement of inflation. They say my 1971 income of $9,900 was equivalent to $49,500 in 2006, but I don't believe it was equivalent to even $30,000 (and my 1956 Buick was *not* equivalent to *any* 2006 car).

Gini coefficient calculator, http://www.poorcity.richcity.org/calculator.htm.

## ECONOMISTS' BLOGS

The Becker-Posner blog (University of Chicago), http://www.becker-posner-blog .com/.

Brad deLong (UC Berkeley), http://www.econbuddy.com/.

Café Hayek (George Mason), http://cafehayek.typepad.com/.

Cato Institute blog, http://www.cato-at-liberty.org/.

EconoPundit (Roosevelt University), http://www.econopundit.com/.

Greg Mankiw (Harvard), http://gregmankiw.blogspot.com/.

Reform Club, http://www.reformclub.blogspot.com/.

The Skeptical Optimist, http://optimist123.com/.

Steve Bainbridge (UCLA), http://www.professorbainbridge.com/.

# Index

## About the Author

**ALAN REYNOLDS** is a Senior Fellow at the Cato Institute and was formerly Director of Economic Research at the Hudson Institute. He served as Research Director with the National Commission on Tax Reform and Economic Growth, as advisor to the National Commission on the Cost of Higher Education, and as a member of the OMB transition team in 1981. His studies have been published by the Organization for Economic Co-operation and Development, the Joint Economic Committee, the Federal Reserve Banks of Atlanta and St. Louis, and the Australian Stock Exchange. Author of *The Microsoft Antitrust Appeal* (2001), he has written for numerous publications since 1971, including *The Wall Street Journal, The New York Times, National Review, The New Republic, Fortune*, and the *Harvard Business Review*. A former columnist with *Forbes* and *Reason*, his weekly column is now nationally syndicated.